13.75

THE W

OTHER BOOKS BY R. B. Y. SCOTT

The Relevance of the Prophets
The Psalms as Christian Praise
Proverbs-Ecclesiastes (Anchor Bible)
Treasures from Judaean Caves
Towards the Christian Revolution
   (editor with Gregory Vlastos)

The Way of Wisdom

IN THE OLD TESTAMENT

R. B. Y. SCOTT

Macmillan Publishing Co., Inc.
New York

Collier Macmillan Publishers
London

Whence then comes wisdom?

. . . God understands the way to it.

Copyright © 1971 by R. B. Y. Scott
All rights reserved. No part of this book
may be reproduced or transmitted in
any form or by any means, electronic or
mechanical, including photocopying,
recording or by any information storage
and retrieval system, without permission
in writing from the Publisher.

Macmillan Publishing Co., Inc.
866 Third Avenue, New York, N.Y. 10022
Collier Macmillan Canada, Ltd.

Library of Congress Catalog Card Number: 71-150075

First Macmillan Paperbacks Edition 1971
13   12   11   10   9   8   7   6   5
Printed in the United States of America

TO
Mary and Jamie
John and Janet
Gavin and Sue

Contents

	Preface	*ix*
	List of Abbreviations	*xiii*
1	Wisdom in the Bible	1
2	The International Context	23
3	Precepts and Proverbs	48
4	Wisdom in Stories and Word Pictures	72
5	Prophecy and Wisdom	101
6	Wisdom in Revolt: *Job*	136
7	Wisdom in Revolt: *Agur and Qoheleth*	165
8	Wisdom Piety	190
EPILOGUE	The Role of Wisdom	223
	Index of Subjects	*230*
	Index of Authors	*232*
	Index of Biblical References	*233*

Preface

This book has been written as a companion piece to the author's *The Relevance of the Prophets* (New York, The Macmillan Company: 1944; rev. ed., 1968). Its claim to attention is similarly modest. But since that book has proved of some use to ministers and to college and seminary students, it is hoped that they and perhaps others who have seen the earlier work may find room on their shelves for the sequel.

An almost inevitable defect of general introductions to wide areas of study is, of course, a certain superficiality. Thoroughness tends to be sacrificed to comprehensiveness, and selectivity to distort proportion. Difficulties may be ignored or too easily glossed over. The author has written in constant awareness of these dangers and cannot claim to have escaped them entirely. He has tried, however, to do more than summarize and coordinate the views of others in an all-inclusive account. He hopes that his colleagues may find here some evidences of original work that may warrant their attention.

The book he would like to have written would have been two or three times as long and possibly less useful to those he has had principally in mind as readers. Particularly to be regretted is the omission of a full treatment of the theology of the wisdom writers in relationship to the theology of the Old Testament as a whole, of their contribution to the creation of apocalyptic literature, and of the heritage of wisdom in the New Testament. *ars longa, vita brevis*; and, as a tired instructor once warned his students, *lahag harbeh yegiʿath basar*.

Needless to say, any use this book may have will depend largely on constant reference to the biblical texts, including those of the English Apocrypha that belong with the religious writings of pre-Christian Judaism which were received into the ancient canon of Christian scripture. Biblical quotations have been taken with few exceptions from the Revised Standard Version, the New English Bible or the Anchor Bible; less often from the New American Bible, the Complete Bible, an American Translation, and the Jerusalem Bible. Some renderings have been quoted from William McKane in Proverbs, and from Robert Gordis in Qoheleth and Job. In general it has seemed preferable to utilize versions which the reader is likely to have at hand for comparison, rather than to substitute everywhere the author's individual rendering for the consensus of the learned companies responsible for widely distributed versions. The translation chosen in each case is that which seems to convey most successfully the sense of the Hebrew and Greek texts. Unless otherwise indicated, the translations are from the Revised Standard Version or, in a few cases, are the author's own. When Hebrew or Greek words are transliterated a simplified system is used which should nevertheless be adequate for their identification. Where the numbering of chapters and verses differs in the English versions from that of the Hebrew Bible, this is indicated by giving in parenthesis the Hebrew numbering, or by subjoining the letters 'EVV' to the reference.

The author's indebtedness to the writings of previous workers will be evident to those familiar with this particular corner of the vineyard. It is acknowledged chiefly, though far from completely, in the footnotes. He particularly regrets that Gerhard von Rad's important work *Weisheit in Israel*, 1970, came to hand too late to be utilized in the discussion. His gratitude for the patience and helpfulness of his wife goes without saying.

One suggestion to the reader may be hazarded here—that he read the brief Epilogue before reading the rest of the book and again after doing so—if indeed he has managed to reach its end, "faint, yet pursuing." The role of Old Testament wisdom becomes more apparent and relevant if one can see it as a significant part of a much needed wisdom for life today.

Princeton University R. B. Y. SCOTT
November 1970

Abbreviations

AB	*Anchor Bible*, ed. W. F. Albright and D. N. Freedman, 1964–
alt.	altered
ANET	*Ancient Near Eastern Texts*, ed. J. B. Pritchard, 2d ed. 1955
ANET Supp.	*The Ancient Near East, Supplementary Texts and Pictures*, ed. J. B. Pritchard, 1969
AT	*The Complete Bible, an American Translation*, 1939
Bib. Or.	*Bibliotheca Orientalis*
BJRL	*Bulletin of the John Rylands Library*
BWANT	Beiträge zur Wissenschaft von Alten und Neuen Testament
BWL	*Babylonian Wisdom Literature*, by W. G. Lambert, 1960
chap.	chapter
EVV	English Versions
Heb.	Hebrew text (N.B. Ep. Heb.—Epistle to the Hebrews)
HTR	*Harvard Theological Review*
IB	*The Interpreter's Bible*, ed. G. A. Buttrick, 1952–57

Abbreviations

ICC	International Critical Commentary
IDB	*The Interpreter's Dictionary of the Bible*, ed. G. A. Buttrick, 1962
JB	*The Jerusalem Bible*, ed. A. Jones, 1966
JBL	*Journal of Biblical Literature*
KJV	The Holy Bible, King James or Authorized Version, 1611 and later
LXX	The Septuagint or Old Greek translation of the Old Testament
MT	The standard Massoretic Text of the Hebrew Bible
NAB	The New American Bible, 1970
NEB	The New English Bible, 1970
RB	*Revue Biblique*
RSV	Revised Standard Version, 1952
Syr.	Syriac
Targ.	Targum
TLZ	*Theologische Literaturzeitung*
v., vv.	verse, verses
VT	*Vetus Testamentum*
VT Supp.	*Vetus Testamentum Supplement*
Vulg.	Vulgate Latin version
ZAW	*Zeitschrift für die Alttestamentliche Wissenschaft*

Books of the Bible referred to with abbreviations

Chron.	*Chronicles*	Ep. Heb.	*Epistle to the Hebrews*
Dan.	*Daniel*		
Deut.	*Deuteronomy*	Esd.	*Esdras*
Eccles.	*Ecclesiastes (see Qoheleth)*	Exod.	*Exodus*
		Ezek.	*Ezekiel*
Ecclus.	*Ecclesiasticus (see Sirach)*	Gen.	*Genesis*
		Hab.	*Habakkuk*

Hos.	*Hosea*	Ps., Pss.	*Psalm, Psalms*
Isa.	*Isaiah*	Qoh.	*Qoheleth*
Jer.	*Jeremiah*		*(see Ecclesiastes)*
Jon.	*Jonah*	Rev.	*Revelation*
Josh.	*Joshua*	Sam.	*Samuel*
Judg.	*Judges*	Sir.	*Sirach (see*
Lev.	*Leviticus*		*Ecclesiasticus)*
Macc.	*Maccabees*	Song of S.	*Song of Songs, or,*
Mal.	*Malachi*		*of Solomon*
Matt.	*Matthew*	Tob.	*Tobit*
Mic.	*Micah*	Wis. Sol.	*Wisdom of*
Neh.	*Nehemiah*		*Solomon*
Num.	*Numbers*	Zech.	*Zechariah*
Obad.	*Obadiah*	Zeph.	*Zephaniah*
Prov.	*Proverbs*		

THE WAY OF WISDOM

1
Wisdom in the Bible

ONE OF THE interesting features of the Old Testament is its remarkable diversity of content. It is a selection from a wider literature, the rest of which has perished.[1] As a literature it took form over a period of something like eleven centuries. Even the selection made toward the end of this period of what was peculiarly significant for Israelite faith bears the marks of a long and often tumultuous historical experience. Early material appears side by side with what is clearly from later times, though exact dating is impossible because of insufficient evidence. In fact, the Old Testament itself provides a very incomplete historical outline into which its literature can be fitted; the historian must piece together the story from many sources, biblical and extrabiblical. By far the most important are the former, even when their interest is not primarily historical; for the literature reflects the life and faith, the religious experience and thought of the historical Israel.

The dominant theme of these sacred writings is the

---

[1] Such as the Book of the Wars of Yahweh (Num. 21:14) and the Book of Jashar (Josh. 10:13; 2 Sam. 1:18). Note in 1 and 2 Kings the frequent referral of the reader to royal chronicles for additional information (1 Kings 11:41; 14:29; 22:39; 2 Kings 20:20).

age-long dialogue between Yahweh, Israel's covenant God, and this people which he had chosen to hear his call, obey his commandments, and serve his purposes on earth.[2] Israel knew herself as the people that God had delivered from Egyptian slavery, made covenant with through Moses, and brought into the promised land. Her religion—this special relationship with a unique deity—established her identity, as a separate political existence could never do. The five books of Moses elaborate this theme of promise, Exodus deliverance and covenant, together with their celebration in cultic worship. The Former Prophets —Joshua through 2 Kings—tell the story of the occupation of Canaan and of Yahweh's dealings with her there until the end of the monarchy. The books of the Prophets record the powerful words of this succession of messengers from Yahweh who recalled Israel to a God who was ever-present in his demands for loyal obedience to his covenant. The Psalms echo the same beliefs and faith of the worshipping community and its individual members.

Over against this dominant theme and within the same canon of sacred scripture stands a different theme in a smaller group of writings known as the Wisdom books. When we read Proverbs, Job, and Ecclesiastes it is clear at once that we are in another realm of discourse altogether. One modern scholar (Gese) has spoken of these works as having the appearance of a "foreign body" in the Old Testament. The remark is true in more than one sense: not only are the Wisdom books so different in manner and substance from the covenant people theme that they have often been the despair of theologians; they also turn out to have much in common with the wisdom writings of foreign peoples like the Egyptians and the Babylonians.

---

[2] Cf. Exod. 19:5–6.

The Meaning of Wisdom

What, then, is the meaning of 'wisdom' in the biblical sense? For one thing, it corresponds only in part to what we usually think of today as wisdom—sagacity, insight, good judgment as to what one should do in a given situation, in the light of human values and goals. The line between wisdom and knowledge was not so sharply drawn in ancient Israel as with the Greek philosophers and with us. The wise man then was, in the first instance, the knowledgeable man, the man with some special skill, above all the man who could teach others because he had superior understanding about how life should be lived and what it means. There is no quick and simple answer to the question of what wisdom means in the writings of the Bible. It has many facets, coming as it does from a long and by no means static tradition. If the student would understand its wealth of meaning he must know something of the story of the Wisdom movement, or school of thought, and ponder the ideas associated with it and the literature it produced.

It may be misleading to speak of a 'Wisdom' movement if this suggests the existence of a self-conscious group within society working deliberately for social change and to forward objectives not generally accepted. Wisdom was rather the fine fruit of a tradition originally rooted in the mores of family and tribe and local community, and hence to a degree was as old as the society itself. Right was the way of wisdom, wrong the way of folly. "Such a thing is not done in Israel," protested a girl threatened with rape "do not commit this folly" (2 Sam. 13:12). That "wickedness comes from wicked men" is identified as an ancient proverb (1 Sam. 24:13 [Heb. 24:14]). Apt quotations of such folk sayings appear here and there in the narrative and prophetic books; Jeremiah and Ezekiel both quote "[When] the fathers have eaten sour grapes, the children's teeth are set on edge" (Jer. 31:29; Ezek. 18:2). Such anonymous folk wisdom appears spontaneously in traditional societies, from the Sumerians onward.

The wisdom tradition, however, was much more than the flowering of proverbial sayings among the common people. We need only recall the reputation of King Solomon as the wisest man in the world, formulated in extravagant terms in 1 Kings 4:29–34 (Heb. 5:9–14). Proverb collections in later times continued to be entitled "Proverbs of Solomon."[3] A late Hebrew work like Ecclesiastes is ascribed to him, and even a book composed in Greek in the first century B.C. is entitled the Wisdom of Solomon.[4] The wisdom movement or tradition was a powerful factor in Israel's religious culture that has had insufficient recognition because other factors have preempted the foreground. In Jeremiah 18:18 and Ezekiel 7:26 the wise man, or elder, is named along with the priest and the prophet as one of the three sources of authoritative guidance possessed by the community: "The priest's *torah* [instruction] must not cease, nor the wise man's counsel, nor the prophet's message." The priest not only conducted the cult of sacrifice and festival; part of his duty was to proclaim the fundamental beliefs and to instruct in the consequent obligations of the people of God.[5] So with the prophet's word, "against the whole family which I brought up out of the land of Egypt, . . . I will punish you for all your iniquities" (Amos 3:1–2).

The spokesmen of wisdom take another line. They have little or nothing to say about institutional religion or a special relationship between Yahweh and Israel, past or present.[6] They do not address the collective Israel, as the

[3] See Prov. 1:1; 10:1, 25:1.
[4] See below, pp. 172–73 and 212–14.
[5] Cf. Deut. 26:1–9; 33:8–10; 2 Chron. 15:3; Mal. 2:4–7.
[6] This statement must be qualified with respect to the later wisdom books, Sirach and Wisdom, in which the streams of wisdom and prophecy have mingled.

prophets do, nor appeal to the authority of revelation. Their concern is with men as individuals, or, more exactly, with man in his individuality and social relationships, and in his private thoughts. Their counsel has to do with how men ought to act in the workaday world, with personal character, and with a way of life that can be called good because it has coherence, value, and meaning. The authority with which they speak is that of the moral experience and trained intelligence of genuinely religious men. Their method is counsel and instruction, and, at a later stage, persuasion and debate.

What has just been said is an attempt to sum up the meaning of wisdom in its mainstream as represented by the Hebrew canonical works, Proverbs, Job, and Ecclesiastes (Qoheleth).[7] But it gives no indication of the extraordinary variety of meanings and shades of meaning of the term in other Old Testament contexts. It could not and did not mean the same thing in the wise woman's bargain with Joab, Ahithophel's counsel to Absalom, Solomon's encyclopedic knowledge and his clever solution of a court case, the spirit-endowed qualities of the messianic king, the teacher's goal for his charges, the divine principle which eluded man's search, the instrument of God in creation, the learning of the scribes, the surpassing brilliance of Joseph and Daniel at foreign courts, and the effect of man's eating the forbidden fruit.[8] How can all these be related to a central idea?

Three converging lines lead toward an answer to this question: (1) the senses in which the terms *wise* and

---

[7] The confusing similarity of the Latinized titles Ecclesiastes for Qoheleth and Ecclesiasticus for Sirach (ben Sira), especially in the abbreviations Eccles. and Ecclus., makes it preferable to use the alternative names from the Hebrew and Greek versions respectively. The author does so henceforward in this book.

[8] 2 Sam. 20:15–22; 16:20–23; 1 Kings 4:29–34 (Heb. 5:9–14); 3:16–28; Isa. 11:1–3; Prov. 2:1–15; Job 28:1–28; Prov. 8:22–31; Ezra 7:11; Gen. 41:39; Dan. 1:17–20; Gen. 3:1–7.

6 / *The Way of Wisdom*

wisdom are used in various contexts; (2) the line of historical developments in the tradition, so far as these can be traced in our sources; and (3) the distinctive content, language, and viewpoint of the Wisdom literature itself. At this point only a preliminary outline will be given. The remaining chapters will be devoted to adding flesh to the skeleton.

The Terms Wise *and* Wisdom

When we speak of Hebrew Wisdom or the Wisdom literature we are using the term *wisdom* in a technical sense for a cultural and religious phenomenon in the life of ancient Israel. This had its own distinctive ways of thought and forms of expression. But confusion will result if we fail to discriminate among the various senses in which ḥokmah ("wisdom") and hākām ("wise") are used in different contexts in the Old Testament.

A striking illustration of this is to be seen in the four different ways in which the famous wisdom of Solomon is presented in the narratives of that king's reign in 1 Kings 1–11: (1) the cunning required for Solomon to settle David's old grudge against Joab (2:1–2, 5–6); (2) the moral discernment necessary for the administration of true justice (3:9, 12);[9] (3) the intellectual brilliance and encyclopedic knowledge that found expression in Solomon's thousands of proverbs and songs (4:29–34 [Heb. 5:9–14]); (4) the special competence of a ruler and administrator (5:7, 12 [Heb. 5:21, 26]).

The primary meaning of ḥokmāh is "superior mental ability or special skill," with no necessary moral reference. Broadly speaking, the moral and religious element is a later enlargement of the meaning of the term.[10] In the

[9] In 3:16–28 the clever stratagem by which Solomon discovers the real mother is intended by the editor to illustrate (2), but in fact it is better seen as an example of (1).
[10] The older sense persists in Job 5:13 with its reference to the craftiness of the wise.

older sources the disgraceful stratagem suggested to Amnon by Jonadab is explained by attributing great wisdom to the latter.[11] The ruse proposed by Joab to the wise woman of Tekoa and the scheme carried out at the suggestion of the wise woman of Abel are clever solutions applied to difficult situations.[12] In Job 38:36 and 39:17 ḥokmah means simply "intelligence," as affirmed or denied to natural objects. In Psalm 107:27 the storm-tossed sailors "were at their wits' end" (RSV)—literally, "their wisdom was swallowed up, overwhelmed." *Wisdom* here clearly designates the special skill of seamanship, which was unable to cope with the gale.[13]

The term is applied also to other particular skills in this general sense of knowing what to do and how to do it. A parade example is that of the master craftsman Bezalel who "was filled with divine spirit, making him skillful (*beḥokmāh*) and ingenious, expert in every craft, and a master of design, whether in gold, silver and copper, or cutting precious stones, or carving wood."[14] Bezalel's associate, Oholiab, was similarly gifted with respect to textiles. We read of the specialized wisdom of farmers, merchants, woodsmen, professional mourners, political counselors, and soldiers, of astrologers, scribes, and priests, and of judges and kings.[15] Only of the last three of these are moral qualities predicated, and not always to them! Royal counselors are difficult to distinguish from courtiers in general; the female attendants on Sisera's queen mother are called "the

---

[11] 2 Sam. 13:3. RSV translates *ḥākām* "crafty"; JB and NEB, "shrewd"; NAB, "clever."
[12] 2 Sam. 14:1–24; 20:16–22. Cf. Qoh. 9:13–16.
[13] As recognized in the NAB, JB, and NEB translations. Cf. 1 Kings 9:27; 22:48–49; Ezek. 27:8.
[14] Exod. 35:31–33, NEB.
[15] Isa. 28:24–29; Ezek. 28:4–5; 1 Kings 5:6 (Heb. 5:20); Jer. 9:17 (Heb. 9:16); 2 Sam. 16:23; Prov. 21:22; Isa. 47:9–13; Jer. 8:8; Mal. 2:4–7; Deut. 16:18; 2 Sam. 14:20; Isa. 10:13; 11:2.

wisest of her princesses."[16] Indeed, in Jeremiah 9:23 (Heb. 9:22) the wise or educated man is associated with the wealthy and powerful simply as members of an elite class.[17]

The skills enumerated above demanded special knowledge acquired through training and experience, in addition to superior intelligence. Wisdom and knowledge (da^cath) are so frequently associated as to be almost synonymous. It is noteworthy that Bezalel was inspired also to teach.[18] One of the specialized skills was that of the scribe, who doubtless taught it to others as well as putting it at the service of the illiterate and, at a higher level, of the courts, the temple, and the political administration.[19] The scribe became the wise man par excellence.

Since literary materials were scarce and costly, education was largely oral; "what wise men have told, and their fathers have not hidden." Parents were the child's earliest instructors in the customs, moral standards and traditions of a family-oriented society. The teacher of young men urged them to obey their fathers' instruction and not to reject their mothers' teaching. Like the beliefs and obligations of religion, these constituted the special qualities of wisdom and understanding that should distinguish this people.[20]

In adult life the council of elders at the town gate adjudicated disputes according to the custom and right of the community. Judges appointed were to be "wise, understanding and of repute," "capable, God-fearing men, . . .

---

[16] Judg. 5:29, NEB.
[17] Cf. Isa. 5:21 in the context of vv. 18–23; Jer. 51:57; Isa. 19:11.
[18] Exod. 35:34.
[19] Isa. 29:12; Jer. 32:9–14; 8:8; 2 Kings 22:3–12; 25:19; Prov. 25:1.
[20] Job 15:18; Exod. 13:14; Prov. 1:8; Deut. 4:5–6.

honest and incorruptible."[21] Since the king was the court of last appeal he must, above all, be just and wise enough to distinguish right from wrong. The ideal king would be endowed by Yahweh with "wisdom and discernment, sound judgment and strength of character, knowledge and true religion."[22]

The idea of wisdom as a fundamentally ethical and religious quality comes to the fore most prominently in Proverbs, Job, the wisdom Psalms, and to a lesser degree in Qoheleth, whose author displays an intellectualist cast of mind. Proverbs 10–31 is a source book of older materials for the study of wisdom, prefaced in chapters 1–9 by ten discourses and some remarkable theological poetry, in light of which the adages and precepts of the later chapters were to be interpreted. The keynote is struck at the outset with a firm declaration of principle: "Reverence for the Lord is the beginning of knowledge; fools despise wisdom and instruction."[23] Here knowledge and wisdom are synonymous. They are rooted in religion, as is the process of instruction. In similar fashion the introductory verses which preface the collection of precepts in 22:17–24:22 stress the teacher's religious and ethical objectives: "that your trust may be in the Lord, . . . to show you what is right and true."

The frequently recurring contrast of the wise man and the fool exhibits the latter as stupid and ignorant, or at the best naïve; but also as headstrong, passionate, malicious, quarrelsome, and morally debased.[24] The wise man, on the other hand, is diligent, prudent, trustworthy, patient, gen-

---

[21] Deut. 1:13; Exod. 18:21, NEB.
[22] 1 Kings 3:9; Isa. 11:2 (author's translation).
[23] Prov. 1:7, NAB. The first clause is repeated in slightly different forms in 9:10; 15:33; Job 28:28; and Ps. 111:10.
[24] See Prov. 1:22; 6:6–19; 14:14–18; 26:1–26; 27:3; 29:9.

erous, modest, peaceable, and self-controlled.[25] Above all, he is aware of the limitations to human autonomy under God's guidance and overruling Providence.[26] The school of wisdom represented in Proverbs believed that there is a divinely directed moral order at work in human life, under which the wise and good are rewarded, and the foolish and wicked bring on themselves appropriate punishment. "No harm shall befall the just man," they said, but "the wicked have their hands full of trouble"; and, again, "The consequence of humility and reverence for the Lord is wealth and honor and life."[27]

This established view of the nature of religious wisdom is directly challenged by Job in the book which bears his name. To the three wise men who debate with him it is axiomatic. "What innocent man has ever perished?" demands Eliphaz. "Those who sow trouble reap as they have sown." Bildad declares that what has been handed down by wise men of the past is certain: "God will not spurn the blameless man, nor will he grasp the hand of the wrongdoer."[28]

Job understands this traditional view very well, even as he subjects it to radical criticism. "I have a mind as well as you," he retorts. "If I could only go back to the old days, to the time when God was watching over me. . . . But now. . . ."[29] The general rule cannot be applied indiscriminately, for in his case it results in injustice. The friends' syllogism is fallacious—suffering is the result of sin; Job suffers, therefore Job has sinned. The poet knows that not all suffering is the result of sin, nor even propor-

[25] See Prov. 10:17; 11:15; 13:17; 14:29; 15:18; 16:32; 17:27; 19:17; 20:13.
[26] See Prov. 2:5–8; 3:5–7; 15:3; 16:1–7, 33; 20:24; 27:1; 28:25; 21:30–31.
[27] Prov. 12:21; 22:4, AB. Cf. 3:33; 10:3, 27; 14:11; 15:6.
[28] Job 4:7–8, NEB; 8:8–10, 20, NEB.
[29] Job 12:2, AB; 29:2, 30:1, NEB.

tionate to man's fault. Failure to recognize this calls into question divine justice, since God's power cannot be doubted. There must be depths in the divine-human relationship which traditional wisdom has not glimpsed, an ultimate mystery beyond its ken. The final wisdom is to recognize and accept the strangeness of the ways of God, and yet to trust that he is good.[30]

Qoheleth also finds the traditional doctrine of reward and punishment unsatisfactory, but he looks at the problem from a different angle, that of the observer rather than the victim of life's anomalies. So far as he can see, the righteous and the wicked, the sage and the fool, fare much the same in this world and die the same death. "How alike in death are the wise man and the fool!" "Just and wise men and what they do are in God's power; whether he will favor them or not, no one knows." God's ways are an insoluble mystery.[31]

Qoheleth uses the word *wisdom* in two closely related senses: (1) intelligence, reason, the philosophic temper, and (2) the rational grasp of meanings. In the experiments he conducted in search of meaning, his "reason remained in control."[32] But his attempt at understanding the moral meaning of human life as a whole proved to be beyond him, "a grasping at the wind." Only in a relative and limited way is the wise man better off than the fool; he is aware of the problem and of his own ignorance. In default of understanding "there is nothing better for a man than to eat and drink and find satisfaction in his work." God has put a darkness in the human mind, and man is in no position to dispute with omnipotence.[33]

---

[30] See further on Job pp. 152–64 below.
[31] Qoh. 2:16; 9:1, AB. Cf. 7:23–24; 8:17.
[32] Qoh. 2:3, AB. Cf. 1:13; 2:9, 12.
[33] Qoh. 2:24, AB. Cf. 3:11; 6:10; 7:13; and see further below, pp. 176–84.

The Wisdom Tradition in Israel

Wisdom in some form was a continuous factor in the common life and consciousness of Israel through more than a millennium of her history in Canaan. In that long time there were many changes in the social, political, cultural, and religious environments. The Wisdom tradition was played upon by many cultural forces as time went on.

Any attempt to trace the history of this tradition is handicapped by the relative paucity and selective nature of Old Testament historical sources. The editors of the primary narrative account of Israel's history from the conquest of Canaan to the Babylonian exile are concerned chiefly with a prophetic interpretation of that history. Indeed, the books Joshua to 2 Kings are classified in the Hebrew Bible as the Former Prophets. The second historical corpus, Chronicles-Ezra-Nehemiah, summarizes and supplements the same story, carrying it down to the restoration of the community after the exile, around the rebuilt temple. Here the emphasis is on the temple cult and King David as its founder. In neither history are there more than incidental references to activities of the sages, with the single exception of what is said about the wisdom of Solomon.

Folk wisdom appears spontaneously in traditional societies. We have evidence for it in the popular proverbs quoted here and there in the narrative and prophetic books, as well as in the distinctive wisdom literature that emerged from the tradition in its later stages.[34] Local sages were consulted for advice, and there were respected counselors at the royal court.[35]

[34] See Gen. 10:9; 1 Sam. 24:13; 2 Sam. 20:18; 1 Kings 20:11; Jer. 13:23.
[35] 2 Sam. 14:2; 20:16, 18; 15:31; 16:15–17:14.

As the monarchy became more firmly established, an organized administrative structure became necessary to maintain social order, adjudicate disputes, and assist the king in forming and carrying out his policies. The royal counselors became in effect cabinet officers. For the courts of David and Solomon these are listed in 2 Samuel 8:16–18; 20:23–26; and 1 Kings 4:1–6. Three of these are of interest for our purpose: the Remembrancer (RSV, "Recorder"; NEB, "Secretary of State"), the Scribe (RSV, "Secretary"; NEB, "Adjutant general") and the King's Friend.[36] The first two of these, and possibly the third (like the army commander), must have had large numbers of subordinates for record-keeping, correspondence, and similar tasks. The point here is that together these formed at the court a corps of 'wise men,' masters of the scribal art. In Proverbs 25:1 the publication of a collection of Solomonic proverbs is ascribed to "the men of Hezekiah, king of Judah."

Solomon's principal wife was an Egyptian princess and he seems to have modeled his court organization on that of the pharaohs, where for many centuries scribes had been engaged in literary composition, as well as serving in the conduct of official business. Their presence at Solomon's court explains, at least in part, that king's later reputation as the composer of thousands of proverbs and songs. The account in 1 Kings 4:29–34 clothes in the hues of legend what was evidently a remarkable flowering of literary activity at Solomon's court and under his patronage. It is of a piece with the story of his intellectual brilliance which so bedazzled the Queen of Sheba and pictures a different kind of wisdom from that of the just

[36] It is impossible to do more than guess from their titles the particular duties of these functionaries. From 2 Sam. 16:17 it would seem that the third was the king's personal adviser.

judge and competent ruler which, we are told, had been granted him in answer to his prayer.[37]

That there is historical substance beneath the legend, however, is indicated by the observations of Alt and von Rad. The former points to the curious fact that the subject matter of Solomon's proverbs according to 1 Kings—trees, birds, animals, reptiles, and fish—is more akin to that of the Egyptian 'classification lists' of natural knowledge than to the adages and precepts concerning human character and behavior called Solomonic in Proverbs 10:1 and 25:1. If the legend were not based on a distinct and inherently probable tradition, this diversity would be most unlikely. Von Rad, in turn, has shown that the Joseph story in Genesis (incorporated in both the J and E documents of the Pentateuch and hence from the early monarchy) is a kind of didactic novel with a wisdom theme, of the youth who learns wisdom and prudence, and triumphs through his virtue and the Providence of God.[38]

In addition to such wisdom writings, the scribes of Solomon's court may well have been responsible for the collection of songs or poems related to the national tradition. Here and there in the narrative books from Genesis to 2 Samuel, short excerpts in verse or longer compositions are quoted. They are of various types—blessings, oracles, laments, liturgical chants, and especially war cries, incantations, and victory songs related to Israel's battles, from the deliverance at the Sea of Reeds to the establishment

---

[37] 1 Kings 10:1–10, 13; 3:5–14. See also R. B. Y. Scott, "Solomon and the Beginnings of Wisdom in Israel," in *Wisdom in Israel and in the Ancient Near East*, eds. M. Noth and D. W. Thomas, *VT Supp. III* (1955), pp. 262–79; M. Noth, *Könige*, Biblischer Kommentar IX, no. 2 (1965), p. 81.

[38] A. Alt, "Die Weisheit Salomos," *TLZ* 76 (1951): pp. 139–44; G. von Rad, "Josephgeschichte und ältere Chokma," *VT Supp. 1* (1953): pp. 120–27.

of David's throne.[39] One of these is said to have been taken from the Book of the Wars of Yahweh and two others from the Book of Jashar.[40] These "books" seem to have been anthologies of poems and war ballads previously transmitted orally, as suggested by the heading of one of them in Numbers 21:17. The collecting of poems on themes central to the national tradition would be a likely activity of the royal scribes.

Another point to be kept in mind is that Solomon's temple, as a dynastic shrine in the new national capital, was an innovation. Scribes were associated with temples as well as with royal courts in the ancient Near East. Some of the literary activity during Solomon's reign may have been the composition or adaptation of liturgical material for use in the new temple, the formal beginnings of psalmody in Israel.

Our next glimpse of the continuing wisdom tradition is in the eighth and seventh centuries B.C., the time of the classical prophets. Two of the three courtiers who parleyed with the Assyrians for King Hezekiah were the Scribe and the Remembrancer. Hezekiah was the first Judean king since Solomon to reign without a rival king in northern Israel; Chronicles reports that he took measures to reunite the religious life of the long-sundered kingdoms.[41] As part of this undertaking a significant portion of the two religious literatures was brought together. This would be done by scribes of the royal establishment, such

---

[39] Gen. 9:24–27; 25:23; 49:2–27; Exod. 15:1–18, 21; 17:16; Num. 10:35–36; 21:14–15, 17–18, 27–30; 23:7–10, 18–24; 24:3–9, 15–24; Deut. 32:1–43; Josh. 6:26; 10:12–13; Judg. 5:2–31; 15:16; 1 Sam. 18:7 = 29:5; 2 Sam. 1:19–27; 23:1–7; 1 Kings 8:12–13.

[40] Num. 21:14; Josh. 10:13; 2 Sam. 1:18. *Jashar* means "upright," and is used as an epithet of Yahweh in Deut. 32:4; Pss. 25:8; 92:15 (Heb. 92:16).

[41] Isa. 36:3, 22; cf. Jer. 36:10–12, 20; 2 Chron. 29–32.

as those referred to (as noted above) in Proverbs 25:1: "These are additional proverbs of Solomon which the men of Hezekiah king of Judah copied out [or took over, transmitted]."

Both Isaiah and Jeremiah denounced the politically minded court counselors for their pro-Egyptian policies that implied distrust of the power of Yahweh to protect his people.[42] And Jeremiah, in 8:8, accuses the temple scribes of having falsified the law of Yahweh, while boasting of their professional status as wise men. There are some hints that in this period schools existed for the instruction of children and youth. His opponents mock Isaiah as a teacher of infants, "precept upon precept . . . line upon line." God is sometimes pictured as a teacher.[43] Isaiah himself is assigned this role in the heavily ironical words of his call to prophesy. Again, there are glimpses of an ordinary scribe at work in the person of Baruch; at one point he is put in charge of business documents, and at another he takes dictation from the prophet.[44]

When Jerusalem fell to Nebuchadnezzar in 597 B.C., King Jehoiachin and his court were exiled to Babylonia. Along with the *sarim*, or high officers of state, the lesser officials known as *sarisim* were taken.[45] Priests, prophets, and scribes must have carried with them in their baggage much of what has survived of preexilic Hebrew writings. Undoubtedly parts of Proverbs and possibly the Book of Job were included.

After Babylon in turn had been conquered by Cyrus the

---

[42] Isa. 29:13–16; 30:1–5; 31:1–3; Jer. 2:17–18; 4:22; 9:23–24 (Heb. 9:22–23).
[43] Isa. 28:9–10, 26. The Hebrew of v. 10 may refer to teaching of the alphabet. See also for the exilic period, Isa. 50:4–6; 54:13.
[44] Isa. 6:9–10; Jer. 32:11–14.
[45] 2 Kings 24:12. The *sarisim* were not necessarily eunuchs, as de Vaux points out in *Ancient Israel* (1961), p. 121.

Persian in 538, many of the Jewish exiles returned at intervals to Jerusalem. Judah became a semi-independent temple state. Now the temple scribes and the wisdom teachers of the schools assumed new prominence. Supreme political authority was of course retained by the Persian state, but local and religious authority devolved largely upon the custodians of the national religious tradition. That tradition, moreover, was beginning to take form in sacred books, with all that this implied for the importance of learning.

Soon after Nehemiah had served as governor in the fifth century B.C. and had rebuilt the city walls, the priest Ezra appeared on the scene bearing the official title "secretary of the law of the God of heaven," and bringing with him a copy of the Torah in approximately its present form. He had been commissioned by the imperial authorities to proclaim the Torah as obligatory on all Jews and to enact heavy penalties for those who transgressed its provisions. But the Torah was much more than a code of laws; it was the book of Israel's covenant with her God, of her fundamental beliefs, of her identity as a people. It was the source and summation of her religious wisdom.[46]

At this point the religious wing of the older wisdom tradition, which, like the secular wing, had retained its orientation toward individuals and had stood aloof from the concern of priests and prophets with their "salvation history," now began to abandon this aloofness. Wise men and scribes turned to the study and exposition of the written Torah as their primary professional interest. A new kind of personal piety emerged which found its delight in meditating on the divine will and wisdom embodied in the sacred writings. A more specifically religious (and, indeed,

[46] Ezra 7:11–26; Neh. 8:1–9:3; 9:38 (Heb. 10:1); cf. Deut. 4:6.

Yahwistic) note was introduced into the wisdom materials used by teachers for the instruction of youth. And finally, though this did not become fully evident until the Hellenistic period, theological reflection on the origin and nature of wisdom as an objective entity connected this creative divine reality with the revelation of the Torah to Israel.[47]

These developments, however, did not bring an end to the secular wisdom of the common life. Not all men were religious, and of those who were, then as now, many would be inarticulate and quite content to leave theology to the experts. Popular sayings and maxims expressing the shrewd common sense of the anonymous observer continued to appear and pass into use under the changing conditions in society. The teachers' epigrams took on a more contemporary dress. In Sirach there is an awareness that man in the Hellenistic period now lived in a cosmopolitan society rather than within the confines of his ancestral land.[48] For example, the most probable meaning of the saying in Qoheleth 11:1 (RSV), "Cast your bread upon the waters," is embodied in the NEB translation "Send your grain across the seas," with its reference to the risks that must be taken in maritime commerce. Furthermore, the old conflict between secular and religious interpretations of wisdom emerged again as an antithesis between revelational theology and philosophical humanism, the former represented by wisdom Psalms, Sirach, and the Wisdom of Solomon, the latter by Agur and Qoheleth. That Qoheleth's radical questioning of traditional beliefs won a response among scholars, as well as among the laity, is evident from the encomiums appended in 12:9–11 to the edition of his teachings. On the other hand, the cautionary postscript in verses 13–14 is clearly from the hand of a more orthodox copyist.

[47] Neh. 8:7–8; Sir. 39:1–8; Pss. 1:2; 19:7–11 (Heb. 19:8–12); 119; Prov. 1–9; 16:1–11; 30:5–6; 8:22–31; Sir. 24:1–12, 23–29.
[48] Sir. 10:8; 11:5; 13:16; 34:10; 39:4.

The Biblical Wisdom Literature

The Wisdom literature of the Old Testament is marked by distinctive interests and characteristic literary forms and vocabulary. To immerse oneself in these writings of the Hebrew sages is the best way to come to understand the wisdom phenomenon.

The principal works in question are three, five, or seven in number, according to different reckonings. Proverbs, Job, and Qoheleth are found in the Hebrew Bible. The larger canon of the Old Testament in Greek[49] includes also Sirach and the Wisdom of Solomon.[50] The number seven of ancient church tradition adds Psalms and the Song of Songs, which are grouped with the other five as poetic works in the Septuagint. Possibly the reason was that Solomon was credited with the composition of songs as well as proverbs. Again, certain wisdom Psalms[51] stand out as bearing the distinctive marks of that tradition in thought and language.

It may be significant that those of the above works that are preserved in the Hebrew Bible all belong to the last of its three divisions, Law, Prophets, and Writings. This division was the latest to be officially accepted (at the end of the first century A.D.) as canonical scripture. It is also the most miscellaneous in its contents. In addition to the three principal wisdom books and the two poetic books named above, most of the remainder have some connec-

---

[49] The oldest translation of the Hebrew Bible was made for Greek-speaking Jews of the Diaspora before the Christian era and before the outer limits of the canon had been set. It is known as the Septuagint and was the form of the Bible most widely used by the early Christian church.

[50] More appropriately known simply as *Sapientia (Wisdom)* in the Vulg., since (as Jerome recognized) a work written in Greek in the first century B.C. could have had no direct connection with the Solomon of history.

[51] Pss. 1, 32, 34, 37, 49, 112, some others. See below, pp. 192–201.

tion with the wisdom tradition. Ezra-Nehemiah recounts the arrival of the priest-scribe Ezra with his scroll(s) of the Torah, and the beginnings of scribal activities in its study and exposition. Ruth can be read as a parable on the acceptance of Moabites. The stories in Esther and Daniel 1–6 turn in part on the superior wisdom of Jewish piety, and in Daniel 7–12 the secret meaning of his visions comes to the seer by revelation.

To these must be added from the Greek and Latin Bibles several other works: Tobit, a morality tale including two short collections of proverbs and precepts; Baruch, the second part of which is a poem urging Israel to relearn the wisdom whose neglect has led to her misfortunes; and three highly colored parabolic tales added in Greek to the canonical book of Daniel. The last appear in the English Apocrypha under the titles Susanna and Bel and the Dragon.

Why is it that by far the greater part of the wisdom literature is thus concentrated in the third division of the Hebrew canon? One reason is that, although the wisdom tradition is as old as Israel's life as a people in Canaan, its literary products are late preexilic or postexilic in date. The second reason may be the explanation of the first, namely, that the older wisdom tradition was quite remote in its interests and methods from the religiously dominant priestly and prophetic traditions. Even in the existing books such passages as Proverbs 16:6 and 21:3 have almost the appearance of a polemic against formal cultic requirements: "By loyalty and integrity guilt is atoned for," and "the doing of right and justice is more acceptable to Yahweh than [the offering of] sacrifice." (AB). Similar independence of the historical theology of Israel is evident in the freedom with which the writers of Job and Qoheleth raise philosophic and theological questions.

At the same time there was a profound cleavage within

the wisdom tradition itself. Proverbs is basically conservative, pragmatic, optimistic, and life-affirming. Job and Qoheleth challenge traditional concepts on the grounds of moral and intellectual integrity. Yet both sides are in search of understanding and of a structural principle that would provide a satisfactory basis for life and thought. By generalizing from common human experience, the first tried to formulate guidelines for a good life. But for intellectually acute and morally sensitive individuals this was not enough. These sought to understand the meaning of life for man, the meaning of the anomalies of suffering and injustice, and the possibility of the knowledge of God. The quest led the poet of Job, as it was later to lead the writers of chapter 8 in the introduction to Proverbs and of the Wisdom of Solomon, to daring exploration of new theological ideas. Wisdom was for them no longer simply the state of being prudent and reflective. It was conceptualized as a structure of meaning, a divine order, a creative power that was God's agent in his relationship to man and the universe.

The chief literary forms found in Proverbs, Job, and Qoheleth are: the sentence saying or proverb; the rhetorical question; the short admonitory precept and its expansion into longer discourses; soliloquy and debate; descriptive, metaphorical, and contemplative poetry; the imaginative tale and the illustrative anecdote. The two major works from the Hellenistic period show many of the same forms and add others. Sirach resembles Proverbs in its use of proverbs, precepts, and questions for purposes of instruction, together with contemplative poems and prayers. The Wisdom of Solomon is farther from the traditional forms. Written in Greek, its form is that of a diatribe or controversial discourse, stating the case for Judaism by relating it to Greek philosophical thought. The author affirms that righteousness is the source of the cardinal virtues, and wisdom is spoken of in terms of the universal reason.

Thus wisdom in Israel was a way of thinking and speaking, with a distinctive vocabulary and literary forms. It sought, in the first place, to provide guidance for living by propounding rules of moral order and, in the second place, to explore the meaning of life through reflection, speculation, and debate. It was a striving for a structure of order, meaning, and value through cultivation of the mind and conscience. Its authority might be compared to that of the prophet's words, or the inspired decision of a king.[52] Yet it was primarily internal, the disciplined intelligence and integrity of men who sought to understand what they had observed and experienced, and to persuade others of the truth they saw.

[52] Jer. 18:18; 1 Sam. 14:20; Isa. 11:1–2. See P.A.H. deBoer, "The Counsellor," *VT Supp. III* (1955), p. 56.

2
The International Context

HEBREW WISDOM was by no means a unique phenomenon in the ancient world. On the contrary, its literature has been found to have much in common with similar records from contemporary and older cultures, notably those of Egypt and Mesopotamia. As already observed, the Old Testament Wisdom books bear few marks of the distinctively Israelite beliefs found in the Law and the Prophets. They have been called "documents of Hebrew humanism."[1] Their oldest roots are in a "lay" folk wisdom concerning human experiences and relationships that had been handed down from immemorial antiquity, as in other traditional societies. More sophisticated developments had to await the dissemination of the art of writing[2] and the growth of literatures.

The discovery that "from the Nile to the Tigris an essentially similar Wisdom literature came into existence and was cultivated"[3] is comparatively recent. It was prompted by the publication in 1923 of an Egyptian work, the In-

---
[1] O. S. Rankin, *Israel's Wisdom Literature* (1936), p. 3.
[2] Writing came into use in the fourth millennium B.C. Alphabetic scripts were invented ca. 1500 B.C. See R. J. Williams, "Writing," *IDB* (1962).
[3] W. Baumgartner, *Israelitische und altorientalische Weisheit* (1933), p. 19.

struction of Amen-em-ope, which proved to have a close yet problematical relationship to a distinct section of the Book of Proverbs, 22:17–24:22. This opened the eyes of scholars to the fact that the Egyptian and Mesopotamian literatures display a wide range of parallels to Job and Qoheleth as well as to Proverbs. The basic work of critical comparison was carried out by a group of scholars between 1925 and 1936. It has continued to the present, with constantly expanding supporting evidence.[4]

"Palestine was a corridor for ideas as well as for armies," as Gressmann remarks.[5] The ideas were transmitted by men, in their heads and, increasingly, in documents which they carried either in the form of clay tablets from Mesopotamia or of papyrus scrolls from Egypt. The evidence suggests that the mysterious skill of writing brought into existence something like an international corps of professional scribes, who traveled from the chief centers of the literary art and offered their services in localities where this was less developed.[6] As a result, the ideas as well as the skills they taught took root outside their places of origin. Local scribes, having learned the rudiments of the profession, would migrate to the more ancient and famous centers for more advanced instruction. The explanation of the resemblance between Proverbs 22:17–24:22 and the Instructions of Amen-em-ope, as well as the differences, may well be that a Hebrew scribe reproduced with modifications what he could remember of the Egyptian work, filling out the sayings to the identical number of thirty with material of his own.[7]

The Old Testament itself fully recognizes this interna-

[4] See R. B. Y. Scott, "The Study of the Wisdom Literature," *Interpretation* xxiv, no. 1 (January 1970): 20–45.
[5] H. Gressmann, *Israels Spruchweisheit im Zusammenhang der Weltliteratur* (1925), p. 7.
[6] Note the presence of a Babylonian scribe at an Assyrian court; Lambert, *BWL*, p. 20.
[7] See below, pp. 29–30, 33, 45, 57.

tional feature of Wisdom and its more famous centers in other lands. Solomon's wisdom is said to have been superior to that of "the people of the east" and of Egypt, superior indeed to that "of all men,"[8] some of the more famous of whom are then named. The "people of the east" were the peoples of the steppe and desert country east of Palestine and not, as might have been expected, of the city states of Mesopotamia. This is clear from Job 1:3 where Job is pictured as one of their great sheiks.[9] When "the wise men of Babylon" are mentioned, as in Isaiah 47:9 ff. and Daniel 5:7 ff., the reference is to magicians, astrologers, and experts in the interpretation of omens and dreams rather than to the authors of wisdom writings in the Hebrew sense, of which also there were a good many.[10] The same restricted sense is found also in some biblical references to Egyptian wise men (see Gen. 41:8 and Exod. 7:11) and to those of the Persian court (Esther 1:13). On the other hand, the term as used in Isaiah 19:11–12 denotes political counselors of the pharaoh. Coming nearer home, the wisdom or special skills of the Phoenicians is drawn attention to in Ezekiel 27:8–9 and 28:4–5.[11] The Edomites, Israel's cousins, and immediate neighbors, won her grudging respect for sapience.[12]

[8] 1 Kings 4:30–31, EVV. The plausible suggestion to read here "all the Edomites" is rejected with good reason by M. Noth, *Könige*, Biblischer Kommentar ix, no. 2 (1965): p. 82.
[9] See also Gen. 29:1; Judg. 6:3; Isa. 11:14; Ezek. 25:4.
[10] See Isa. 44:25; Dan. 1:20; 2:12. The distinction in terminology is historically correct. "Generally 'wisdom' refers to skill in cult and magic lore. . . . Though this term is thus foreign to ancient Mesopotamia, it has been used for a group of texts which correspond in subject matter with the Hebrew Wisdom books." Lambert, *BWL*, p. 1.
[11] Note also the mythological wisdom ascribed in Ezek. 28:11 ff. to the king of Tyre. This will be discussed in another connection, see p. 100.
[12] See Jer. 49:7; Obad. 8; Job 2:11. Extensive Edomite influence in the Old Testament is posited by R. H. Pfeiffer, *Introduction to the Old Testament* (1941), pp. 35, 669 and passim.

The Wisdom Literature of Egypt

For comparative purposes the most important extrabiblical literature in the area under discussion is the Egyptian. The proximity of Egypt, one of the superpowers, meant that from the middle of the second millennium B.C. Palestine was at most periods either directly under Egyptian political control or threatened by it. Trade relations were close and relatively constant. Not surprisingly, therefore, the Egyptian was the most pervasive of all external cultural influences, at least until the Hellenistic period. Among these influences was that of the ancient and famous Egyptian wisdom tradition.

In Egypt, as in Israel, two divergent and almost contradictory tendencies are found in wisdom writings. The first, and undoubtedly older, type is conservative in outlook and purpose, seeking to pass on and inculcate the moral code and beliefs of social tradition. The second (of which Job and Qoheleth are the chief biblical examples) is more intellectual and sophisticated; it questions traditional values and beliefs on the grounds of moral integrity. Both types, however, are parts of the same urgent striving for an order of meaning and values that would illuminate understanding and provide guidance for human behavior. In Egypt this was more than a quest, it was a faith. *Ma'at*, the comprehensive idea of order, truth, goodness, justice, was regarded as a divine reality creating and supporting the cosmos and the world of men. The cosmic order and the moral order were one, to be realized by men in wise thought and speech and act.[13]

It follows that in Egyptian wisdom writing the teaching function was primary. The most characteristic documents

---

[13] See H. H. Schmid, *Wesen und Geschichte der Weisheit* (1966), pp. 17–22; H. Frankfort and others, *The Intellectual Adventure of Ancient Man* (1946), pp. 14, 108–09.

are the so-called Instructions, which usually take the form of admonitions and advice given by a king or high officer to his son and prospective successor. The oldest of more than a dozen examples dates back to the Pyramid Age, and the latest to the fifth and fourth centuries B.C. One of the earliest is that of Ptah-hotep, vizier of a Fifth Dynasty pharaoh. He draws the king's attention to his own advancing age and petitions that his son be designated as his successor. The king agrees on condition that the son be suitably trained to "set an example for the children of officials." "Teach him first about speaking."[14] This refers not merely to the ability to use language correctly and effectively, but also to prudence and integrity in dealing with all kinds of persons and situations in the course of official duties.

The vizier responds by instructing his son (and those who will later ponder his words), "about wisdom and about the rules of good speech, as of advantage to him who will hearken." The young man must be modest, reliable, self-controlled, honest, teachable, respectful to superiors, and of good moral behavior. Above all he must order his life according to justice and truth, for "the strength of justice is that it lasts." The breadth and depth of the concept *good speaking* is indicated in the maxim: "Good speech is more hidden than the emerald, but it may be found with maidservants at the grindstones."

An example of the same genre from the Middle Kingdom is the Instruction made by his father for the pharaoh Meri-ka-re. This was a time when political instability had shaken confidence in the old order of things and the old king's counsel is concerned with practical measures for

[14] The translations of the Instructions excerpted are those of John A. Wilson in *ANET*, pp. 412 ff. and, for 'Onchsheshonqy, of S. R. K. Glanville in his *Catalogue of Demotic Papyri in the British Museum*, II (1955).

defense of the state, as well as with the qualities of character needed by the holder of "a goodly office, the kingship." Once more, emphasis is laid on craftsmanship in speech as a mark of intelligence, firmness, and wisdom. "The tongue is a sword . . . and speech is more valorous than any fighting." The king's strength rests on the love of his people and the support of his nobles, but even more on his own justice and integrity. Therefore, "do justice whilst thou endurest upon earth. . . . Do not oppress the widow. . . . Do not slaughter. . . . Thou shouldst punish with beatings and with arrests." The king's behavior will have eternal consequences when, "after death . . . his deeds are placed beside him in heaps." He must "act for the god," remembering that "more acceptable is the character of one upright in heart than the [sacrifice of an] ox [by] the evildoer."[15] The expectation of judgment after death is here a decisive consideration.

Under the New Kingdom a work of the same type appeared, ascribed this time to a scribe, Ani, rather than to a king. The prized qualities of the older writings are echoed, as in the counsel, "Do not talk a lot. Be silent and thou wilt be happy. . . . Thou shouldst not express thy [whole] heart to the stranger"; and again, "Thou shouldst not sit when another who is older than thou is standing." There is a new emphasis on family obligations, "Take to thyself a wife while thou art [still] a youth, that she may produce a son for thee. . . . Thou shouldst not supervise [too closely] thy wife in her [own] house. . . . Let thy eye have regard, while thou art silent, that thou mayest recognize her abilities. . . . Set thy eye on how thy mother gave birth to thee, and all [her] bringing thee up as well." Restraint in speech has its place also in prayer, "The dwell-

---

[15] See 1 Sam. 15:22; Hos. 6:6, quoted in Matt. 9:13; cf. Prov. 21:3.

ing of God, its abomination is clamor. Pray thou with a loving heart, all the words of which are hidden . . . and he will accept thy offering."[16]

The Instruction of Amen-em-ope is the best known of this type of Egyptian wisdom writings because of its close resemblance to parts of Proverbs 22:17 ff. The reputed author is a royal official who addresses his youngest son, also an official. A new feature in the literary form is extensive use of proverbial sayings and figurative illustrations in addition to the precepts and admonitions characteristic of the aforementioned works. For example,

Better is bread when the heart is happy, than riches with sorrow.
The ship of the covetous is left [in] the mud, while the boat of the silent man [has] a fair breeze.
As for the heated man . . . he is like a tree growing in the open . . . its end is reached in the shipyards, [or] it is floated far from its place, and the flame is its burial shroud. [But] the truly silent man holds himself apart.[17] He is like a tree growing in a [garden]. . . . Its fruit is sweet; its shade is pleasant; and its end is reached in the garden.

Many of the precepts and adages of Amen-em-ope resemble in form and spirit those of the Hebrew wisdom teachers, as the following examples show:

Do not carry off the landmark . . . nor encroach upon the boundaries of a widow.
Do not cry out against him whom thou hast attacked.
Better is a measure that the god gives thee than five thousand [taken] illegally.

---

[16] See Qoh. 5:1 (Heb. 4:17); Matt. 6:1–8.
[17] The "silent" man is master of his tongue and of his thought and action; the "heated" or passionate man has no self-control. The contrast corresponds to that of the wise man and the fool in the Book of Proverbs.

30 / *The Way of Wisdom*

Better is poverty in the hand of the god than riches in a storehouse.

Cast not thy heart in pursuit of riches.

Do not associate to thyself the heated man.

Do not talk with a man falsely; [it is] the abomination of the god.

One thing are the words which men say, another is that which the god does.[18]

It will be noticed how religion has become a powerful sanction for morality.

In a later work, the Instruction of 'Onchsheshonqy of the fifth century B.C., the proverbial form is still more prominent. The saying "He who digs a pit [for another man] will fall into it [himself]" is included here as well as four times in the Bible.[19] Many others of 'Onchsheshonqy's proverbs have a familiar ring: "Better a statue of stone for a son than a fool." "Do not send a fool on a large matter." "Do not undertake expense until you have set up your storehouse." "Do not speak hastily lest you give offense." "He who does not gather wood in summer will not be warm in winter." "If a woman is at peace with her husband, it is the will of God." "No man knows the day of misfortune." "Do a good deed and throw it into the river; when this dries up you shall find it."[20]

It is evident that this work is a collection of proverbs and precepts current in Egypt at the time of writing, even though its composition is ascribed to a father facing a long term of imprisonment and wishing to counsel his son. The

[18] Cf. Prov. 22:28; 23:10; 19:28; 24:28; 10:2; 19:1; 23:4; 22:24; 12:22; 16:9.

[19] Prov. 26:27; Ps. 7:15 (Heb. 7:16); Qoh. 10:8; Sir. 27:26. Cf. the story of Haman hanged on the gallows he built for Mordecai (Esther 7:9–10) and the "engineer hoist with his own petar" (*Hamlet*, act 3, sc. 4).

[20] Cf. Prov. 17:21; 26:6; 24:27; 18:6; 20:4; 19:14; Qoh. 8:7–8; 11:1.

theme of advice given at parting recurs in Tobit, chapter 4, and in a story from the Middle Kingdom in Egypt in which a sailor encourages his son leaving for school by comparing various occupations unfavorably with the scribal profession.[21]

Other compositions that can be classed as Wisdom literature because of their didactic or philosophic tone are the poem on the Divine Attributes of Pharaoh, addressed to a man's children that they might know "a manner of living aright," and the Song of the Harper which expresses a philosophy of *carpe diem* not unlike that of Horace and Qoheleth: "Follow thy desire as long as thou shalt live. Put myrrh upon thy head and clothing of fine linen upon thee. . . . Make holiday, and weary not therein. Behold, it is not given to a man to take his property with him. Behold, there is not one who departs who comes back again."[22]

The entertaining Protests of the Eloquent Peasant[23] who appealed for justice against a man who had wronged him, is wisdom literature of a distinct type—that of instruction through the telling of a story which holds the pupils' interest.[24] The peasant's trenchant and epigrammatic speeches of protest arouse sympathy and admiration, and at the same time underline the necessity of justice and moral behavior. "Doing justice is the breath of the nose. . . . The great man who is covetous is not really great. . . . If thou veilest thy face against violence, who then will punish meanness? . . . His property is the breath of the suffering man, and he who takes it away stops up his nose. . . . Cheating diminishes justice. . . . Do justice for the

[21] For this Satire on the Trades see *ANET*, pp. 432–34.
[22] *ANET*, pp. 432–34. Cf. Horace *Odes* 1.11; Qoh. 9:7–10.
[23] *ANET*, pp. 407b–10b.
[24] On such stories and political "novels," cf. R. N. Whybray, *The Succession Narrative* (1968), pp. 103–05.

sake of the Lord of justice.... Now justice lasts to eternity; it goes down into the necropolis with him who does it ... he is remembered for goodness. That is a principle of the word of god. Is it the hand-scales [?]—[then] it does not tilt.... The balance of men is their tongue."

The above story has some bearing also on the theme of a suffering just man's cry for justice, found in the Book of Job. Another feature of Job, the radical questioning of traditional religious beliefs, appears in an Egyptian work known as A Dispute over Suicide (or "the argument with his soul of the man weary of life").[25] "Goodness is rejected everywhere.... The land is left to those who do wrong. ... I am laden with wretchedness.... Death is in my sight today like the odor of myrrh, like sitting under an awning on a breezy day ... like the clearing of the sky ... like the longing of a man to see his house [again] after he has spent many years held in captivity." Such yearning for release through death recalls the anguished outcry with which the Joban dialogue begins in chapter 3: "Why did I not die from birth? For then I should have lain down and been quiet ... [where] the wicked cease from troubling, and the weary are at rest; ... the small and the great are there, and the slave is free from his master.... Why is light given to him who is in misery, and life to the bitter in soul?" In the Egyptian work, however, despair is not followed by an outcry against divine injustice.

Egyptian wisdom thus shows some real similarities and points of contact with Old Testament wisdom in both its conservative and radical aspects. The father-to-son form of moral instruction, the didactic use of proverbs and precepts, the high value placed on the scribe as a wise and learned man, the idea of human wisdom as conformity to

[25] *ANET*, pp. 405–07.

a divinely established cosmic and moral order, the grounding of ethics in religion, and the exploration of problems of the value of life and the meaning of justice—these comprise a common element. The virtues and vices about which young men are counseled are much the same and are judged in similar fashion. In addition to the apparently direct relationship of Proverbs 22:17 ff. to the Instruction of Amen-em-ope, there is evidence of Egyptian influence in the ideas of the restrained speech of the "silent" man, and of Yahweh's "weighing of the heart." The latter idiom is derived ultimately from the Egyptian picture of judgment after death, when a man's heart is weighed in the balance against *Ma'at* or truth.[26]

The differences here between Hebrew and Egyptian wisdom are chiefly theological. They are most obvious in the contrast between Hebrew ideas of reward and punishment in this life and the Egyptian view that judgment will take place in the hereafter. There is also no close counterpart in Egyptian wisdom to the radical probing of problems of justice, theodicy, and faith in the Book of Job, or to the rationalist agnosticism of Qoheleth.

A quite different area of comparison is brought to our attention by what is said in 1 Kings 4:33 (Heb. 5:13) about the subject matter of Solomon's proverbs and songs: "He spoke of trees . . . beasts . . . birds . . . reptiles . . . and fish." Yet the proverbs of Solomon[27] in the later collections deal almost exclusively with human character and behavior rather than with such natural phenomena. An explanation of this striking contrast is suggested by the fact that included under the same heading, "Teaching," are writings like those discussed above, and also writings concerned with phenomena external to man. The latter

---

[26] See Prov. 10:19; 11:12; 13:3; 17:27; 16:2; Job 31:6.
[27] Note the headings in Prov. 10:1 and 25:1.

are natural science and natural philosophy in embryo. In other words, the Egyptians distinguished knowledge from wisdom, though not explicitly and though both were forms of teaching or learning. There is other evidence in the Old Testament, in addition to the passage in Kings already mentioned, that somewhat the same situation existed in Israel under Egyptian influence.

The principal documentary representatives of this Egyptian protoscience are known as *Onomastica* or "noun lists."[28] One of these from about 1100 B.C., that of Amenope, is headed "Beginning of the Teaching about all that is, which Ptah has created." There follows a list of 610 subjects, each represented by a noun or nominal phrase "about the heaven and what pertains thereto, about the earth and what is in it," and so on through an orderly classification of divine and human beings, animate creatures, inanimate objects, natural features, meteorological phenomena, cities, buildings, food and drink, et cetera. There are no definitions or descriptions. The point is that these "names" provide a comprehensive outline of knowledge. The comparable feature in the Old Testament is the series of phenomena in heaven and earth referred to in poems found in Job 38–39, Psalm 148, Sirach 43, and the Song of the Three Youths inserted in the Greek version of Daniel 3.[29]

The Wisdom Literature of Mesopotamia

The second extensive wisdom literature forming part of the cultural context of Hebrew wisdom was that of the

[28] Cf. A. H. Gardiner, *Ancient Egyptian Onomastica* (1947); A. Alt, "Die Weisheit Salomos," *TLZ* 76 (1951): pp. 139–44.

[29] As pointed out by G. von Rad in his article "Hiob xxxviii und die altägyptische Weisheit," *VT Supp. III* (1955): pp. 293–301. The Creation story in Gen. 1 also may have been influenced by the classification lists of natural phenomena; cf. S. Herrmann in *TLZ* 76 (1951): pp. 413 ff.

Sumerians, Babylonians, and Assyrians. Mesopotamia was physically more remote from Israel than Egypt, and its direct cultural influence in Canaan was more intermittent. Nevertheless it is a fact, however this is to be accounted for, that in several important areas such as mythology, law codes, and wisdom writings, the Old Testament has greater affinities with Mesopotamian than with Egyptian literature.

One reason for this was perhaps a cultural affinity. The Hebrew patriarchs were remembered as having migrated to Canaan from an earlier home on the upper Euphrates, whereas, in the national tradition, Egypt had been the oppressor nation from which Yahweh had delivered his people. More important, in the second millennium, Akkadian, the language of Babylonia, had become an international language current in Canaan.[30] This again must be connected with the fact that Babylonian scribes served abroad and carried with them their knowledge of Babylonian literature.[31] There can be no question but that this literature was known among the Canaanites and was passed on by them to the Israelites. When in the eighth to sixth centuries Palestine successively became part of the Assyrian and neo-Babylonian empires, the influence of Mesopotamian culture was again felt; not least after the fall of Jerusalem in 587 B.C. and the transportation to Babylonia of the upper stratum of Judaean society, including its intelligentsia. In the Persian period and later the formative influence on Judaism of the continuing Jewish community resident in Babylonia was profound.

The wisdom tradition in Babylonia was very ancient.

---

[30] As it was in the Amarna letters, official correspondence from Canaan actually addressed to the Egyptian court! See W. F. Albright and T. O. Lambdin, in *Cambridge Ancient History*, vol. 1, chap. iv, fasc. 54, rev. ed. (1966), p. 16; chap. xx, fasc. 51, pp. 1–23.

[31] See Lambert, *BWL*, p. 20.

Its beginnings, and indeed its basic developments, can be traced back to the Sumerians who created the first civilization of Mesopotamia, 3300–2300 B.C., in a group of city-states near the mouths of the two rivers. They invented the cuneiform method of writing on clay tablets which was taken over, together with a good deal of their literature, by the later Babylonians and Assyrians. In fact, most Sumerian literature is known from copies made by Babylonian scholars after 1700 B.C. In the area of what in particular can be called "Wisdom literature," though the Babylonians made modifications and introduced new ideas, the literary forms typical of Mesopotamia were mostly originated by the Sumerians.[32]

The first of these is the Noun List, or inventory of phenomena, corresponding to the Egyptian *Onomasticon*.[33] This has been aptly called "a continuous book-keeping of the state of knowledge"[34] because these lists were constantly being revised and expanded. Their significance is that they undertook to classify phenomena in related groups—plants, animals, utensils, occupations, towns, stars, and gods—and thus to begin the process of rational thought concerning man's relationship to the world external to himself.

The next step was to discriminate between related concepts and to compare and evaluate them, noting that some occur in pairs of opposites such as light and darkness, cold and heat.[35] In this connection the Sumerians created a

[32] See Lambert, *BWL*, pp. xix (Time Chart), 1–20; S. N. Kramer, *History Begins at Sumer* (1959); — art. "Sumer," *IDB* iv, pp. 454–63.

[33] See pp. 33–34 above. The form probably originated with the Sumerians.

[34] H. H. Schmid, *Wesen und Geschichte*, p. 97. The present writer is much indebted to Schmid's illuminating discussion.

[35] See for such pairs of opposites, Gen. 8:22; Qoh. 3:2–8, Sir. 42:24, and von Rad's comments on "Twin-formulae" in his *Old Testament Theology, I*, Eng. trans. (1962), p. 418.

special literary form, the disputation fable, in which their claims to superiority are debated by summer and winter, cattle and grain, the bird and the fish. In one example there are four contestants, the fox, the dog, the wolf, and the lion. The genre was taken over by the Babylonians, as in the fables of the tamarisk and the date palm,[36] and of the ox and the horse. The closest biblical parallel is Jotham's fable of the trees and the thornbush in Judges 9:7–15.

The major category of proverbs includes, along with pithy observations on human character and experience, short anecdotes, parables, and even fables, metaphorical of human experiences and situations. An example of the last-named is the episode of the dog who went to a banquet, but, when he saw the bones they had for him, decided he could do better elsewhere.[37] The same satirical note appears in the anecdotes of the fox who pretended to be a lion or a wolf, but fled from dogs, and of the mosquito who apologized to an elephant for stealing a ride.[38] Popular sayings which comment on human character and behavior, as well as more sophisticated adages and maxims, were assembled by Babylonian scribes in standard collections. Some examples will illustrate their tone and typical content:

The dog recognizes a man who loves him.
The poor man is always curious about what he will have to eat.

[36] See *ANET Supp.* (1969), pp. 156–57; Lambert, *BWL*, pp. 150–64, 175–89; Kramer, *History Begins*, pp. 136–42.
[37] E. I. Gordon, "A New Look at the Wisdom of Sumer and Akkad," *Bib. Or.* xvii, nos. 3–4 (1960): p. 149.
[38] See Lambert, *BWL*, pp. 217, 219. The second of these reappears in Aesop, and Gordon has identified over one hundred Aesopic fables in the Sumerian collections. See Gordon, "A New Look," pp. 138–39.

Tell a lie, [then] tell the truth—it will be considered a lie.
Wealth is distant, poverty is close by.
Winter is evil; summer has sense.
A shepherd should not [try to] be a farmer.
In a city without dogs, the fox is overseer.
The wise man is girded with a loin-cloth; the fool is clad in a scarlet cloak.
A house without an owner is [like] a woman without a husband.[39]

Fables, parables, and metaphors partake to some degree of the nature of riddles in that their meaning has to be read beneath the surface of the words used or the picture drawn. Such verbal or logical puzzles deliberately constructed to require ingenuity for discovery of their meaning, as, for example, the riddle propounded by Samson to the wedding guests in Judges 14:10–18, are uncommon in Sumerian literature. Gordon gives a sample from Ur: "One whose eyes are not open enters it, one whose eyes have been opened comes out from it. Its solution—the Academy."[40]

Corresponding broadly to the Egyptian father-to-son Instructions are two groups of Mesopotamian wisdom texts. Both of these contain moral and practical counsel; the distinction is that in one case the counselor is given a prehistoric mythological setting. In one form of the Sumerian deluge myth the Noah of the story, Ziusudra, is instructed in the right conduct which will ensure against a new destruction. Unfortunately only a fragment of these Instructions of Šuruppak (Ziusudra's father) has been published. A more fully preserved composition has been called by Kramer "The Farmer's Almanac." In it a farmer of ancient times instructs his son about irrigation, plowing,

[39] See Lambert, *BWL*, pp. 213–82; E. I. Gordon, *Sumerian Proverbs* (1959).
[40] Gordon, "A New Look," p. 142.

sowing, and harvesting; the writer declares that his agricultural expertness has come to the farmer from the god Ninurta.[41] The parallel with the wisdom oracle in Isaiah 28:23–29 is remarkable.

The second group of texts more closely resembles the Egyptian Instructions in their content and setting. In the Counsels of Wisdom from the mid-second millennium, the son addressed is expected to hold high office at court; he is warned against dishonesty, improper speech, bad companions, and unsuitable wives. Such admonitions as the following recall both the Egyptian Instructions and biblical proverbs:

Let your mouth be controlled and your speech guarded; let insolence and blasphemy be your abomination; speak nothing profane nor any untrue report. A talebearer is accursed. . . . Do not return evil to the man who disputes with you; requite with kindness your evil-doer, maintain justice to your enemy, smile on your adversary. . . . Every day worship your god. . . . In your wisdom study the tablet. . . . Sacrifice prolongs life, and prayer atones for guilt."[42]

A similar text has been called Counsels of a Pessimist because of its emphasis on the brevity of life: "Mankind and their achievements alike come to an end." The person addressed is exhorted to offer prayers and free will offerings, to attend to his livestock and his family, and to "banish misery and suffering from your side" because these produce bad dreams. One is reminded of Qoheleth's philosophy.[43] The Advice to a Prince recalls the queen mother's vigorous exhortations in Proverbs 31:1–9. The

[41] Lambert, *BWL*, pp. 92–94; Kramer, *History Begins*, pp. 65–69.
[42] Lambert, *BWL*, pp. 96–107; *ANET Supp.*, pp. 159–60.
[43] *BWL*, pp. 107–09; cf. Qoh. 2:15–25; 5:1–7 (Heb. 4:17–5:6).

Babylonian work couches its warnings more deferentially in the third person, and as a general hypothesis; for instance, "If a king does not heed justice, his people will be thrown into chaos, and his land will be devastated."[44]

Among the Aramaic papyri of the fifth century B.C. found at Elephantine in Egypt was a version of the Words of Ahiqar,[45] a quasi-legendary Assyrian court sage. The teachings are a collection of proverbs, precepts, riddles, short fables, and religious observations, all having points of contact with some Egyptian sayings, but even more with the biblical Book of Proverbs. Examples of the latter are,

Withhold not thy son from the rod, else thou wilt not be able to save [him] (cf. Proverbs 13:24; 23:13–14).
More than all watchfulness, watch thy mouth (cf. Proverbs 4:23–24; 13:3).
The wrath of a king, if thou be commanded, is a burning fire (cf. Proverbs 16:14).
If thou take a loan, give no rest to thyself until [thou repay] the loan (cf. Proverbs 6:1–5).
From thee is the arrow, but from God the [guidance] (cf. Proverbs 16:1).
Hunger makes bitterness sweet (cf. Proverbs 27:7).

As the positive, conservative, and didactic aspect of biblical wisdom is paralleled in such proverbs, the radical questioning of traditional ethics and beliefs that distinguishes Job and Qoheleth also has its counterpart in the Babylonian problem literature. The two issues that stand out most prominently are those of death and of the good man's unmerited suffering. The root difficulty was in reconciling these with the firmly established ethical doctrine that a man is rewarded or punished in this life according to

[44] *BWL*, pp. 110–15.
[45] *ANET*, pp. 427b–30b; A. Cowley, *Aramaic Papyri of the Fifth Century B.C.* (1923), pp. 204–48.

his behavior and his devotion to the gods. The goddess Ishtar is praised in hymns as the giver of joy, who guides mankind aright and causes the oppressed and mistreated to prosper. The beneficent sun god Shamash punishes evil-doers, protects fugitives, and favors the honest merchant and the doer of kind deeds.[46]

Why then must men die so soon, and why should they suffer when not conscious of wrongdoing? In the Epic of Gilgamesh the prehistoric hero, shocked by the death of his friend, endures incredible hardships in search of the secret of immortality—only to learn that "when the gods created mankind they assigned death to men, but held life in their keeping."[47] Far removed from the epic in tone and form is the satirical dialogue of a master with his obsequious servant, wrongly entitled the Dialogue of Pessimism.[48] The subject is the ambiguity of morals for master and slave, with death as the great equalizer. The dialogue is concluded with the master's question "What [then] is good?" and the slave's no longer subservient answer, "To have my neck broken and your neck broken and to be thrown into the river!"

More significant are the compositions dealing with the ethical and theological problem of the suffering of the innocent. The issue was first raised by Sumerian thinkers. Lambert quotes from an unpublished Sumero-Babylonian text which declares, "I have been treated as one who has committed a sin against his god," and notes the occurrence of the name Mina-arni, meaning "what is my guilt?"[49] Kramer has translated a Sumerian poem with the Joban

---

[46] See the Hymn to Ishtar, the Prayer of Lamentation to Ishtar, and the Hymn to Shamash, *ANET* pp. 383–85, 387–89; Lambert, *BWL*, pp. 121–38.
[47] *BWL*, pp. 11–12; *ANET*, pp. 72–99, esp. 88, 90.
[48] *BWL*, pp. 139–49; *ANET*, pp. 437–38.
[49] *BWL*, pp. 10–11.

motif under the title "Man and his God." In this a formerly rich, wise, and upright man is afflicted with suffering and illness. Since he apparently accepts as right the dictum of the sages that "never has a sinless child been born to its mother," his only recourse is to continue to praise his god and humbly pour out his supplications for deliverance. Finally "his god accepted the words which the man prayerfully confessed . . . the [?] which had smitten him like a [?] he dissipated."[50] No challenge is made to the justice of the god's dealing with man. The justice of the god is axiomatic, and so is the traditional belief in the causal relationship of deed and consequence. It is the argument of Eliphaz to Job, "Is not your fear of God your confidence? . . . Think now, who that was innocent ever perished? . . . Can mortal man be righteous before God? . . . Man is born to trouble. . . . As for me, I would seek God, and to God would I commit my cause."[51]

Two other extensive treatments of the same theme come from the Cassite period (1500–1200 B.C.) in Babylonia. The first of these is a monologue known by its opening line as "I will Praise the Lord of Wisdom."[52] In it the sufferer recounts how he has been forsaken by gods and men, has been afflicted by dreadful illnesses, and has found no succour in answer to his prayers and sacrifices. Yet, he says, "I gave attention to supplication and prayer; sacrifice [was] my rule; the day for reverencing the god was a joy to my heart." Like Job, he feels that he is being treated as a sinner, in spite of his piety. "I wish I knew that these things were pleasing to one's god! . . . Who

---

[50] S. N. Kramer, "Man and his God," *VT Supp. III* (1955): pp. 170–82; Kramer, *History Begins*, pp. 114–18; *ANET Supp.*, pp. 153–55.
[51] Job 4:6–7, 17; 5:7–8.
[52] Lambert, *BWL*, pp. 21–62; cf. p. 15; R. D. Biggs, in *ANET Supp.*, pp. 160–64.

knows the will of the gods in heaven?" He wonders why circumstances change suddenly without apparent reason: "He who was alive yesterday is dead today; for a minute he was dejected, suddenly he is exuberant. . . . [But] my god has not come to the rescue. . . . my grave was waiting." At last Marduk relents and sends messengers who appear in successive dreams to promise deliverance. Then "the Lord took hold of me, the Lord set me on my feet, the Lord gave me life, . . Marduk, he restored me." But the writer offers no explanation of why Marduk has allowed his faithful servant to suffer, and why he was inexplicably restored.

The second work, the so-called Babylonian Theodicy, resembles the Book of Job in presenting the issues in the form of a debate, in this case with a single friend instead of with three.[53] In broad outline the positions taken by the two sages correspond to those of Job and his counselors. The sufferer asserts that it is the wicked oppressors who prosper in this world, while he has been left an orphan and suffers ill health and poverty in spite of his piety. His opponent defends the traditional teaching of reward and punishment according to a man's deserts. He asserts dogmatically that this moral law of consequences is invariable, at least in general. "When you consider mankind as a whole . . . he who waits on his god has a protecting angel." (This is a significant qualification, since the injustice arises when the general law is taken as applying in every individual case.) Like Job, the sufferer here is desperate and without hope. He cries out for understanding of his predicament, "Can a life of bliss be assured? I wish I knew how!" The friend counsels patience and faith; the prosperity of the wicked is impermanent, and "the way of the gods is remote, . . . knowledge of it is difficult." The suf-

[53] *BWL*, pp. 63–91; Biggs, in *ANET Supp.*, pp. 165–68.

ferer is accused of perversity and blasphemy. But the friend is led into a further damaging admission; if the wicked are powerful it is because lies and injustice belong to the nature of man as the gods made him, so that the gods are ultimately responsible. The sufferer thus wins his point, yet still has no recourse except to continue to pray for divine mercy.

Before leaving the topic of Mesopotamian wisdom literature two other matters remain to be mentioned. Lambert remarks that Akkadian has no general term corresponding to the Hebrew word *ḥokmah*, "wisdom," and covering the broad spectrum of literature that has been discussed. The word *nēmequ*, "wisdom," is "rarely used with a moral content," but normally refers to skills in incantation and interpretation of omens.[54] The clarification of this linguistic point at the same time draws attention to the negative biblical view of the Babylonian expertise in magic, omens, and esoteric knowledge generally. Isaiah 47:9, 12–13 speaks of incantations and spells that will not be able to save Babylon from disaster. In 47:13 the counsels are not the advice of wise men but the omen readings of astrologers. In the Persian period and later, the term *Chaldaeans* had largely lost its ethnic sense and had come to mean Babylonian specialists in magical and cultic lore. This usage appears in Daniel 2:12, 10, 12, where (strangely enough) in Babylon itself "Chaldaeans" are listed as one type of such specialists who together form the class of wise men.[55]

A word should be said in conclusion about the institution through which Sumero-Babylonian wisdom writings were composed and transmitted—the Academy, *ē-dubba* (literally, "the house of tablets"). The invention of writing

---

[54] *BWL*, p. 1. See n. 10 above.
[55] In the fifth century B.C. Herodotus (1:181, 183) speaks of the Chaldaeans as a priestly class in Babylon.

required centers of instruction in this new skill, with its enormous importance for the development of civilized social life. By the middle of the third millennium such schools for scribes were well established in Sumer. The institution continued under the first dynasty of Babylon and was replaced in the Cassite period by hereditary scribal guilds. The significance of the *ē-dubba* for literature was twofold: Pupils were set to the copying and study of traditional texts, resulting in their preservation, and new compositions were produced by the master scribes. Thus "the Sumerian school came to be the center of culture and learning. Within its walls flourished the scholar, the 'scientist,' and the writer of poetry and prose."[56]

The Wisdom of the Peoples

The foregoing survey of wisdom writings from the two major civilizations which long antedated the rise of Israel demonstrates that the study of Hebrew wisdom must take place against a broad intercultural background. It will have shown also that there were differences as well as similarities in this matter between the Egyptians and the Sumero-Babylonians, and between both of them and Israel. Each tradition had its own distinctiveness due to living conditions, social structure, history, and religious beliefs. The only known example of direct literary dependence is that of Proverbs 22:17 ff. on the Instruction of Amen-em-ope, although some of the proverbs are so alike[57] that they

---

[56] S. N. Kramer, "Sumer," *IDB*, iv, pp. 462–63; see also, Kramer, *History Begins*, pp. 1–11; E. I. Gordon, *Sumerian Proverbs*, pp. 19–20; J. Nougayrol, in *Les Sagesses du Proche-Orient ancien* (1963), pp. 43 ff.

[57] E.g. "Hunger makes bitterness sweet" (The Words of Ahiqar, 188, *ANET*, p. 430); "To one who is hungry everything bitter is sweet" (Prov. 27:7).

may have migrated across cultural frontiers, as is the habit of proverbs.

Among the features shared by the wisdom traditions of the two great riverine civilizations are the extended Instructions or Counsels dealing with the proper behavior of youths aspiring to high position, cast in the father-to-son form; the encyclopedic noun lists; collections of proverbs and precepts; the high value placed on the scribal profession; and the feeling for a cosmic order with which the moral life of man ought to conform. But here a distinction must be made. To the Egyptians *Maʿat*—truth, right, justice—was the ultimate reality to which even the gods were subject. In Babylonia, right was what the gods willed, and this must be discovered through the study of omens. Man had been created to serve the gods and must not offend them. The Sumerian gods represented natural forces with which mankind must come to terms; they were not governed by moral standards as were the Babylonian gods who were conceived on the analogy of human beings. The Babylonian theologians "tried to reduce the conflicting elements in the universe to parts of a harmonious whole . . . [with] moral laws springing from the human conscience."[58]

In this later development, as in Egypt, religious belief became a sanction helping to enforce morality among men. Here again a difference emerges. The Egyptians expected judgment in the afterlife, whereas, in Mesopotamia as in Israel, reward or punishment by the gods in consequence of a man's deeds was looked for here and now. Because this did not square with experience, the problem of divine justice was raised in these two wisdom literatures as it was not in Egypt. This radical questioning, moreover, was also in both cases the challenging of a strongly held conserva-

[58] Lambert, *BWL*, p. 7.

tive belief to the contrary, enshrined in the cult and the community's laws and taught in the schools. In both Israel and Mesopotamia emphasis was laid on the collecting of anonymous proverbs and precepts for purposes of moral instruction. Such popular adages were supplemented by proverbs composed for the specific purpose of inculcating ethical standards related to religious belief.

The comparison of the wisdom literatures of Mesopotamia and Egypt with that of the Bible is possible because so much of these literatures has been preserved. There are no surviving documents of the wisdom of Edom and of Phoenicia which the biblical writers refer to in terms suggesting that these too were significant.[59] The loss is probably due to the predominant use of perishable papyrus as writing material; at Ugarit and Alalakh on the north Syrian coast the use, in addition, of baked clay tablets on the Mesopotamian model has preserved records, and, at the former, an extensive literature. Included in this literature are collections of maxims in the familiar father-to-son form.[60] Philological and stylistic evidence of Ugaritic (i.e., Canaanite) influence on biblical Hebrew has been traced particularly in Psalms and Proverbs,[61] and it is reasonable to conclude that there once existed an extensive Canaanite poetic and wisdom literature of which these echoes remain.

---

[59] See nn. 11 and 12 above.

[60] C. F. A. Schaeffer, *Comptes rendus de l'Académie des Inscriptions et Belles-Lettres* (1961), p. 236; cf. also the Akkadian proverbs and a text about innocent suffering, found at Ras Sharma—*Ugaritica* V (1968), pp. 265-30.

[61] Cf. W. F. Albright, "The Role of the Canaanites in the History of Civilization," in *The Bible and the Ancient Near East*, ed. G. Ernest Wright (1961), pp. 328-62; ———— "Canaanite-Phoenician Sources of Hebrew Wisdom," in *VT Supp. III* (1955): pp. 1-15; M. Dahood, *Proverbs and Northwest Semitic Philology* (1963); *Psalms I–III* (Anchor Bible), 1966-1970, passim.

3
Precepts and Proverbs

INHERENT IN the idea of wisdom was that it could be taught, whether as a technical craft, as rules for the good life, or as a profound understanding of the meaning of human existence.[1]

Israel's teachers were well aware that people vary in native intelligence, and that their pupils might be open to instruction or might resist it. Some were ignorant and unskilled simply because they had not been taught. Others were unteachable because they could not learn, and still others because they would not.

These differences are reflected in the usages of the several Hebrew words for *fool*, antithesis of the wise man. The *pethi* is the naïve, untutored youth whose intelligence has not been awakened. He is simple, but not, as some translations put it, "a simpleton." The *kᵉsil* is stupid. The *'ᵉwil* or *sakal* is obstinate in his folly. The *baʿar* is crude, the *nabal* brutal and depraved, the *holel* irrational to the point of madness. The *leṣ* is the foolish talker, opinionated and insolent.[2]

---

[1] See Exod. 35:34; Prov. 1:2–6; Qoh. 12:9; Ps. 90:12; Job 6:24.
[2] See Prov. 1:4; 14:15; 12:23; 17:16; 15:2; 27:12; Qoh. 10:3; Prov. 30:2; Judg. 19:23; Qoh. 10:13; Prov. 3:34; 15:12.

Counselors and Teachers

Two principal ways in which wisdom was propagated can be distinguished: instruction, training (*musar*) and counsel or persuasion (*'eṣah*). The difference lies primarily in the relation of the recipient to the authority of the teacher. In the first case we have to do with the natural authority of parents and of tribal or community custom, but also with judicial authority in the administration of justice, with priestly authority in the sphere of cultic religion, and with political authority. In the second case, counsel was sought voluntarily from men and women whose only authority lay in the prestige derived from special competence. Such were the royal counselors and the local sages who could be consulted by the common people. Their advice might be rejected, as with Ahithophel who was so chagrined that he went out and hanged himself.[3] The wisdom teacher's authority was of both kinds because his task was both to instruct and to persuade, "to sharpen the wits of the ignorant, to give to youth knowledge and foresight."[4]

Parental instruction naturally came first. The teacher built on it, and indeed resumed the paternal role. "My son," he said, "attend to your father's instruction and do not reject the teaching of your mother."[5] A child's curiosity was to be satisfied. "When your children shall say to you, 'What do you mean by this service?' you shall say 'It is the sacrifice of the Lord's passover.'" Such religious beliefs and moral standards, as well as instruction in practical skills, were of course not simply those of a single household, but the common tradition of clan and community.[6]

[3] 2 Sam. 17:23.
[4] Prov. 1:4, AB. Cf. 19:20; 22:15.
[5] Prov. 1:8, NEB. Cf. 3:11–12; 4:3–5; 6:20; 13:1; 15:5; 23:22.
[6] Exod. 12:26–27; cf. Jer. 35:5–10.

An outstanding example is that of the Rechabites, whose way of life as a mobile tent-dwelling clan in a settled agrarian and urban society was held by them to be an ancestral duty.

Even in the smaller family circle, teaching had a mandatory quality. It was a commandment (*miṣwah*), often with the negative emphasis of many "don'ts." It entailed frequent correction and rebuke, including physical punishment. "Do not withhold discipline from a boy; take the stick to him, and save him from death."[7]

The categorical prohibitions of the type familiar from the Ten Commandments have been traced back by scholars to the unconditional obligations of tribal life. Alt has made a basic distinction between case law, like that in Exodus 21:1 ff., and the imperious commands and prohibitions related to the sacral sphere. Gerstenberger in turn argues that the original setting of such laws was the inviolable ethos of a tribal community, so that by transference they were wholly appropriate as commandments for the people of God. Richter thinks rather of the schools for court officials under the early monarchy as the source of both the "must" and "should" types of prohibitions, the former predominating in the law codes and the latter in other contexts.[8] These professional schools seem to have contributed to the materials preserved in Proverbs some sayings particularly apposite for such specialized training; for instance,

---

[7] Prov. 23:13, NEB. Cf. Prov. 13:1, 24; 15:5; 29:15. The historian notes how David had failed in this respect, 1 Kings 1:6.

[8] A. Alt, *Essays on Old Testament History and Religion*, Eng. trans. R. A. Wilson (1967); E. Gerstenberger, *Wesen und Herkunft des "Apodiktischen Rechts"* (1961, 1965); W. Richter, *Recht und Ethos* (1966). H. W. Wolff in *Amos' geistige Heimat* (1964) adopts Gerstenberger's position.

Without a hand at the helm a people will perish, but safety lies in having many counselors.[9]

A king's rage is like a lion's roar. . . . Do not put yourself forward in the king's presence or take your place among the great; for it is better that he should say to you, 'Come up here,' than move you down to make room for a nobleman.[10]

Precepts and Proverbs as Teaching Tools

Evidence for the existence and nature of schools for the training of youth during the monarchical period is slight and inconclusive, as noted above in Chapter 1. Their existence probably may be inferred from what is said about the royal establishments of David, Solomon, and Hezekiah, and from possible allusions in Isaiah to schools.[11] A third piece of evidence is more substantial, though remaining in the realm of inference. This is the preservation in Proverbs and Qoheleth of sayings which apparently were used for teaching purposes and which in themselves are quite secular in tone, yet are without special reference to training for a position in the king's service. They would be at home on all levels of society, for they embody the shrewd observations and counsels of folk wisdom. For example, "A toiler's appetite toils for him, for his hunger drives him," "Endless dripping on a rainy day—that is what a nagging wife is like," "A man charged with bloodshed will jump into a well to escape arrest."[12]

While these proverbs could indeed be used in a school

---

[9] Prov. 11:14. Probably two distinct maxims are here combined, since in 15:22 the second line is different. "A hand at the helm" is, literally, "steering, guidance."
[10] Prov. 19:12; 25:6–7, NEB. See also 20:2; 14:28; 34, 35; 16:12, 14, 15, etc.
[11] See above, p. 16.
[12] Prov. 16:26; 27:15; 28:17, all NEB.

for officials as well as among the general populace, there are others that express resentment against the rich and powerful (even the king), or the hopelessness of the poor. "A poor man must speak as a suppliant, but the rich man answers roughly," "The rich lord it over the poor, and the borrower becomes the lender's slave," "Like a starving lion or a thirsty bear is a wicked man ruling a helpless people," "Wealth brings many new friends, but the needy is parted from the one friend he has."[13]

Precepts were authoritative instruction and regulations for behavior, based on the imperatives of social order and values or on religious belief. Proverbs were rules in another sense, generalizations from experience about how "the world wags" and men behave, with the good or bad consequences that have been observed to follow. Their purpose is not indoctrination but illumination and education in the true meaning of the word, to awaken the mind, kindle the imagination and train the judgment. The teachers sought to bring to bear on unformed minds and new situations the values derived from experience. Where the precept speaks in the imperative, the proverb speaks in the indicative. The first calls for obedience, the second seeks to evoke a freely given response.

Proverbs, Qoheleth, and Sirach are the three wisdom books most evidently associated with schools or academies for the education of young men.[14] Qoheleth stands apart from the other two as a more philosophical work which its final editor warns must be studied with caution.[15] All three make use in various ways of the primary tools of precepts and proverbs.

Proverbs is best described as a source book of wisdom

[13] Prov. 18:23, AB; 22:7, NEB; 28:15, NEB; 19:4, AB.
[14] Cf. Prov. 1:2–7; 2:1 ff.; 3:1 ff.; 22:17–21; Qoh. 11:7–12:1; 12:9–14; Sir. 24:32–34; 38:24–39:16; 51:23–28.
[15] Qoh. 12:12–14. On this book, see below, Chap. 7.

materials assembled and edited by a teacher for use in his school. It contains two collections of Solomonic proverbs (10:1–22:16, and 25–29), two shorter documents described as "words of wise men" (22:17–24:22, and 24:23–34), and four appendixes in chapters 30–31. All this is preceded in chapters 1–9 by the teacher's own more religiously oriented introduction, with a foreword and motto in 1:2–7 stating his objectives and methods. Four terms in verse 6 call for special comment at this point, "proverb[s] [*mashal*] and parable[s] [*mᵉliṣah*], the words of the wise and their riddles [*ḥidoth*]" (NEB).

This looks like a broadly comprehensive indication of the various literary forms found in Proverbs. *Mashal* appears at 10:1 and 25:1 in the titles of the two major collections of sentence sayings and precepts.[16] The two shorter pieces which come between these are headed "words of the wise" (22:17 and 24:23). The numerical proverbs in 30:15–31 are riddles of a sort.

The most important of these terms is *mashal*. The basic meaning of this word is "likeness, comparison," as in proverbs like "As the mother, so her daughter" and "Like Nimrod, a mighty hunter."[17] Sayings of this type, expanded into verse couplets, are common in Proverbs. Other examples emphasize contrast, dissimilarity, the parallel in reverse: "A wise son makes his father happy, but a son who is a fool is a grief to his mother" (10:1). Still other proverbs compare values, as "A poor man is better than a liar" (19:22). The point is that the essential nature of something is brought out by comparing it with something else.

---

[16] And also, of course, in the present title of the whole book, where it probably has been transferred from 10:1 when the introductory chapters were inserted.

[17] Ezek. 16:44; Gen. 10:9. A. R. Johnson, "Mashal," *VT Supp. III* (1955), pp. 162–69.

Hence, the *mashal* is a kind of 'model' or 'paradigm'[18] of hidden truth. We can understand why it is used elsewhere in the Old Testament of a profound, mysterious, prophetic oracle (Num. 23:7), of an allegory or riddle (Ezek. 17:2), and even of Job's solemn oath that he is speaking the truth (Job 27:1). Through the mysterious power of the spoken word, the *mashal* reaches the reality and expresses the meaning of an experience. Von Rad emphasizes that the philosophical and the gnomic are "two completely different forms of the apperception of truth," and quotes with approval a saying of Herder's that one does not learn from such maxims, but with their help.[19]

The second term, *mᵉliṣah*, is more difficult to explain because it is a rare word, found in only two other Old Testament passages. In Habakkuk 2:6 it introduces a denunciation of a tyrant nation and is paralleled with *mashal* (which is used in the same way in Isaiah 14:4).[20] In Sirach 47:17 it is associated with "proverbs and parables" as compositions of Solomon, and is translated "interpretations" (RSV) or "answers" (NEB), from the Septuagint.[21] The meaning here in Proverbs may be taken to be "criticism" or "warning speech." The reference could then well be to the ten discourses of chapters 1–7, to the appeals and denunciations of personified wisdom in 1:20–33 and chapters 8 and 9, and possibly to the queen mother's diatribe in 31:1–9.[22]

---

[18] The terms are those of W. McKane, *Proverbs* (1970), p. 26.

[19] G. von Rad, *Old Testament Theology*, Eng. trans. (1962), I: 421.

[20] In Hab. 2:6 *mᵉliṣah* is glossed with the word *ḥidoth*, "riddles."

[21] Other modern English versions translate it variously in Prov. 1:6: "figure" (RSV), "parable[s]" (NEB, NAB, AT), "metaphor" (AB), "obscure saying[s]" (JB), "allusion" (McKane).

[22] Note that the related word *meliṣ* in Job 16:20; 33:23; Gen. 42:23; means "critic," "interpreter," "spokesman."

Attention has been drawn already to the two short collections of personal admonitions and negative precepts in Proverbs 22:17 ff. and 24:23 ff., that are headed "words of the wise."

The fourth category in Proverbs 1:6 is riddles (*ḥidoth*). This word, like its English equivalent, has the primary meaning of a verbal puzzle calling for mental acuteness to solve it. Its purpose is entertainment, as in the stories of Samson's wager with the wedding guests, of the Queen of Sheba's testing of Solomon's knowledge and wit, and of the contest among the three guardsmen at Darius's court.[23] The simple verbal puzzle, however, can be developed into other forms such as metaphor, parable, and allegory, where the meaning is concealed beneath the literal sense of the language used. Riddles can thus be of value in the educational process, by arousing curiosity and stimulating thought and imagination.

The frequent obscurity of prophetic oracles is reflected in the statement in Numbers 12:8 that Yahweh spoke to Moses "plainly, not in riddles." In Ezekiel 17:2 *ḥidah* is an allegory. In the wisdom Psalms it connotes a problem of understanding.[24] The word is not used again in Proverbs, but what it represents may be recognized in the numerical proverbs of 30:15–31, which pose the problem to the hearer of identifying and explaining the common element in the phenomena described: "How an eagle soars in the sky, how a snake glides across a rock, how a ship moves over the sea, and how a man wins his way with a girl" (30:18–19, AB).

The four literary forms we have been discussing served in different ways the primary objectives of the teacher mentioned earlier: precept, instruction (*musar*), counsel, and persuasion (*ʿeṣah*). A *mashal* might convey a precept

---

[23] Judg. 14:10–18; 1 Kings 10:1–3; 1 Esd. 3:1–4:47.
[24] Pss. 49:4 (Heb. 49:5); 78:2.

directly, "Do not be fond of sleep lest you lose your inheritance" (20:13, AB), or indirectly, "A little sleep, a little slumber, a little folding of the hands to rest—and poverty will come upon you like a vagabond" (24:33–34). The m^{e}liṣah or speech of warning is imperative in tone, but includes the element of persuasion by citing the benefits of response and the penalties of refusal.[25] The preemptory injunctions of the "thirty precepts" are varied in number 18 with a graphic description of drunkenness, in place of a direct warning against it.[26] Only the riddles lack a moralizing note.

The precepts of the wisdom teachers are less imperious than the categorical commands and prohibitions of the familial, cultic, and legal spheres. Unlike these, their characteristic form is exhortation, coupled with a statement of the motive or result that commends it.[27] It thus becomes an appeal to reason and conscience: "Listen to advice and accept instruction, and you will die a wise man" (Prov. 19:20, NEB) and "Be sparing in visits to your neighbor's house, if he sees too much of you, he will dislike you" (25:17, NEB). For every precept introduced by an imperative verb there are a dozen where the imperative is clearly implied, as may be seen from two similar sayings in Proverbs 25: "If you find honey, eat only what you need, too much of it will make you sick" (25:16, NEB) and "Eating too much honey is bad [for you]" (25:27a).

In the first of the two parts of Proverbs headed "words of the wise," 22:17–24:22, a whole series of direct imperative admonitions or instructions make this section

---

[25] See Prov. 2; 3:1–12, 21–35; and the preamble in 22:17–21 to the "thirty precepts" of the wise men.

[26] Prov. 23:29–35.

[27] Where motive or purpose clauses are attached to absolute commands, as in Exod. 20:4–12, there is good reason to believe that these are secondary additions. See Richter, *Recht und Ethos*, p. 116.

stand out from the unorganized collections, chiefly of sentence proverbs, that precede and follow it. The section shows such a close literary relationship to one of the Egyptian Instructions ascribed to a certain Amen-em-ope, that it seems to have been based on it.[28] It has the same formal organization, in which an introduction is followed by thirty precepts or implied precepts, with their motive or purpose clauses. At some points the verbal similarity is close, with slight changes to make it fit the Palestinian scene:

Cast not thy heart in pursuit of riches . . . they will not spend the night with thee . . . they [will] have made themselves wings like geese and are flown away to the heavens (Amen-em-ope, chap. 7).[29]

Do not wear yourself out in pursuit of wealth . . . when you look for it, will it not have vanished? It will have grown itself wings and like an eagle will have flown away into the heavens (Prov. 23:4-5, AB).

Again, in the third of the four appendixes to Proverbs (31:1-9), a queen mother harangues her son at some length on the responsibilities he is neglecting through his dissolute behavior. *"Precept"* and *"instruction"* are terms too colorless for a piece in such vigorous language, but they belong in the same general category.

A more academic tone pervades the ten discourses[30] which form the framework and provide much of the substance of the opening section of Proverbs in chapters 1-9. Yet here, too, especially in the tenth discourse (chapter 7)

---

[28] On the Egyptian Instructions, in which a pharaoh or high government official admonishes his son or prospective successor, see above, pp. 26-31.
[29] See *ANET*, p. 422b.
[30] See R. N. Whybray, *Wisdom in Proverbs* (1965), pp. 33-52, 61-71; R. B. Y. Scott, *Proverbs-Ecclesiastes AB* (1965), pp. 14-17, 23-24, 33-65.

and other passages warning against adultery, the teacher's feelings kindle his imagination and the warning is developed into a vivid word picture. Recent scholarship has pointed out the affinity of these discourses also, in form and substance, with the Egyptian Instructions.[31] They begin with the same call for attention, "My son!" There follows (usually) an imperative verb or verbs, with accompanying circumstantial and motive clauses as, "My son, if vicious men entice you, do not consent, . . . do not go their way; . . . these men are setting a bloody ambush—for themselves!"[32]

Unlike the teacher's discourses, yet similarly admonitory in tone, are three poems in which a personified Wisdom cries aloud to men and one which includes a similar address from personified Folly. In 1:20–33 Wisdom berates fools for their refusal to listen to her. In chapter 8, and more briefly in 9:1–6, 11–12, she appeals for a hearing on the grounds of her priceless worth and of her prime place in the divinely created order of the world. Folly tempts men in 9:13–18 with what looks like a colloquial saying, "Stolen water tastes sweet!"

The second principal teaching tool was the proverb. A proverb is a short, pregnant sentence or phrase whose meaning is applicable in many situations, with imagery or striking verbal form to assist the memory. It has been well described as having shortness, sense, and salt.[33] Most of those in Proverbs and Qoheleth have their verbs in the

[31] R. N. Whybray, *Wisdom in Proverbs*; C. Kayatz, *Studien zu Proverbien 1–9* (1966); McKane, *Proverbs*, pp. 6–10, 267–72.

[32] Prov. 1:10–19, AB. The remaining discourses begin at 2:1; 3:1; 3:21; 4:1; 4:10; 4:20; 5:1; 6:20; 7:1. It is less certain how far each extends.

[33] McKane, *Proverbs*, pp. 123 ff., 183, 414–15 distinguishes empirical generalizations to be taken literally from true proverbs having "representative potential and openness to interpretation."

indicative mood. Others take the form of rhetorical questions or exclamations, and a very few the direct or indirect imperative (Hebrew jussive). An example of the last-named is the sarcastic, "Let not one who is girding on [his armor] boast like one who is unfastening [it afterwards]."[34]

In addition to the two collections of proverbs of Solomon, smaller groups of sayings appear in Proverbs 6:12–19 and 30:10–33. In Qoheleth individual sayings are quoted (or in some cases composed as epigrams by the author), mainly in chapters 7 and 10, and incidentally elsewhere in the course of his argument.[35] Sirach is essentially a prolonged instruction, in which meditations and prayers are interspersed with precepts and instructional sentence proverbs. Among the latter, some echo those of Proverbs and Qoheleth, often in an expanded form.[36] In Tobit two brief speeches of admonition incorporate proverbs as implied precepts, 4:13b and 12:7–10.

Proverb Patterns

Certain common patterns are discernible in the anonymous folk sayings of many peoples, ancient and modern. Some examples of these are found in biblical wisdom writings, and even in those of Egyptian and Babylonian origin. In various ways they express the idea of an order of life which ought to be, of right values and due proportions. Norms of human behavior and relationships are not just arbitrary regulations to preserve the status quo, but expressions of the shape and structure of a successful and

[34] 1 Kings 20:11.
[35] In 1:15, 18; 4:5–6; 5:1, 3, 7, 10–12 (Heb. 4:17; 5:2, 6, 9–11); 6:11; 9:17–18; 11:3–4.
[36] 13:3, 26a, cf. Prov. 18:23; 15:13a. With 21:20, cf. Qoh. 7:5–6.

meaningful common life. Many sayings are scornful or reproachful, drawing attention to what is contrary to the way things ought to be, to what is absurd, paradoxical, or, in the ethical realm, wrong. Still others express the pathos of inexplicable misfortune. Together they represent an attempt to sort out the multitudinous phenomena with which a man is confronted in this life.

The first of these types or patterns of folk sayings points to those things that appear distinct and yet really are identical or equivalent: "A penny saved is a penny earned," "One man's meat is another man's poison" (Aesop), "A worker's appetite works for him" (Prov. 16:26), "A man who flatters his neighbor is [really] spreading a net for his feet" (Prov. 29:5, NEB).

The second proverb pattern distinguishes among things that seem the same but are in fact different, contrasting, or paradoxical: "Much noise, few eggs," "Good fences make good neighbors," "A stranger's ox eats grass, but one's own ox lies down in hunger" (Babylonian), "The fool . . . regards knowledge as ignorance, and profit as loss" (Ptahhotep), "To the hungry man even the bitter tastes sweet" (Prov. 27:7, AB), "The more he talks, the more meaningless it becomes" (Qoh. 6:11, AB).

The third pattern, of similarity or analogy, is the most prominent in biblical wisdom sayings, as might be expected from the meaning of *mashal*, "proverb."[37] "Like people, like priest" (Hos. 4:9), "Like arrows in the hands of a warrior are the sons of one's youth" (Ps. 127:4), "Good news from a distant land is like cold water to a parched throat" (Prov. 25:25), "Like a dog returning to its vomit is a stupid man who repeats his folly" (Prov. 26:11, NEB). Simile, metaphor, and parable abound in the Bible.

A fourth pattern is focused on what is futile or absurd.

[37] See pp. 53–54 above.

"You are a scribe and you don't even know your own name!" said the Sumerians.[38] The Hebrews often gave this the form of a mocking question, "Is Saul also among the [raving] prophets?" (1 Sam. 10:11), "Can the sea be ploughed with oxen?" (Amos 6:12b, NEB), "Can the Ethiopian change his skin [color], or the leopard his spots?" (Jer. 13:23). In Proverbs 17:16 a teacher of privileged youth reflects ruefully, "Why ever does a fool come, fee in hand, to buy wisdom—when he lacks brains?"

Many sayings classify persons according to their characteristic behavior: "Children and fools speak the truth," "A rolling stone gathers no moss." Proverbs 26 holds up to scorn successively the fool, the loafer, the quarrelsome man, the slanderer, and the dissembler. So, for Qoheleth, the fool "shows no sense . . . but announces to all and sundry that he is a fool . . . his tongue is his undoing; he begins by talking nonsense, and ends in dreadful frenzy" (Qoh. 10:3, 12–13, AB). As for the indolent, his "roof beams sag, and a lazy man has a leaky house" (10:18, AB).

A sixth pattern is that of relative values or proportion: "Better this than that," or "this is bad, but that is worse." The former, which becomes one of the stylistic marks of Hebrew wisdom writing, appears also in the Instruction of Amen-em-ope, "Better is bread, when the heart is happy, than riches with sorrow."[39] Similarly in Proverbs 15:17, NEB, "Better a dish of vegetables if love go with it, than a fat ox eaten in hatred."[40] The converse in climactic form is found both in the Words of Ahiqar and in Proverbs, "I have lifted sand, and I have carried salt; but there is naught which is heavier than [rage]," "The weight of

---

[38] E. I. Gordon, *Sumerian Proverbs* (1959), p. 200.
[39] *ANET*, pp. 422b, 423b.
[40] Prov. 15:16 is another variant of the same proverb.

stone, the heaviness of sand, the vexation of a fool is heavier than both."[41] The dismal conclusion of Qoheleth that "When riches multiply, so do those who live off them" (5:11, NEB [Heb. 5:10]) may be classed with these statements of relative value: what is better in one way is worse in another.

Another common pattern in wisdom sayings points to the consequences of human behavior. Many of these are implied precepts, others are simply observations of the way things work out in an organized community. Examples of the former are: "A lazy man does not plough in autumn; he expects crops at harvest and there is nothing," "Anxiety in a man's heart weighs him down, yet an encouraging word will make him happier," "He who guards the fig-tree will eat its fruit, and he who watches his master's interests will come to honor."[42] The second type of consequential sayings may be illustrated by, "Where there is no expertise a nation falls, but safety lies in many advisers," "A king's majesty is derived from a populous nation; without [his] people a prince is nothing."[43]

The proverb of appropriate retribution is a special type of the proverb of consequence. "The biter bit," or the Shakespearian "hoist with his own petar," expresses originally the satisfaction of the onlookers when a man brings on himself the calamity he has planned for someone else. Two of these sayings are combined as parallels in Proverbs 26:27, "He who digs a pit [for another] falls into it [himself]," and "he who sets a stone rolling is caught up by it" (McKane's trans.). The first line expresses the thought in a favorite image which reappears in Qoheleth, Sirach, and, in a slightly different form, in Proverbs 28:10; it is alluded

[41] *ANET*, p. 429a; Prov. 27:3 (McKane's trans.).
[42] Prov. 20:4, McKane's trans.; 12:25, AB; 27:18, NEB.
[43] Prov. 11:14, McKane's trans.; 14:28, AB.

to also in Jeremiah and the Psalms.[44] The second image is found with other variants in the same contexts in Qoheleth and Sirach, and also in the Egyptian ʿOnchsheshonqy (22:5).

Underlying the thought of appropriate retribution is the belief in a superhuman justice at work to keep the world in balance—the ma^cat of the Egyptians and the nemesis of the Greeks and Romans.[45] Later this was made specific in theological terms, "God punishes for a transgression, he rewards for a good deed" (Papyrus Insinger).[46] The dominant teaching of biblical wisdom is similar; appropriate punishments and rewards are paired, and both attributed to Yahweh's action. "The Lord will not let a good man starve, but he rebuffs the craving of the wicked," "The fruit of humility is the fear of God with riches and honor and life. The crooked man's path is set with snares and pitfalls." "Who that was innocent ever perished?" demands Eliphaz of Job, "as I have seen, those who plow iniquity and sow trouble reap the same. By the breath of God they perish."[47]

Folk Sayings and Literary Proverbs

The colloquial sayings cited in the narrative and prophetic books are markedly different in form from the balanced lines and monotonous rhythm of the Proverbs of Solomon, 10:1 ff. and 25:1 ff. They are terse and con-

[44] Qoh. 10:8a; Sir. 27:26a; Jer. 18:22b; Pss. 7:15; 9:15; 57:6 (Heb. 7:16; 9:16; 57:7).
[45] This is not meant to suggest that Ma^cat and Nemesis are comparable in other respects. Ma^cat was the divine order behind phenomena, Nemesis a goddess of vengeance, and so, vengeance itself.
[46] Section 25. Cf. H. H. Schmid, *Wesen und Geshichte der Weisheit* (1966), p. 221.
[47] Prov. 10:3, AB; 22:4–5a, NEB; Job 4:7–9.

densed to the point of obscurity when isolated from their context in a life situation. Usually they consist of only two or three Hebrew words:

kᵉnimrod gibbor ṣayid (*Like Nimrod, a mighty hunter!*) (Gen. 10:9)[48]

bᵉhar YHWH yera'eh (*In the mount of Yahweh he appears [?]*) (Gen. 22:14)
hᵃgam shaul bannᵉbi'im (*Is Saul too among the prophets?*) (1 Sam. 10:11)
merᵉsha'im yese' resha' (*Wickedness comes from wicked men*) (1 Sam. 24:13 [Heb. 24:14])
kᵉ'immah bittah (*As a mother, so her daughter*) (Ezek. 16:44)
ka'am kakkohen (*As a people, so [its] priest*) (Hos. 4:9)
'al yithhallel ḥoger kimᵉpatteaḥ (*Let not one arming boast like one disarming*) (1 Kings 20:11)
sha'ol yish'ᵃlu bᵉ'abel (*The proper place to ask counsel is in Abel*) (2 Sam. 20:18)

In Genesis 16:12 the scornful comment on Ishmael has all the marks of a folk saying or a combination of two sayings:

pere' 'adam (*A wild ass of the steppe!*)
yado bakkol wᵉyad kol bo (*His hand against everyone and everyone's hand against him*)

The alliteration and assonance in this last example are to be noticed, as in Genesis 22:14 and 1 Samuel 24:14 above.

Contrasted with these terse sayings are the two-line literary proverbs exhibiting the several kinds of poetic parallelism, familiar from the Book of Proverbs and traditionally known as proverbs of Solomon. Each line usually

---

[48] The added words *before Yahweh* may or may not have been included in the original saying.

consists of three or four stressed words; these accents, and hence the rhythm, often can be recognized even in translation. For example,

a four/four beat   "A wíse són delíghts [his] fáther, but a fóolish són is a gríef to his móther"

a three/three beat   "The memóry of a goód man is a bléssing, but the reputátion of wícked men will rót"

a four/three beat   "He who líves blámelessly will líve sáfely, but one whose wáys are croóked will be expósed"

These three examples juxtapose contrasting statements in similar sentence structures; that is, in antithetical parallelism. A variant of this type is the proverb of comparative value, such as, "Better a pittance honestly earned than great gains ill gotten" (16:8, NEB). A succinct comparison may be repeated in synonymous parallelism, "Better be slow to anger than a fighter, better govern one's temper than capture a city," "Pride leads to disaster, and arrogance to downfall." Sometimes the second line carries forward the substance of the first line instead of providing a formal balance, "Gracious words are liquid honey, sweet to the taste and refreshing to the body." A variant of this requires both lines to complete the sentence, "An attentive ear and an observant eye, Yahweh is the maker of them both."[49]

There are many possible varieties of these three basic types of poetic parallelism. The first line may provide the

[49] Prov. 16:32, NEB; 16:18, 24; 20:12, McKane's trans.

protasis of a conditional sentence and the second line the apodosis, as in 16:7, "When Yahweh is pleased with a man's conduct, he makes even his enemies to be at peace with him" (AB). Again, the second line may give the reason for what is said in the first, "Wrongdoing is hateful to kings, for through the right a throne stands secure" (16:12, AB). Or the second line may give the result of the first line, "Bread got by fraud tastes good, but afterwards it fills the mouth with grit" (20:17, NEB).

This parallelism is a notable feature of Semitic poetry and rhetoric, and is characteristic in Psalms and the prophets. The above examples show that the form is flexible and capable of many kinds of artistic variations. The collections in Proverbs make a sophisticated use of many of these. Yet the individual two-line proverbs with parallelism are seldom poetic in themselves. Nor do they have the sustained rhetorical air of the discourses found in chapters 1-9. Why then is this form, rather than the compact and prosaic form of the folk sayings, adopted by the sages for teaching purposes?

The main reason may simply be the obvious one that the wisdom teachers were highly literate men, not village sages, hence they would naturally follow in the literary tradition. On the other hand, it may be that the parallel structure of these 'Solomonic' proverbs proved itself useful in schoolroom instruction. It would add a measure of sonorous dignity in keeping with the prestige of learning. Moreover, it can be assumed that memorization played a large part in the process of learning, and this would be aided by the repetitions and contrasts of parallel lines. In recitation these would provide also the opportunity for antiphonal reading and oral responses.

At this point the question arises whether or not the teachers deliberately made use of sayings from traditional folk wisdom, or composed dicta or epigrams modeled on them. It would be strange if they did not. Certainly there is a wide variety in tone and in the topics included. At one extreme are the exhortations to personal piety and the affirmations that Yahweh is master of men's lives and guarantor of the moral order.[50] With these are associated the recurrent encomiums on wisdom and wise men,[51] and the identification of wise men with the righteous and of fools with the wicked.[52] At the other extreme are the caustic or pathetic comments on the way things are, which have no evident bearing on matters of wisdom or religion, like, "One man pretends to be rich, yet has nothing; another pretends to be poor, yet has great wealth" (13:7); "Even in laughter the heart may grieve, and mirth may end in sorrow" (14:13, NEB); "'It is no good, no good!' says the buyer, but as he goes away he congratulates himself" (20:14, AB).

The sentiments expressed in these verses could well have originated in colloquial sayings, perhaps more compact in form. If so, they have been recast in the standard parallelism, since both lines are needed to express the thought. In other cases, however, we find what appear to be folk sayings which are complete in themselves, quoted in one line and then expanded or commented upon to create a didactic couplet.[53]

---

[50] Prov. 10:3, 22, 29; 11:1, 20; 12:2, 22; 14:2, 26, 27; 15:3, 8; etc.

[51] Prov. 10:8, 14; 12:1; 13:20; 14:6, 8, 33; 15:7, 12, 24; 16:16; etc.

[52] Originally *righteous* meant "innocent" or "in the right," as judged in a court of law, and *wicked* meant "in the wrong," "guilty." See Deut. 25:1. For the more generalized sense, see Gen. 18:23–25; Ps. 1:5–6.

[53] Gordis has illuminated many difficult passages by showing that apparent incongruities in a writer's thought may be due to the introduction of quotations without any external sign that this is what they are. See R. Gordis, *Koheleth: The Man and his World*, 3d ed. (1968), chap. xii; ——— *The Book of God and Man* (1965), chap. xiii.

In addition to some instances of proverbs repeated almost verbatim,[54] there are others of which only one line is identical, the balancing line of the couplet providing a different parallel or comment. For example, "A rich man's wealth is his strong city, but poverty is the undoing of the helpless" (10:15, NEB), "A rich man's wealth is his strong city, a towering wall, so he supposes" (18:11, NEB). The identical first lines form an independent sentence with a striking image, and make a general observation from experience which is applicable on many occasions. This has been turned into a poetic couplet, in one case by providing an antithesis and in the other by extending the metaphor. In 12:14 the second compensating line is broadly synonymous, but in 13:2 it is antithetical. In 22:28a we have a clear example of an ancient maxim, having almost the force of law, to which a lame second line has been added, "Do not remove an ancient landmark,[55] which your fathers have set." Later, in 23:10–11, the same maxim is made into a quatrain, adding the sanction of divine vengeance, "Do not remove an ancient landmark, or enter the fields of the fatherless, for their guardian is powerful, and he will plead their cause against you." Sometimes it is the second line of the couplet that is a duplicate, "Pride is the precursor of ruin, and humility must come before honors" (18:12, AB); "The fear of the Lord is the foundation of wisdom, and humility must come before honors" (15:33, AB). What originally could have been a simple parental admonition has been given in the one case a moral counterpart, and in the other a religious dimension.[56]

[54] 18:8 and 26:22; 21:9 and 25:24; 6:10–11 and 24:33–34; 22:3 and 27:12.

[55] In Deut. 19:14 and 27:17 it is stated as a law. Cf. Amen-em-ope, chap. 6, in *ANET*, p. 422b.

[56] For other examples, see 10:6, 11; 26:7, 9; 11:14 and 24:6; 13:9 and 24:20.

A particularly good example of a maxim that stands out from its present context is, "Partiality in giving judgment is wrong." In 24:23b it has no balancing line, but in this case is explicated in two following couplets which contrast good and bad judges. Where it occurs in altered forms in 18:5 and 28:21, the balancing lines differ. This alone is enough to suggest that it is a quotation, which is confirmed by its appearance in legal formulations, "You shall not be partial in giving judgment; you shall listen to high and low alike."[57]

In view, then, of general probability and of what seem to be clear examples of single-line quotations in Proverbs, we may expect to find other single-line sayings of traditional origin that have been utilized in the same way. They would be compact, pointed, picturesque, derivative from common experience, and expressing a widely applicable idea or viewpoint. Moreover, they will be unmarked by the special interests and terminology of the wisdom teachers.[58] Some will show alliteration and assonance, but the majority will be prosaic. The following are possible examples:

First comes insolence, then comes disgrace (Prov. 11:2a).
He who tills his land will have enough to eat (12:11a).
Walk with the wise and be wise (13:20a, NEB).
The fellow of fools will fare ill (13:20b, AB).
No oxen—a bare barn! (14:4a).
The toiler's appetite toils for him (16:26a, AB).
Letting water escape starts a quarrel (17:14a).
[Casting] the lot puts an end to disputes (18:18a).
To observe a law is to preserve yourself (19:16a, AB).
The man who sows injustice reaps trouble (22:8a, NEB).

[57] Deut. 1:17. Cf. Lev. 19:15; Deut. 16:19.
[58] The last-named feature is properly insisted on by H.-J. Hermisson, *Studien zur israelitische Spruchweisheit* (1968), p. 52.

Even bitter food tastes sweet to a hungry man (27:7b, NEB).
A door turns on its hinges, a sluggard on his bed (26:14, NEB).
Better is fame than fine ointment (Qoh. 7:1a, AB).
Dead flies will make a bottle of perfume stink (Qoh. 10:1a, AB).

Numerical Proverbs

A distinct proverb type which appears sophisticated but may, on the contrary, belong to the early stages of proverb making, takes the form of a culminating numerical progression, as in, "There are three things that will not be satisfied, four that will never cry 'Enough!'—Sheol, a barren womb, a land short of water, and fire which never cries 'Enough'" (30:15b–16, AB).

The explanation of the idiom (which occurs also in Ugaritic poetry) lies in the fact that it is found in synonymous parallels; yet, since a whole number cannot have a synonym, it is paired with the number next below it.[59] This kind of proverb belongs with the efforts of the older wisdom thinkers to classify phenomena by their common characteristics. The adage on four insatiable things is followed in Proverbs 30 by companion pieces on four mysterious things, four intolerable types of people, four remarkable small creatures, and four proud walkers. These are a kind of riddle: What is it that explains the apparent similarities? What do they portend for man's understanding of the order of the world about him?

In Proverbs 30:11–14 four sorts of sinners are similarly listed, but the introductory formula is missing. That there

---

[59] W. M. W. Roth writes of "The Numerical Sequence $x/x+1$ in the Old Testament," *VT* 12 (1962): pp. 300–11. The formula would be more exactly described as $x-1/x$, since the items enumerated always total the higher of the two numbers.

was once such an introduction can be inferred from 6:16: "there are six things which the Lord hates, seven which are an abomination to him." In these two cases we see how the ancient classification formula was reused in later times for moral and religious instruction. The riddle form remains, but its original purpose and significance have evaporated. There is nothing puzzling and mysterious about the various kinds of sinners, they are simply listed.

This is a far cry from the riddle Samson set the wedding guests, "Out of the eater came something to eat, out of the strong came something sweet" (Judg. 14:14). The solution, which also has the form of a riddle (and may originally have been a separate one), was obtained only by suborning the bride with threats, "What is sweeter than honey? What is stronger than a lion?" (v. 18) Samson's famous retort is a metaphor whose meaning is obvious; yet like all metaphor is part way to a riddle, "If you had not plowed with my heifer, you would not have found out my riddle." Indeed, the imagery in many proverbs gives them a riddle-like quality, as in Proverbs 27:17, NEB, "As iron sharpens iron, so one man sharpens the wits of another," or in 25:21–22, (NEB), "If your enemy is hungry give him bread to eat; if he is thirsty give him water to drink; so you will heap glowing coals on his head."

4
Wisdom in Stories and Word Pictures

C. S. LEWIS MAY be right that the appeal of the Bible (he was speaking particularly of the King James Version) will always be primarily to those for whom it is a sacred book, and that its literary influence has been overstated. "It contains good literature and bad literature," he says, "but even the good literature is so written that we can seldom disregard its sacred character."[1]

It may well be true that the Bible would not have had the influence which it has had on English literature if it had not first come to be widely read as a sacred book. It may be true also, as Lewis says, that few turn to it today simply for its literary value. But what needs to be stressed in reply is that the English Bible translations preserve certain remarkable literary characteristics of Hebrew origin that contribute to its impact on the reader, whatever his motive in reading.

One such characteristic is the unstudied directness and simplicity of the Hebrew prose sentence structure, which gives it force and lucidity. This can be recognized in anything like a faithful translation. Nouns and verbs predominate. Attributive adjectives and adverbs are used sparingly.

---

[1] C. S. Lewis, *The Literary Impact of the Authorized Version* (1950), p. 25.

There is no multiplying and balancing of subordinate clauses to distract attention from the main thrust of the sentence. It is a plain speech, without syntactical frills: "Pride comes before disaster, and arrogance before a fall" (Prov. 16:18, NEB). "When Job's three friends . . . first saw him from a distance, they did not recognize him; and they wept aloud, rent their cloaks and tossed dust into the air over their heads. For seven days and seven nights they sat beside him on the ground, and none of them said a word to him; for they saw that his suffering was very great" (Job 2:11–13, NEB).

A second feature is poetic, the parallelism of the semitic verse form producing an echo in the mind. The poet's thought is repeated in different language, but with the same or very similar sentence structure, so that the second line balances the first: "Unless the Lord builds the house, its builders will have toiled in vain, Unless the Lord keeps watch over a city, in vain the watchman stands on guard" (Ps. 127:1, NEB). The parallel may point a contrast, like the obverse and reverse of a coin: "What a faint whisper we hear of him! Who could attend his mighty roar?" (Job 26:14, AB). Again, the second line may extend or amplify the thought, while maintaining the rhythmic balance: "How beautiful you are, my dearest, O how beautiful, your eyes are like doves!" (Song of Songs 1:15, NEB).

A third feature is characteristic of both poetry and rhetorical prose—the luxuriant use of concrete imagery, especially of visual imagery, in simile and metaphor; and conversely the rarity of abstract expressions. For example,

> The ongoing life of good men is like the light of dawn that grows ever brighter until full day; the wicked walk in a deep darkness where they cannot perceive what it is that trips them up. (Prov. 4:18–19, AB)

As I have seen, those who plow iniquity and sow trouble

reap the same. By the breath of God they perish, and by the blast of his anger they are consumed. (Job 4:8–9)

Consider God's handiwork; who can straighten what he has made crooked? (Qoh. 7:13, NEB)

Finally, there is the supreme Hebrew gift of storytelling and the creation in words of dramatic scenes where the actors live and move and speak. This gift was a heritage from royal courts and innumerable tribal and village conclaves, honed to perfection by the writers of Genesis, Samuel, Kings, and the parable of Ruth. Quiller-Couch speaks of the interest of "the whole splendid barbaric story; . . . the flocks of Abraham and Laban; the trek of Jacob's sons to Egypt for corn; the figures of Rebekah at the well, Ruth at the gleaning, and Rizpah beneath the gibbet; Sisera bowing in weariness; Saul—great Saul—by the tent-prop with the jewels in his turban."[2]

The word pictures are painted with remarkable economy of line and color. What the participants say is told, but what they are thinking and feeling is left to the imagination. The effectiveness of the writing is all the greater because of such restraint and dignity. Rebekah, coming from a distant land, catches her first glimpse of her future husband: "When she saw Isaac, she alighted from her camel, and said to the servant, 'Who is the man yonder, walking in the field to meet us?' The servant said, 'It is my master'" (Gen. 24:64–65). The aged Jacob, hearing the news that the loved son he had given up for dead is now a ruler in the land of Egypt, cries out, "'It is enough; Joseph my son is still alive. I will go and see him before I die'" (Gen. 45:25–28). David, fleeing unarmed from King Saul's jealous wrath, stops at a sanctuary for food, and asks the priest, "'Have you not here a spear or a sword at hand?' . . . And the priest said, 'The sword of Goliath

---

[2] Sir A. Quiller-Couch, *On the Art of Reading* (1920) pp. 149–50.

the Philistine . . . is here, wrapped in a cloth behind the ephod; if you will take that, take it, for there is none but that here.' And David said, 'There is none like that; give it to me.' "³

Such stories were, of course, told for entertainment; but there was more to them than that. They were cultural instruments, forming and confirming the values and purposes of those who listened. They memorialized heroes, antiheroes and events of continuing significance in the community. They belonged to a living tradition whose highlights were tales of Abraham's migration to the land of promise, of Jacob's dream of a stairway between earth and heaven, and of a miraculous deliverance under Moses at the Sea of Reeds. From remote or recent history they illustrated with imaginative embellishments what the storyteller was really saying beneath the surface of his tale.

It is, therefore, not surprising that the wisdom teachers, in their turn, drew on this inherited gift of lively narrative for purposes of instruction and persuasion, as in the schematized folk tale in Job 1–2. Admittedly they fell short of the mastery of the historians, and their didactic, moralizing purpose was too obvious. Their use of imagery cannot be compared with that of prophecy at its most powerful, or of psalmody at its most deeply felt. Inevitably their word pictures were less charged with feeling, for to them control of emotion in the service of reason and sound judgment was an ideal. Even in the supreme poetry of the Book of Job, it can be argued that the wealth of imagery, metaphor, and simile appeals more to the mind and the aesthetic sense than to the emotions of the reader.

Similes and Metaphors

As noted in the preceding chapter, the word *mashal*, usually translated "proverb," has a wider connotation than

³ 1 Sam. 21:1–9 [Heb. 21:2–10].

the metrical couplets of the Book of Proverbs. Its basic meaning is "likeness," "comparison." Its commonest form is the simile.

A comparison may be made directly or indirectly, in a phrase, a sentence, or a complete story. The terse saying "As the mother, so her daughter" (Ezek. 16:44) may refer either to appearance or to behavior, more probably to the latter. Another saying on the same pattern, "As the people, so the priest" (Hos. 4:9), can have different meanings in different contexts. In Hosea the meaning is "People and priest alike will be punished." But in other contexts the saying could mean "A people is no better than its priest(s)," or even "A priest takes his tune from the people," that is, rather than from his obligations to God.

When the two members of the comparison are sufficiently expanded the ambiguity disappears, as in "Like clouds and wind that bring no rain is the man who boasts of gifts he never gives" (Prov. 25:14, NEB).

Sometimes a comparison is made in order to affirm that one thing is preferable to another on moral or other grounds. "Better not vow at all than vow and fail to pay" (Qoh. 5:5 [Heb. 5:4], NEB), "Better to possess little and have religious faith than to be rich and live in turmoil" (Prov. 15:16, AB).

Proverbs that cite famous names imply a complimentary comparison with a living person, "May the Lord make [Ruth] . . . like Rachel and Leah, who together built up the house of Israel." Similarly, "[He is] like Nimrod, a mighty hunter in the Lord's sight."[4] It will be noticed that in these examples the identifying relative clause might have been further expanded in terms of the story alluded to. Thus, in Sirach, one of the several variants of the saying about the nagging wife[5] adds two descriptive coup-

[4] Ruth 4:11; Gen. 10:9.
[5] Prov. 21:9, 19; 25:24; Sir. 25:16.

lets to round out the picture, "I would sooner share a home with a lion or a snake than keep house with a spiteful wife. Her spite changes her expression, making her look surly as a bear. Her husband goes to a neighbor for his meals, and cannot repress a bitter sigh" (Sir. 25:16–18, NEB).

The description here could be recast in story form; that is, it has the makings of a parable. This can be illustrated by considering how easily a parable like that of the Pharisee and the tax collector[6] can be turned into a gnomic couplet, "Better to be a tax collector who acknowledges his sin than a Pharisee who is self-righteous before God."

Whereas the simile compares two things in plain language, the metaphor does this, so to speak, in code, in figurative language whose key words or phrases represent something other than their literal meaning. A metaphor gives striking expression to an idea which, if the metaphor is to be effective, must be understandable from the context in which it is used. In the wisdom books simple metaphors are not found as often as might be expected. The poem of Job opens with one in 3:3–10, where the afflicted hero invokes dreadful curses on the day of his birth, to convey the thought, Why ever was I born? Again, in 29:14–16, he affirms his innocence by declaring, "I put on righteousness and it clothed me; justice, like a cloak or a turban, wrapped me round. I was eyes to the blind and feet to the lame; I was a father to the needy" (NEB). Once more, in 31:6, "Let God weigh me in the scales of justice" (NEB).

A metaphor and its meaning appear in parallel lines in Prov. 25:15, "With patient persistence a high official may be persuaded, and a soft tongue can break a bone" (AB). Micah's dreadful metaphor of cannibalism, for oppression of the poor, becomes in Qoheleth a figure for the self-

---

[6] Luke 18:9–14. For the proverb form, see Prov. 19:1; 28:6.

destruction of the indolent, "The fool with folded hands is devouring his own flesh."[7]

The meaning of some metaphors from an ancient setting which we know so imperfectly, naturally enough, can only be guessed at. For instance, "If the snake bites before [or without] being charmed, the snake-charmer has no value [or profit]" (Qoh. 10:11). Does this mean 'Prevention is better than cure'? Or, 'Knowledge unused is no use'? Or what?

Many ingenious explanations, none conclusive, have been offered for the oxymoron in the second part of the famous injunction, "If your enemy is hungry, give him bread to eat, and if he is thirsty, give him water to drink; For you will heap coals of fire on his head, and the Lord will reward you" (Prov. 25:21–22). Perhaps even in ancient times the point of the metaphor was deliberately made obscure, so as to provoke discussion. Is it any more startling than the counsel to treat an enemy as one would treat a friend?

Parables, Allegories, and Illustrations

A parable is an imaginative story or a single scene drawn from daily life, which is intended to suggest by analogy the point the speaker wishes to make.[8] The best known examples are the parables of Jesus reported in the Synoptic Gospels. Some of these are explicitly identified as similes: "The kingdom of heaven is like leaven . . . , like treasure hidden in a field . . . , like a merchant in search of fine pearls . . . , like a net which was thrown into the sea. . . ."[9] In each example the metaphor is expanded, but

[7] Mic. 3:1–3; Qoh. 4:5.
[8] The Greek word *parabole*, lit. "what is put beside something," represents the basic meaning of the Hebrew *mashal*. Cf. above, pp. 53–54.
[9] Matt. 13:33, 44, 45, 47.

without being developed into a full-fledged story or single scene. On the other hand, the story of the sower in the same chapter,[10] though it lacks the comparative conjunction, is identified by the editor as a parable. In fact, it is a kind of riddle, as we learn from the conclusion, "He who has ears, let him hear," or "understand."[11] Neither of the two supreme parables of the Good Samaritan and the Prodigal Son is expressly identified as such, but they are teaching stories complete with plot, character portrayal, revealing incidents, and climax. The former ends with a challenge to the hearer to make his own decision as to the identity of the neighbor.

In the Old Testament the full-fledged parable is rare. The best-known example is the juridical parable of the rich man's seizure of the poor man's solitary lamb, by which the prophet Nathan brought home to David the nature of his offence in the matter of Uriah's wife. Isaiah's 'Song of the Vineyard' is another example. Hosea's experiences with his promiscuous wife became a parable to him and, through him, to Israel.[12] The books of Ruth and Jonah can be read as parables.

Curiously enough, the single, fully developed wisdom parable appears not in the wisdom books but in the Book of Isaiah. In Isaiah 28:23–29 the prophet casts his oracle into the form and language of the wisdom teachers. Just as the farmer is wise in the ways of agriculture because "he is instructed aright, his God teaches him," so Yahweh's all-powerful shaping of events displays a wisdom transcending the man-centered calculations of the court counsclors.[13]

---

[10] Matt. 13:3–9.
[11] There may be an allusion to Isa. 6:10, "lest they hear with their ears and understand with their minds." Cf. Matt. 13:13–16.
[12] 2 Sam. 12:1–14; Isa. 5:1–7; Hos. chaps. 1 and 3. Two other 'juridical' parables resembling Nathan's are found in 2 Sam. 14:4–17; 1 Kings 20:35–42.
[13] See also Isa. 28:9–13; 29:13–16; 30:1–2; 31:1–3.

The little story in Qoheleth 9:13–16 about the forgotten wise man who might have saved his city is sometimes cited as a parable. It is better regarded as an illustration of the observation that the superiority of wisdom over power can be nullified by neglect. The distinction between a parable and an illustration must be recognized: the illustration clarifies and reinforces the teaching being given, whereas in a parable the audience is called upon to see the analogy and draw its own conclusions. In the first case the hearer is passive. In the second he is actively involved in the search for understanding. At any rate, this is the intention of a parable; if the audience, like the disciples of Jesus in Matthew, is not perceptive enough to grasp the point, it may have to be explained.[14]

Although the wisdom teachers do not make much use of the parable proper, they do avail themselves of teaching illustrations. In Proverbs 1:11 ff. we are permitted to overhear the conversation of the thugs who are tempting an unwary youth to share the easy profits of crime, "Come with us! Let us make a bloody ambush! Let us for sport waylay some innocent! . . . We shall lay our hands on all manner of wealth, we shall fill our houses with plunder. Throw in your lot with us! We shall have a common purse!" In another passage a conspiring villain is drawn to the life, "never straightforward, he winks his eyes, makes signs with his feet, points with his fingers."[15]

Warnings against the prostitute and against overindulgence in wine are underlined in Proverbs 7 and 23 with graphic descriptions of the streetwalker's operations and of the fatuous behavior of the drunkard. Qoheleth illustrates one of his proverbs in 4:13–16 by referring to an episode of the rise and fall of successive kings. The first part of Job's final speech of self-defense in chapter 29 is

---

[14] See Matt. 13:10–23.
[15] Prov. 1:11, 13, 14; 6:12–13, AB.

a tableau picturing what his life had been like before the blow fell.

The only two fables found in the Old Testament both serve as parables. The first is told by Jotham in Judges about the trees' search for a king to reign over them; the second by Jehoash in 2 Kings about the impertinence of a thistle that wanted to marry the daughter of a cedar tree.[16] A fable is, strictly speaking, a short story in which non-human characters are pictured as endowed with human traits, including speech. Often it presents a conflict situation.[17] Marks of this genre appear in the accounts of the talking serpent of Eden, and the talking donkey of Balaam.[18] Occasionally in the wisdom books a natural object or non-human creature is represented as speaking. In Job 28:14 and 22 the ocean depths and the underworld deny that they are wisdom's dwelling and in Proverbs 30:15 the leech figuratively cries out "Give! Give!" But these are only incidental figures of speech.

An allegory, broadly speaking, stands to a metaphor as a parable to a simile. There are two types of allegory: in one, a story is told or a scene described whose elements are a series of metaphors or representative figures; in the second, a story or scene is developed from a single metaphor. The allegory of the two eagles, the cedar, and the vine in Ezekiel 17 is a good example of the first. The two eagles are the Babylonian king and the Egyptian pharaoh, the cedar twig is the Jewish King Jehoiachin who was exiled in 597 B.C., and the vine is Zedekiah who intrigued with Egypt and rebelled against Babylon.

Both types of allegory appear in the wisdom books. In the superb allegorical poem in Qoheleth 12 the infirmities of old age and the approach of death are portrayed in

---

[16] Judg. 9:7–15; 2 Kings 14:9.
[17] See R. J. Williams, "The Fable in the Ancient Near East," in *A Stubborn Faith*, ed. E. C. Hobbs (1956), pp. 3–26.
[18] Gen. 3:1–13; Num. 22:21–35.

the teacher's counseling of young men to make the most of their days of youthful vigor:

> Remember . . . before the sunshine turns to darkness,
> > the light fails from moon and stars,
> > and the clouds return with the rain[s];
>
> When that day comes the palace guardians will tremble,
> > and the powerful will stoop;
>
> The grinding women will cease work because they are few,
> > and they who look out from the lattices will find it dark.
>
> The doors to the street will be shut
> > as the sound of the mill becomes low;
>
> The voice of the birds will be silenced,
> > and all singers of songs will be hushed.
>
> When men will grow afraid of a height,
> > and terrors will lurk in the road;
>
> The almond tree will blossom [white],
> > the locust will bend under his load,
> > and the caper berry will stimulate no more.
>
> So man is on the way to his long-lasting home,
> > and already the mourners gather in the street, [waiting]
>
> Until the silver thread is snapped and the golden bowl is broken,
> > the pitcher is shattered at the spring,
> > and the water-jar[19] broken at the cistern. (AB, alt.)

In the second type of allegory the appeal of wisdom to men is pictured as that of a female figure, "Length of days is in her right hand, in her left hand wealth and honor. Her ways are pure delight, and all her paths are peace."[20] The feminine possessive pronouns (pronominal suffixes)

---

[19] The word *galgal* here, from the parallelism and from Ugaritic cognates, almost certainly refers not to a wheel, but to a round pottery vessel of some sort, as my colleague J. S. Holladay, Jr., pointed out to me. See M. Dahood, *Ugaritic-Hebrew Philology* (1965), p. 54; J. Gray, *The Legacy of Canaan* (1957), p. 201.

[20] Prov. 3:16–17, as translated by W. McKane, *Proverbs* (1970), pp. 214–15. Cf. 4:6–9; Sir. 4:11–19; Wis. Sol. 6:12–16.

Wisdom in Stories and Word Pictures / 83

are used because of the feminine gender of the antecedent noun *hokmah*, "wisdom." From this grammatical usage it is a short step to the figure of Wisdom as a female person; "Say to wisdom, 'You are my sister,' and call insight your intimate friend" (Prov. 7:4).

The metaphorical picture is further developed in the allegorical poems in Proverbs 1 and 8 and in Sirach 24. Again, in Proverbs 9:1 ff. and 13 ff., Wisdom and Folly are personified as rival hostesses inviting men to very different kinds of banquets.

In the first of these, Proverbs 1:20–33, Wisdom appears as a prophetess denouncing and threatening those who reject her, "Since you spurn all my advice and will not accept my warning, I in turn will laugh when sudden calamity strikes you, I will mock when terror overtakes you . . . Then men will cry out for me, but I will not answer."[21] Just as the prophet sometimes adopted the role of the wisdom teacher,[22] the latter here tries to reproduce the effect of the prophetic oracles of denunciation and doom. There is no call for repentance, and judgment is not pronounced in the name of Yahweh. Instead, it is by the inexorable working of the moral law that "The waywardness of the wicked will be the death of them, and the carelessness of fools will destroy them" (1:32, AB).

Chapter 8 is a poem of a different order and tone. Formally, it consists of three strophes of equal length, followed by an epilogue. In the first strophe, Wisdom appeals to men to listen to her. The second declares her nature, her contributions to the spiritual and moral fiber of society, and the rewards she brings to those who respond to her. The third strophe, verses 22–31, soars into the empyrean, far beyond anything in its near or remoter contexts. The poet takes his flight from the word *re'shith*, "beginning," the key word in the motto, "The fear of Yahweh is the

[21] Prov. 1:24–26, 28, AB.
[22] See pp. 79, 124–29.

beginning of knowledge."[23] Now Wisdom affirms that she is the beginning in a much more radical sense—as the first principle of the cosmic order, associated with Yahweh himself in its creation:

> Yahweh possessed me from the initiation of his sovereignty,[24] before his acts of long ago, From of old I was poured out [?], from the first, before the beginnings of the world; When there were no deeps I was brought forth . . . before the mountains were set in place; . . . When he established the heavens, I was there; . . . when he set its limits for the sea . . . I was at his side as helper [?],[25] I was his daily joy, playing in his presence continually, playing in the habitable world, and finding joy in humankind. (AB, alt.)

This metaphor of the personified Wisdom recounting her divine origin and cosmic importance recurs in Sirach 24. But the figure has changed significantly. Now she is the Creator's word, "I am the word which was spoken by the Most High, It was I who covered the earth like a mist" (24:3, NEB). The reference to Genesis 1 is clear. Searching for a home among mankind, Wisdom is directed by the Creator, "Make your home in Jacob; find your heritage in Israel" (24:8, NEB).

In the Wisdom of Solomon, the same metaphor is used with still more elaborate imagery, but at the same time wisdom is considered nonmetaphorically as the endowment

---

[23] Prov. 1:7. In 9:10 wisdom is *t*ᵉ*hillath ḥokmah*. See above, p. 9.

[24] Or "Yahweh created me at the beginning of his sovereign acts." The word *qanah* means either "acquire, possess" as always elsewhere in Prov., or (less often) "create," as in Gen. 14:19 and Deut. 32:6. The first meaning is to be preferred here, since wisdom remains an attribute of Yahweh in spite of the metaphorical personification. It is Yahweh who creates in or by his wisdom, as in 3:19.

[25] Or, "confidant" (McKane, *Proverbs*, pp. 223, 356–58). The form of the word *'amon* is unique and its meaning problematical.

necessary for kingship which Solomon receives in answer to his prayer. Metaphorically, she is,

> a pure effluence from the glory of the Almighty, . . . the brightness that streams from everlasting light, the flawless mirror of the active power of God, and the image of his goodness. Wisdom I loved [says Solomon], I . . . longed to win her for my bride . . . So I determined to bring her home to live with me, Knowing that she would be my counselor.[26]

Narratives as Paradigms

Sometimes the gift for lively narrative was utilized as a paradigm, picturing a pattern of behavior to be emulated. This might be done overtly, in which case the story or scene described illustrates and emphasizes an admonition; or it might be done indirectly by arousing admiration of, or contempt for, the principal character in the story. In that case the story assumes some resemblance to a parable.

In the Book of Proverbs the sluggard or loafer is made the object of much scorn and ridicule. He rolls over on his bed and back again, like a door swinging on its hinges. He is too indolent even to feed himself.[27] In addition to these small gems of sarcasm, two longer pieces are built around the saying "A little [more] sleep, a little [more] slumber, A little [longer] with hands folded in repose, And poverty will overtake you like a vagabond" (AB). In 24:30 ff. this is the reflection of a passerby who observes that the property of a lazy man is overgrown with weeds and its walls broken down. In 6:6 ff. the same lesson is drawn from the contrasting industry of the lowly ant, "Go watch an ant, you loafer! Observe her ways and become wise! Though she has no chieftain, overseer or ruler, she makes sure of her [winter's] food in the summer, she stores up her provisions at harvest." (AB, alt.)

[26] Wis. Sol. 7:25–26; 8:2, 9, NEB.
[27] Prov. 26:14–15; cf. 10:26; 13:4; 15:19; 19:24; 22:13.

A quite different mood pervades the portrait of the capable and diligent housewife in Proverbs 31:10–31. Although the sequence and imagery of this poem are noticeably affected by its limiting acrostic structure, the picture is a vivid one and breathes the pride and admiration of its author. It could well have been composed as a paradigm for a prospective bride.[28]

> A capable wife is a rare find, her worth is far greater than jewels, . . . She seeks out wool and flax, and delights in her handiwork; she is like the merchant ships, bringing her provisions from afar. She rises while it is still night . . . She girds herself firmly and goes to work with a will; she feels that her affairs go well, her lamp burns late at night. She stretches out her fingers to the spindle-whorl, while her hands grasp the spindle. She opens her hands to the needy, and stretches out her arms to the poor. She makes her own bed-covers, fine linen and purple wool are her clothing, . . . Her husband is well known in the city gates where he sits with the community's elders, . . . She watches closely what goes on in her household, and permits no one to eat the bread of idleness. Her sons rise and pronounce blessings on her, her husband too, and he sings her praises—"Many women have shown their worth, but you excel them all." (AB, alt.)

Another type of paradigm is the prose narrative which has the purpose (or one purpose among others) of evoking sympathy and admiration for one who shows moral qualities and accomplishments worthy of imitation. The story may be quasi-historical, as in the case of Joseph; or it may be clearly fictional, yet given a historical setting, as with Ruth, Daniel (in chapters 1–6), Esther, and Judith. The prose folktale that introduces the poem of Job has a similar function; indeed, its fictional character is made obvious by

---

[28] The same theme is expressed epigrammatically in 18:22 and 19:14.

the once-upon-a-time tone of the opening verse, and by the alternation of scenes between earth and the heavenly court.

The story of Joseph takes up almost the last quarter of the Book of Genesis. It is unlike the preceding patriarchal narratives in several respects. They are episodic and discontinuous, and deal with tribal movements and with divine manifestations in particular localities. The story of Joseph, on the other hand, is a continuous biographical narrative with many of the characteristics of a novel. It carries Joseph from foolish youth through many vicissitudes to maturity, wisdom, and great success. The story has an overall literary unity[29] and a plot, a natural sequence of incidents, reversals of fortune, and a dramatic climax which resolves the conflicts of the story. The personal characters of the *dramatis personae* are revealed in incident and dialogue against finely painted backgrounds. The whole is filled with human interest and charged with emotion. The treatment is realistic; there no theophanies or divine appearances to Joseph. But the religious factor is there, no less real because it is kept in the background. The pharaoh's dreams and Joseph's ability to explain them are attributed to God. More important is the lesson drawn by Joseph from what has happened to them all when, at the critical moment, he reveals his identity to his brothers: "'I am Joseph your brother, whom you sold into Egypt. And now do not be distressed, or angry with yourselves, because you sold me here; for God sent me before you to preserve life'" (Gen. 45:4–5).

G. von Rad has pointed out the remarkable way in which this story embodies the teaching of the wisdom

---

[29] This can be said without prejudice to the fact that its present form results from the weaving together of the J and E versions.

schools.[30] It pictures the triumph over all adversities of a man of unusual ability, intelligence, and personal integrity. Through his experience of the ups and downs of life, Joseph has learned the values of humility, self-discipline, industry, and foresight. Success does not spoil him, but rather gives opportunity for the exercise of leadership and administration. The arrogant conceit of his youth has vanished. In its place there has come the enduring power of family affection and the magnanimity that does not seek revenge on the brothers who so grievously had wronged him. Now Joseph sees in all that has happened the working of the overruling power of Providence, which can bring good out of evil.

This understanding of religion in noncultic terms and without reference to a theology of the chosen people is characteristic also of Proverbs, Qoheleth, and Job. Joseph's refusal to commit adultery with Potiphar's wife and his achievement as an honored counselor at a royal court are further links with the special concerns of Israel's sages.

A second extended narrative with some features of a novel and of didactic narrative is the account of the events which led to Solomon's succession to David's throne, rather than one of David's other sons. This is the so-called Succession History, comprising almost all of 2 Samuel 9–20, plus 1 Kings 1–2, and possibly some of the background material now found in earlier parts of 1 and 2 Samuel. This section is marked off from what precedes by the concluding summary in 2 Samuel 8 of the victories which established David's empire. At this point, too, the duplications and inconsistencies which indicate that the pre-

[30] G. von Rad, "Josephgeschichte und ältere Chokma," *VT* Supp. I (1953), pp. 120–27; ——— *Old Testament Theology, I* (1962); pp. 172–73. This view raises problems for Pentateuchal criticism, as pointed out by R. N. Whybray, *VT* xviii, 4 (1968); pp. 522–28, and is criticized on stylistic and other grounds by J. L. Crenshaw, *JBL* 78 (1969), pp. 129–37.

ceding narrative has been put together from two principal sources come to an end. The Succession History is one continuous document, beautifully organized and brilliantly written. The author keeps his eyes fixed on the historical objective of Solomon's anointing as king (Kings 1–2). He believes that Yahweh has so ordered the course of events that Bathsheba's son came to the throne by divine choice.

The story has been universally recognized as historiography of the first rank, written by someone who had been close to the events and who was convinced of their crucial importance and providential ordering. The episodes of the narrative are described wholly in natural and human terms, without benefit of supernatural interventions of any kind. Effect follows cause; the character and behavior of the principal participants open the channels in which the river of history flows. Yet the river flows inexorably to the sea, in accordance with Yahweh's plan for David's dynasty. The author gives just one specific hint of this underlying theme of his work; when Bathsheba gave birth to her second son, he was named Solomon. "But because Yahweh loved him, he sent word through Nathan the prophet that for Yahweh's sake he should be given the name Jedidiah," (which may mean "Yahweh's favorite").[31]

In a recent study that has carried forward previous investigations of the Succession History, R. N. Whybray[32] affirms that, though its "theme is historical, the treatment is that of the novelist" (p. 11). There is "unity of theme and action, leading . . . to a logical and satisfactory conclusion. . . . Each chapter plays an essential part in the

[31] 2 Sam. 12:24–25; see Deut. 33:12; 1 Kings 1:17–18, 28–30.
[32] R. N. Whybray, *The Succession Narrative* (1968). Cf. L. Rost, "Die Überlieferung von der Thronnachfolge Davids," *BWANT* III, no. 6 (1926); G. von Rad, "The Beginnings of Historical Writing in Ancient Israel," in his *Problem of the Hexateuch and other Essays* (1966).

whole"; there are "convincing and lively dialogue, credible characters . . . and a lively and flexible style" (p. 19). But private scenes which no one but the participants could have witnessed are crucial in the author's portrayal and must have been supplied by him. The objective is clearly that of establishing Solomon's claim to the throne, at a time when others, such as Adonijah and his partisans, were questioning it.

The principal new contribution of Whybray's book is his contention that the writer of the Succession History was a wisdom teacher who set out deliberately to illustrate proverbial teaching (p. 95). He draws attention to the similarity in this respect of the Joseph story, with its idea of God's hidden guidance of human destiny, to the writer's fondness for similes and comparisons and to the way in which wisdom teachings are illustrated (or, as Whybray puts it, "dramatized") in the Succession History. Even the prominence of the rival royal counselors, Hushai and Ahithophel, in the account of Absalom's rebellion, points in the same direction.

If Whybray is right, the author here has been more successful than the author of the Joseph story in concealing his didactic purpose. Neither David nor Solomon, within the limits of this document, is pictured as a model of wisdom and noble character. The overriding issue here is the legitimacy of Solomon's succession, as decided by events which were under Yahweh's direction. As in the Joseph story, the form undoubtedly is that of the historical novel, but this story stands much closer to real persons and events. Its drama has not been contrived by the writer, but emerges from dramatic happenings in recent memory. If, as is quite possible, the author belonged to the wisdom school, the indications of this are incidental to his primary purpose as an apologist and a creative historian. They exhibit the reflective observation of human life and character which precedes, not follows, the formulation of wisdom teachings.

A more convincing case has been made by Talmon for the Book of Esther as a paradigmatic wisdom tale in an historical setting.[33] As in the Joseph story and in Daniel, chapter 1, the setting is the court of a foreign monarch, where Hebrew expatriates rise to prominence through their wisdom. Esther, like Joseph and like Nadin in the Ahiqar story, had been a homeless orphan. The tale turns on dramatic reversals of fortune in which justice and virtue triumph. Both Haman and Mordecai are royal counselors. The former is clever, but wicked, and is gradually unmasked as capable of passionate rage, pride, thoughtless speech, and imprudent conduct. Mordecai the Jew, on the other hand, shows himself prudent and self-controlled. Esther, too, is not only beautiful but good, clever, and courageous. Haman hanged on his own gallows illustrates perfectly the many proverbs about deserved retribution.[34]

As in the Joseph story, and in wisdom writings generally, the special relationship of Israel to her God Yahweh is not mentioned. The story is primarily about individuals whose moral behavior is admirable or otherwise.[35] In Esther God is unmentioned, unless the obscure allusion in 4:14 to possible help "from another quarter" refers to divine intervention. The omission is comparable to the reticence of

---

[33] S. Talmon, "'Wisdom' in the Book of Esther," VT xiii, no. 4 (1963): pp. 419–55. The affinities between the Esther and Joseph stories, even to the point of verbal coincidences, has been noted by earlier scholars such as L. A. Rosenthal, in ZAW 15 (1895) and 17 (1897). J. L. Crenshaw is unconvinced; see footnote 30.

[34] Prov. 26:27; Qoh. 10:8; Ps. 7:14–16, EVV; Sir. 27:25–27; 'Onchsheshonqy 22:5.

[35] The theme of Jewish nationalistic reaction to anti-Semitic persecution comes in only in the sequel, where the account of the institution of the Purim festival is awkwardly appended to the tale of Esther.

many proverbial wisdom writers in ascribing the consequences of human behavior directly to God.

The theme of the Book of Esther is resumed in Judith, the apocryphal tale of another heroic woman who delivered her people at great risk to herself. The historical setting, in a Persian invasion of Judaea, is even more patently fictional. This time the heroine is noted, not only for her beauty and cleverness, but also for her exemplary piety (which proves no hindrance to calculated deception and a bloody deed). The specifically wisdom features of the story are few. Judith is known among her own people as a woman of understanding and she wins Holofernes' unsuspecting compliments for the strategem she proposes. The paradigm of the story is that of patriotism, courage and self-sacrifice, and only incidentally that of wisdom.

Stories about Sages and Their Sayings

Quite a different type of story is one in which the central figure is himself a wise man. Quotable sayings are attributed to him or he is described as exhibiting extraordinary knowledge and understanding. Two such tales from outside Israel may be taken as typical: the Egyptian Tale of the Eloquent Peasant, and the (originally Assyrian) Words of Ahiqar.[36]

The first of these tells how a peasant on a journey is beaten and robbed by a man through whose property he is passing. He appeals for redress to the chief steward, with such unexpected eloquence (a much admired accomplishment in Egypt) that the steward reports it to the pharaoh. The latter suggests that the case be postponed, in order to derive entertainment from the peasant's further

---

[36] *ANET*, pp. 407b–410b; 427b–430b. See also pp. 31–32 above.

complaints. The peasant makes nine successive appeals, exercising all the arts of the suppliant,

> Desire to live long, as it is said: "Doing justice is the [very] breath of the nose." ... Do not plunder of his property a poor man. ... Thou wert appointed to be a dam for the sufferer, guarding lest he drown, [but] behold, thou art his flowing lake. ... Cheating diminishes justice. ... Do justice for the sake of the Lord of Justice. ... Justice lasts for eternity; it goes down into the necropolis with him who does it. ... He is remembered for goodness.

It is pleasant to learn that the peasant's eloquence and persistence won his case.

The story of Ahiqar was widespread in antiquity in varying forms. It tells of a certain Ahiqar, a royal counselor to Sennacherib, king of Assyria, who had adopted his nephew Nadin, only to have the latter falsely accuse him of treason in order to supplant him. Ahiqar manages to escape execution and is later restored to favor and takes vengeance on Nadin. Within this narrative framework is incorporated a large collection of proverbial sayings, supposedly used first in Nadin's education, and later to denounce him.[37] Many of these resemble maxims and adages in the book of Proverbs, "Withhold not thy son from the rod, else thou wilt not be able to save him," "From thee is the arrow, but from God the [guidance]," "Hunger makes bitterness sweet."[38]

The Book of Tobit in the larger canon[39] makes a direct reference in 14:10 to the Ahiqar story; the Assyrian setting and period are the same, and its fictive narrator even claims Ahiqar as his nephew. Tobit is a popular romance about a pious Israelite who lived in Nineveh with his wife and

---

[37] The oldest surviving version is in Aramaic of the fifth century B.C. and is incomplete. Later and fuller versions are extant in Syriac, Arabic, and other languages. The story appears also in a supplement to the *Arabian Nights*.
[38] Cf. Prov. 23:13–14; 16:9; 27:7.
[39] See above, p. 19, n. 49.

son Tobias.[40] Tobit becomes blind and poor. At the same time, in distant Ecbatana, a cousin of theirs named Sarah is in deep trouble, having lost seven husbands in succession, slain by a demon in the bridal chamber. The prayers of both are heard, and an angel is sent to help them.

Tobit now sends his son to Media to collect a sum of money belonging to him. The angel disguises himself and becomes Tobias's traveling companion. En route they catch a fish and, on the angel's instructions, Tobias removes the heart, liver, and gall to serve as amulets. At Ecbatana Tobias meets and marries Sarah, having banished the demon by burning the heart and liver of the fish. Returning home with his new wife and the money, Tobias restores his father's sight by rubbing his eyes with the gall of the fish. The angel then reveals his identity, admonishes father and son and vanishes. Tobit gives thanks to God and all ends happily.

The element of folklore in this story is obvious, but incidental to its purpose, which is to show the power of prayers and good deeds to win divine aid and overcome misfortune. The highest wisdom is seen to be the fear of the Lord. The father's words of counsel to his son on their parting provide the traditional setting for wisdom instruction.[41] The precepts and proverbs here are clearly of more general application than the immediate circumstances,

> Give me decent burial. Show proper respect for your mother. . . . Remember, my son, all the dangers she faced for your sake while you were in her womb.[42] . . . Do not fall into evil ways, for an honest life leads to prosperity. . . . Do not turn your face

---

[40] The familiar forms of the names Tobit and Tobias come from LXX. Both father and son are called Tobias in Vulg. In the Qumran Hebrew and Aramaic mss. they are known respectively as Tobi and Tobiah.
[41] Tob. 4:1–21. See above, p. 31.
[42] Cf. Instruction of Ani, *ANET*, pp. 420b–421a.

away from any poor man, and God will not turn his face away from you. . . . Beware, my son, of fornication. . . . Pride breeds ruin and anarchy. . . . and the waster declines into poverty. . . . Pay your workmen their wages the same day. . . . Be circumspect. . . . and show yourself well-bred in all your behavior. . . . Do not do to anyone what you yourself would hate.[43] Do not drink to excess. . . . Do not despise any advice.

The angel's admonitions in 12:6–10 also are partly in proverbial form.

The stories in 1 Kings about Solomon, the most celebrated wise man in ancient Israel, are partly history, partly fiction. Solomon was, of course, a prominent historical figure, and the tradition associating him or his court with the early flowering of wisdom is firmly rooted in fact. But, as already noted,[44] the fulsome description of Solomon's limitless knowledge and wisdom as surpassing that of any human being past or present, and the ascription to the king himself of the authorship of thousands of proverbs and poems, not to mention his dumbfounding the Queen of Sheba by his instant success in solving every riddle she put to him—is fiction, founded, at most, on a substratum of fact. Otherwise, unlike many of the prophets, the writers of the wisdom books remain anonymous[45] and unlocated in chronological history, until Jeshua' ben Sira' in the second century B.C.

The stories of Daniel and his three friends, in the Book of Daniel, chapters 1–6, belong to a different category. These again are paradigmatic stories. The youths' faith-

---

[43] For other formulations of the Golden Rule, cf. Exod. 23:4–5; Prov. 25:21–22; Matt. 7:12; the Babylonian Counsels of Wisdom, lines 41 ff, *ANET* Supp. p. 159.

[44] See above, pp. 13–14.

[45] With the possible exception of what is said about Qoheleth in the footnote to his collected teachings in Qoh. 12:9–10. We still do not know his name; he is simply called "Teacher" or "Doctor" (in 12:8 with the definite article).

fulness to Jewish dietary rules results in their superiority, both physical and mental, to their fellow trainees. Again, the trio's refusal to worship the golden idol brings divine deliverance from a fiery furnace into which they had been thrown in consequence. Daniel's constancy in praying thrice daily toward Jerusalem causes him to be cast into a pit with lions, from which, similarly, he is delivered.

The kind of wisdom with which the pious Daniel is endowed, however, is not like that attributed to Solomon. Daniel has the gift of interpreting dreams, and such ominous words as *mene mene tekel upharsin* written by a mysterious hand on the palace wall. This gift is not the esoteric skill of the Chaldaean magicians and omen interpreters. "This secret," he says, "has been revealed to me, not because I am wise beyond all living men" (2.30, NEB). True, he is twice spoken of as "master of the magicians"; he had been promoted over them because he received divine revelations, and not as their superior in magic lore. As in the Joseph story, the author lays stress on the fact that the worshiper of the true God was filled with the divine spirit, and hence could understand what lay outside the competence of magicians.[46] "The fear of the Lord," which in Proverbs is the first requirement for acquiring wisdom, has here become the source of understanding of divine mysteries. From this it is but a step to the picture of Daniel, in chapters 7–12, as himself the seer of apocalyptic visions.

Wisdom in Paradise

It is doubtless an exaggeration to claim that the myths of Genesis 1–11, portraying the origins of the world and of the human condition, are wisdom documents. Yet, broadly speaking, that is what they are. Though making

[46] Dan. 4:9 (Aram. 4:6); 5:11; 2:48. Cf. Gen. 41:38.

little use of wisdom phraseology and traditional ideas, they explore ultimate questions about God's relationship to man and his world of a kind that concerned the theological wing of the wisdom teachers. To call these stories 'myths' is to beg the question of the nature and function of myth. They discuss what is, in terms of how it came to be. In doing so, they make use of floating mythological materials from more ancient cultures which dealt with similar questions. The echoes of the Mesopotamian myths of creation and of the great deluge are unmistakeable, even though the biblical stories have been recast in forms compatible with, and indeed instrumental for, Israel's distinctive faith.

At least one of these origin stories, that in Genesis 3 describing the fall of man and his ejection from the garden of Eden, has certain wisdom features. The story can be read as a parable of human alienation from God and from the world as God intended it to be, through man's rebellion against his Creator and the laws of his own being. It also illustrates graphically the subtle process of temptation and the self-justification which accompanies it. But the tale also probes the profound problems of the nature and limitations of human knowledge and of the relation of knowledge to morality. These elements presuppose a highly developed type of wisdom thinking as their background.

To begin with, there is the fabulous feature of the talking snake, like the talking donkey of Balaam.[47] The snake is, of course, not the Devil of later theological speculation, to which, nevertheless, this story undoubtedly contributed.[48] Here it is just one of the wild creatures mentioned in 2:19–20, but the cleverest of them, able to speak and reason like a man. The adjective *'ārūm* means "intelligent,"

---

[47] Num. 22:21–35.
[48] Cf. Wis. Sol. 2:24; 2 Cor. 11:3; Rev. 20:2.

and in a bad sense "crafty."[49] That this word is found elsewhere in the Old Testament only in Proverbs and Job hints at wisdom influence.

The pivot of the tale is the eating of the tree of knowledge, and the consequences that follow this forbidden act. This tree of knowledge belongs primarily to the narrative in chapter 3, and the tree of life (or, of immortality) to the preceding chapter. Two distinct myths have been drawn upon by the biblical author, and some confusion has resulted from their combination.[50] The trees are magic trees, whose fruits, if eaten together, would confer on man the immortality and knowledge which belong to divine beings. "Then Yahweh God said . . . 'Behold, the man has become like one of us, knowing good and evil; what if he now reaches out his hand and takes fruit from the tree of life also, eats it and lives forever?'" (Gen. 3:22, NEB).

What then is this knowledge of good and evil? It would seem at first sight that it means here sexual consciousness, since the serpent was a phallic symbol,[51] the fruit arouses the woman's desire, and the immediate result of eating is the couple's sexual awareness of each other. This may indeed have been the point of the more ancient myth utilized by the biblical writer.[52] To the extent that this theme survives in the present passage, it has been turned into a polemic against the lascivious rites of the Canaanite cults. But this is not the only possible meaning. The verse just quoted precludes it, because biblical religion simply

---

[49] Cf. "wise as serpents" in Matt. 10:16, and the puzzle of their means of locomotion, Prov. 30:19.

[50] See J. L. McKenzie, *Myths and Realities* (1963), pp. 164–70.

[51] Ibid., pp. 166, 265.

[52] Cf. the Sumerian myth of Enki, the gardener, and Ninhursag, the mother goddess. Enki brings on himself a curse for eating certain plants that apparently had been forbidden him. See *ANET*, p. 40; and for the Gilgamesh epic, *ANET*, pp. 75, 77. See also S. N. Kramer, *Mythologies of the Ancient World* (1961), p. 101.

has no place for sex differentiation in its concept of deity.

In most Old Testament contexts the phrase *good and evil* has no moral connotation; it usually means "good and/or bad," that is, (as a hendiadys) "everything," or, when negative, "nothing."[53] In Deuteronomy 1:39 and Isaiah 7:15–16 the words refer to the inexperience of infants. Only in 1 Kings 3:9 (Solomon's prayer) do the words certainly have the moral connotation "right" and "wrong." It is, therefore, at least possible that the meaning in Genesis 3 is that the definition of what is right and what is wrong belongs to God alone. Certainly this question lies at the heart of Job's agonized dilemma, "Dost thou see as man sees?" (10:3–4). Is what man understands by justice not what this means to God? The other interpretation also is possible from the standpoint of translation, namely, that what man gained by eating the fruit was knowledge of everything, like the knowledge of a god. But this hardly fits the moral profundities of Genesis 3, or the subsequent history of man as the Bible tells it.

By choosing to disobey the commandment which was integral to his life in Paradise, man claimed to decide for himself that what he wants is good, his good, and what he does not want is bad. In asserting his freedom and independence, he discovered that he had exiled himself from the world the Creator had called good. He has preferred his own knowledge to trusting the divine goodness. Knowledge is power, the power of self-determination, the power which seeks to impose man's will on other living things, and to remake creation in his own image and likeness. He has become almost a god. In his *hubris* he acts as if he were God, answerable to none. But man is not a god, because he is mortal. The knowledge he has seized, and all that goes with it, is limited and negated by death. Exile from Eden is the price man has paid for his declara-

---

[53] Cf. Gen. 31:24, 29; 2 Sam. 13:22; 19:35; Zeph. 1:12.

tion of independence. "So Yahweh God drove him out of the garden, . . . and to the east of the garden of Eden he stationed the cherubim[54] . . . to guard the way to the tree of life" (3:24).

A related Canaanite myth touching on the theme of primeval man in the Garden of Eden is obscurely alluded to in Ezekiel 28. In his first oracle, verses 2–10, the prophet declares that the pretensions of the king of Tyre to a godlike wisdom and power will bring his overthrow. The same theme is developed in verses 12–19 against the background of a story with striking resemblances to that in Genesis 3, but with equally striking differences.

The Tyrian king is here symbolically identified with archetypal man, accoutered as a king, filled with wisdom and altogether beautiful. This man was in Eden, a divine garden, guarded by a k^erub or "cherub," until he became lawless and was cast out in disgrace; or rather, cast down to earth from the mountain of the gods (where, in this story, Eden was located). Other differences from Genesis 3 are that there is no mention of a serpent or a woman or of a temptation to grasp the fruit of knowledge (since man here was already filled with wisdom). His sin was the use of his wisdom to grasp at divine power.[55] Here the picture resembles another mythological picture in Isaiah 14:12–15, where the morning star sought to set his throne above the stars and make himself the equal of the Highest God, only to be cast down to Sheol.

Unlike Genesis 3, however, these prophetic oracles do not properly belong with didactic stories on the nature and origin of wisdom, but instead with the subject of the next chapter.

[54] The cherubim were supernatural creatures, represented in Mesopotamian art as winged bulls or lions, whose function was to guard access to sanctuaries and to the sacred person of the king. See Ezek. 28:14, 16; Exod. 25:18–20; 1 Kings 6:23–28.

[55] V. 17, "for the sake of your splendor" (RSV); "to increase your dignity" (NEB).

5
Prophecy and Wisdom

PROPHECY WAS the most distinctive single element in ancient Israelite religion, and the most powerful in its permanent effect on the faith that created the Bible. The dramatic challenges of Elijah, the moral passion of Amos and Micah, the eloquent faith of Isaiah in a holy and sovereign God, the agonized personal experiences of Hosea and Jeremiah, the despair and hope of the God-struck Ezekiel, the lyrical joy of Deutero-Isaiah in the Creator's new creation in history—these are Old Testament religion at its most vital. The basic assertion of these men was that their God Yahweh had made himself known to them as a living God whose will they were to declare to his chosen people. He was a God who acted in and through significant events in the continuing historical experience of Israel. His prophetic messengers believed that they knew what Yahweh was doing and was about to do because he had sent them and they were privy to his plans.[1]

Moreover, the narrative histories of Israel's life in Canaan from the conquest to the exile were assembled and edited to illustrate a prophetic theme—that Yahweh's people had received his support and the continuing guidance of prophetic voices, and finally were overthrown as a result of

[1] Amos 3:7; Isa. 29:14; 30:1; 46:8–11; Jer. 1:5–7; 23:18, 22.

their ever-recurring disobedience and disloyalty.[2] This in turn was in keeping with the picture of Moses himself as a prophet, called by Yahweh as his messenger to the incipient Israel, and to be the agent of her historical deliverance. The prophet as an inspired messenger for his god was a religious phenomenon not peculiar to Israel, as we know from the Zakir inscription and the Mari tablets.[3] But there is nothing comparable elsewhere in the range and quality of the literary records of prophecy, or in the profundity and pervasiveness of prophecy's influence on religion.

It is, therefore, at first sight disconcerting to find three of the major prophets vehemently denouncing their contemporaries the wise men. "Shame on you!" cries Isaiah, "you who are wise in your own eyes, and prudent in your own esteem." "I will again do marvelous things with this people, . . . and the wisdom of their wise men shall perish." Jeremiah declares that "the wise men shall be put to shame, . . . they have rejected the word of the Lord, and what wisdom is in them?" To Deutero-Isaiah, Yahweh is the maker of heaven and earth "who turns wise men back and makes their knowledge foolish."[4] It would seem that Fichtner is justified in asserting that prophecy and wisdom are contradictory and worlds apart.[5]

There is some truth in Fichtner's claim, but it is oversimplified and must be qualified in various literary and historical contexts. Prophecy and wisdom are phenomena

---

[2] These books, Joshua to 2 Kings, were later to be called the Former Prophets on account of this theme. Still later they were attributed by some to prophetic authorship.

[3] See *ANET Supp.*, pp. 187–89; J. S. Ross, "Prophecy in Hamath, Israel, and Mari," *HTR* 63 (1970), no. 1, pp. 1–28.

[4] Isa. 5:21, NEB; 29:14; Jer. 8:9; Isa. 44:25.

[5] J. Fichtner, "Jesaja unter den Weisen," in his *Gottes Weisheit* (1965), p. 18. Curiously enough Fichtner points his contrast by comparing Amos with Proverbs, whereas Terrien and Wolff justly draw attention to evidence of wisdom influence on Amos in particular. See n. 47 below.

too complex to be represented by one prophet and one particular type of wisdom writing. Each has its own history and various meanings within a broad area of similarity. The calculating politicians whom Isaiah denounces as self-styled wise men are no more typical of wisdom as a whole than the false prophets who opposed Jeremiah are typical of prophecy. Throughout a long association in the same community the two groups had different objectives and were sometimes in direct and obvious conflict. In them two streams of Israel's cultural and spiritual life flowed side by side for centuries. Inevitably they influenced each other, for they had much in common. Eventually the two streams merged in a piety centered on a holy book. In the second century B.C. Ben Sira' was a wisdom teacher who modeled his work largely on the Book of Proverbs, yet incorporated with his precepts and maxims a deep appreciation of 'holy history' and of temple worship. He even laid claim himself to prophetic inspiration (Sir. 1:10; 24:33).

Thus in considering the interaction of prophecy and wisdom it is necessary both to define our terms and to envisage differing circumstances. Is the word *ḥakam* being used as an adjective, "wise," or as a noun, "wise man," "sage"? If the former, what is the nuance intended—clever? cunning? skilful? sagacious? If a noun, does it refer to a sage in the broad sense, or an educated man as such? to a professional scribe? to a teacher? to a royal counselor? to a member of the secular establishment (as in Jer. 9:23, EVV), or of the religious establishment (as in Jer. 18:18)? Again, when does the noun *sōpēr*, "writer," indicate a man's occupation (as with Jeremiah's amanuensis Baruch), and when is it the title of a high political officer, one of the chief ministers of the king?[6]

[6] Jer. 36:26; 2 Sam. 8:17; 1 Kings 4:1–6; 2 Kings 18:37; Ezra 7:12–26. There was a twofold reason for Ezra's title; he was a scholar and also the deputy of the Persian king.

A Changing Picture

It may be helpful in distinguishing the several currents and crosscurrents to glance at the situations in different historical periods, observing the stages of development in both prophecy and wisdom, with any indications of their interaction.

THE TIMES OF SAMUEL, SAUL AND DAVID

The picture here is not altogether consistent, since the source materials underlying 1 and 2 Samuel interpret the sequence of events and the dramatis personae from different viewpoints. Samuel himself is first introduced as a peripatetic holy man who had the gift of clairvoyance and received divine revelations in dreams. It is explained parenthetically that "he who is now called a prophet (*nabi'*) was formerly called a seer (*ro'eh*)." This equation provides the link with a second portrayal of Samuel as a *nabi'*; he is called by Yahweh, entrusted with a doom oracle on the priestly family of Eli, and later commissioned to summon first Saul, then David, to the kingship. Samuel becomes Saul's prophetic mentor, and is reported to have denounced the king's disobedience in terms reminiscent of Hosea.[7]

When called and proleptically anointed as king, Saul is given as a confirmatory sign the prediction that he would shortly meet a band of spirit-intoxicated prophets and would 'prophesy' with them. When this takes place Saul catches their frenzy, and we see how far removed was this kind of prophecy from that of an Isaiah or a Jeremiah. These were not spokesmen of Yahweh's word, calling on men to obey his will. Instead, by their wild, emotional group behavior they sought to arouse the people

---

[7] 1 Sam. 9:1–10:16; 3:1–21; 9:15–10:1; 16:1–13; 15:17–23; Hos. 6:6.

to militancy in Yahweh's cause, after the fashion of Muslim dervishes.[8]

There were, however, two individual prophets of the word of Yahweh, Gad and Nathan, who were members of David's inner circle. Gad is given, in addition, the special title "David's Seer," presumably as a private consultant who could foresee the future and advise the king accordingly.[9] This function was different from that of the *nabi'*, who was sent by Yahweh to reproach the king on moral grounds and to pronounce Yahweh's judgment.[10] The relationship of Gad and Nathan to the king was probably not an official one, since they are not listed among David's officers of state in 2 Sam. 8:16 ff.

It is strange that no prophet appears in the story of the struggle among David's sons to succeed him, until its climax in 1 Kings 1 when Nathan reemerges to press on David the promise made to Solomon's mother. Even then, Nathan seems to speak on his own behalf rather than as Yahweh's messenger. A possible reason for this is that the 'Succession History' was produced by a writer of the wisdom school who would have no motive to stress the role of prophets.[11] Instead, the pivot of the story is the contradictory advice to Absalom given by the court counselors Hushai and Ahithophel.[12] There is thus no direct conflict here between the representatives of prophecy and wisdom. The one ignores the other.

In addition to royal counselors, wisdom appears in other ways in this early period. A famous female sage from Tekoa

---

[8] 1 Sam. 10:5–13; 19:20–24.

[9] 2 Sam. 24:11; 1 Sam. 22:5. The term *hozeh* seems to mean "one who receives divine revelations in dreams." It may or may not be synonymous with *ro'eh*, used of Samuel in 1 Sam. 9:9. Both words are later used loosely of prophets (*n^{e}bi'im*).

[10] 2 Sam. 12:1–14; 24:10–13.

[11] See above, pp. 88–91.

[12] 2 Sam. 15:31–34; 16:15–17:14.

106 / *The Way of Wisdom*

is induced by Joab to secure by a ruse the king's permission for Absalom's return from banishment. Another wise woman persuades Joab himself to accept a compromise rather than destroy a city. And in the account of the rape of Tamar the epithet "wise" is applied pejoratively to the cunning Jonadab, and the girl protests that such "wanton folly (*n^{e}balah*) is something "not done in Israel."[13] This story clearly reflects established moral standards under the categories of wisdom and folly.

THE REIGN OF SOLOMON

It is a striking fact that, following Nathan's part in setting Solomon on the throne, there is no further mention of prophets until, at the end of the reign, Ahijah, in Yahweh's name, commissions the revolt of the northern tribes.[14] The biblical account of the reign is, in fact, not consecutive but topical, with more space given to the building and dedication of the temple than to all other matters put together. Solomon's power and glory, his reputation for wisdom, his administrative and defense measures, his building operations in Jerusalem and other cities, his imperial policies, are dealt with briefly and almost incidentally. In place of prophetic messengers, we are told that Yahweh twice spoke directly to the king himself in dreams.

There must, however, have been extensive literary activity in this period, although this is mentioned only with respect to Solomon's proverbs and songs, as well as to annalistic records. The great epic of Israel's origins, the J strand of the Pentateuch, is a work of consummate artistry and theological penetration. It certainly comes from the early monarchy and probably from the time of Solo-

[13] 2 Sam. 14:1–23; 20:15–22; 13:1–14.
[14] 1 Kings 11:29–31.

mon. The Succession History had told how the dynastic torch was passed to Solomon, without introducing supernatural features other than the workings of divine Providence. Its author's method is that of the wise man who teaches morals and religion indirectly through the creative treatment of observable events. It is quite otherwise with the J author or authors. Their theme is the story of a people who had become a nation by the deliberate purpose of Yahweh. Their God participates personally in that history through successive revelations of himself, of his purpose, and his power. Now, at the climactic moment when "the kingdom was established" and the temple built, the national story is told as *sacred* history. There are wisdom features in the epic, as might be expected from the breadth of the author's interests and intellectual grasp. His primary theme and his theology, however—Yahweh's self-revelation in promise and moral imperative to this people which he had brought into being on the stage of history—are fundamentally prophetic.

The role of Solomon as patron of a flourishing school of gnomic wisdom has already been discussed.[15] In this development the influence of the more ancient and also contemporary foreign wisdom traditions can be recognized. The fact that the king's principal wife was an Egyptian princess is, at least, a hint that Egyptian court organization and administrative bureaucracy also contributed ideas (and perhaps direct assistance) to the rapid organization of Solomon's kingdom. To the extent that Egyptian models were followed, the king's chief advisers would be men trained for high office in wisdom schools. Officials and clerks would require training in the mysteries of writing, calculating, record keeping, and some would be competent in foreign languages and literatures. Indeed, the silence

[15] See above, pp. 13–15, 95.

concerning the activity of prophets in Solomon's reign may be due to the dominance at the court of these professional representatives of a secular and politically oriented wisdom.[16]

THE PERIOD OF THE CLASSICAL PROPHETS FROM AMOS TO JEREMIAH (CA. 750–587 B.C.)

In this period the prophets spoke essentially with one voice, denouncing king and people for apostasy, hypocrisy, and the general moral corruption resulting from failure to conform to Yahweh's demands. Imminent doom was predicted in default of a radical change of heart.

Two things differentiate these men from earlier prophets like Nathan and Ahijah: (1) They were the first whose oracles were preserved extensively in writing, and (2) their messages were addressed, not to the king alone, but to groups in society like the priests, or the rich and powerful, or to the nation as a whole.[17] Their messages were primarily denunciation and the threat of doom. In this they were unlike the later Ezekiel and Deutero-Isaiah who proclaimed a new hope, in the changed circumstances after the doom had fallen on Israel as predicted.

It may be that we gain from the books of the classical prophets an exaggerated impression of the recognition they received from their contemporaries, before events had validated their words. Amos and Isaiah (for a time) were forced into retirement. Jeremiah was constantly at odds with the 'powers that be,' and at the end of his life was completely repudiated by the remnant of his people. Only after disaster had come was it recognized that the prophets

---

[16] As in Isaiah's time. See Isa. 19:11–13; 28:14–22; 30:1–5.

[17] J. S. Holladay, Jr., sees here the pattern of a new Assyrian policy of dealing with whole peoples rather than with kings alone and, hence, requiring publication of their communications. See his "Assyrian Statecraft and the Prophets of Israel," *HTR* 63 (1970): pp. 29–51.

had been right, and men honored their words in so far as these had been preserved by their disciples.

In these records the opposition of certain wise men to the prophets is noted. Who were they, and what was the reason for their antagonism? At one point Isaiah was evidently in conflict with a ruling court circle on critical issues of Judah's foreign policy. The political expediency of worldly wisdom led the court to put its trust in Egyptian military assistance rather than in Yahweh. The prophet pours scorn on their Egyptian counterparts whom these men so greatly admired.[18] Probably he has the same people in view when he denounces the men of rank, "wise in their own eyes," who taunt him with a demand for evidence of Yahweh's greater wisdom. They scoff at what they consider his presumption in "teaching" them as if they were children in school.[19]

Jeremiah, too, confronted "the wise" as a recognized group in the power structure—the wise, the mighty and the rich. More specifically, those who formed the governing council under the king are designated *sarim* "princes," "secular authorities." A different type of "wise men" (probably wisdom teachers), together with the priests and the cult prophets, comprised the religious establishment.[20] Still another group were the temple scribes who were now the custodians and authorized teachers of a written Torah which, in their view, made the prophetic word superfluous.[21] Some of the *sarim* defended Jeremiah against the accusation of sacrilege made by the temple authorities and some of them seem to have been sympathetic, or at least concerned, when Jeremiah's prophecies were written down and read in the temple. But they, too, cry treachery when,

[18] Isa. 19:11–12; 30:1–2; 31:1–2.
[19] Isa. 5:18; 28:9–10.
[20] Jer. 9:12, 23–24, EVV; 26:10–11; 18:18.
[21] The Torah here referred to is undoubtedly the recently published Deuteronomic scroll. See Jer. 8:8–9; 2 Kings 22:8–23:3.

during the final siege of Jerusalem, the prophet counsels surrender as in line with Yahweh's will.[22]

In addition to the secular wisdom of politics and to the gradual spread of literacy through the schools, there are other signs of wisdom activities in this period. This influence on the prophets themselves is discussed below. In Proverbs 25:1 a descriptive heading credits the following collection of sayings to "the men of Hezekiah," which indicates that organized literary work was going on again at the royal court. The old wisdom doctrine of the natural consequences of right and wrong personal behavior[23] was now taken over into the national covenant theology of Deuteronomy as the alternatives of divine promise or curse. This, in turn, was to reinforce the dogma of inevitable individual retribution asserted by Job's opponents. The shattering shock of the sudden death of the 'good' King Josiah may well have precipitated the soul-searching in connection with this doctrine that was to produce the Book of Job.

THE PERIOD OF THE EXILE

The Judaean monarchy was effectively ended when King Jehoiachin was banished to Babylonia in 597 B.C., together with the personnel of government and leading citizens. Further deportations took place ten and fifteen years later. Other Judaeans fled to Egypt. Yet many of the common people remained, for they were not replaced with new settlers as had been done by the Assyrians after the fall of Samaria. Nevertheless, the more literate, articulate, historically and theologically aware Judaeans were now for the most part to be settled in Babylonia for two generations, and in many cases for much longer.

[22] Jer. 26:10, 16; 36:4–26; 37:11–15; 38:1–6.
[23] See above, pp. 10–11, 63.

Two major prophets were among the exiles. Ezekiel was both a priest and a prophet, and his messages touched the wisdom theme only in the oracles on the proud semimythical wisdom of the king of Tyre. Deutero-Isaiah arose as spokesman among the exiles of a new hope in the creative power of Yahweh, which would be displayed in a triumphant return to Zion. In contrast to this he scorns the impotence of the divination and priestly magic which passed as wisdom in Babylonian religion. It is Yahweh's plan and purpose of Israel's salvation that will succeed, for his wisdom no other man or god can match.[24]

Neither Ezekiel nor Deutero-Isaiah concerns himself with the wise men of Israel, or is much influenced by them. This was a time and place where the scriptural scribe and teacher came into his own. Torn up by the roots and no longer a territorial nation, the Judaean Israel began the consolidation of her national and religious literary inheritance. On the basis of the Deuteronomic covenant theology the society's traditions from conquest to exile were linked in a continuous history that showed how Israel had been led by Yahweh, delivered by his power, but finally ruined through persistent disloyalty to his covenant. For this theologically motivated history, Joshua to 2 Kings, a new historical introduction with accompanying homily was prepared, to precede the Book of Deuteronomy.[25] The homily incorporates a novel and significant theological thought, that the covenant laws embody a divine wisdom concerning human life in society, which other peoples will come to recognize as intrinsically superior because of its inherent rightness.[26]

---

[24] Ezek. 28:2–6, 12, 17; Isa. 44:25; 47:9–13.
[25] Deut. 1–4, according to the widely accepted view of M. Noth in his *Überlieferungsgeschichtliche Studien* (1957).
[26] Deut. 4:5–8; cf. Sir. 24:1–12, 23–29.

AFTER THE EXILE

The fire of prophecy flared up briefly in Haggai, 1 and 2 Zechariah, and Malachi, then flickered and went out. Even these men stood in the shadow of "the former [i.e., preexilic] prophets."[27] According to Talmudic tradition "from the day the temple was destroyed the prophetic gift was taken from the prophets and given to the sages."[28] The sages meant here are the scribes and interpreters of the Torah in the tradition of Ezra and his assistants, together with their heirs, the "doctors of the Law" mentioned in the New Testament, and the rabbinic sages of the Mishnah.[29]

The wisdom tradition found expression in other ways as well. In the Persian period a wisdom teacher and theologian assembled the older materials of the Book of Proverbs for use in his school and contributed an introduction to these in chapters 1–9. This contains ten admonitory discourses and also theological explorations of the origin and nature of wisdom as a concept and as a living, divine reality confronting mankind. In the second century B.C. Sirach (ben Sira') is constructed largely on the model of Proverbs. Another work comes from an anonymous teacher known as Qoheleth; as we have seen, he presented a very different view, philosophically agnostic and determinist. The work known as the Wisdom of Solomon, or simply as Wisdom, is a manifesto by an Alexandrian Jew of the first century B.C. who sought to steady the faith of Jews living in an alien environment, and to make a case for the Jewish idea of wisdom in the face of Hellenistic thought. Finally there are the midrashic stories in Daniel 1–6 about the wisdom revealed to the pious and faithful hero who

[27] Zech. 1:4; 7:7.
[28] T. Bab., Baba bathra 12a.
[29] Neh. 8:1–8; Luke 5:17; Acts 5:34.

was thus enabled to surpass the esoteric wisdom of the Babylonians.

The Differences between Prophecy and Wisdom

From the foregoing historical outline it will be seen that prophecy and wisdom were markedly distinct cultural and religious phenomena, each with its own history concurrent with the other's. Prophecy was at its most intense and most articulate in the eighth to the sixth centuries B.C. The course of the wisdom tradition was more continuous and long drawn-out; it flourished particularly in the early monarchy and again after the exile when prophecy fell silent. There was constant interaction between the two, and sometimes conflict. Here it is necessary to notice the difference between the secular and the religious forms of wisdom, and between the self-serving and conforming prophets and the prophets of Yahweh's word, whose messages were eventually to be validated by history and religious experience. Like must be compared with like— in kind and quality. We are enabled to do this through the more important literature which wisdom and prophecy each have contributed to the Bible.

The basic differences between these two are: (1) in their respective presuppositions and angles of approach; (2) in their distinct theologies; (3) in their immediate concerns, objectives, and methods; and (4) in their characteristic ways of thought, vocabularies, and developed literary forms.

Broadly speaking, the prophet speaks from the standpoint of revelation, the wise man from that of reason working from the data of experience and observation. The prophet feels a compulsion to declare a word from God to his contemporaries. He is one sent with a message, a man set apart. "Before you were born I consecrated you," says Yahweh to Jeremiah; "I appointed you a prophet to the nations."[30] This is not to say that every separate oracle introduced with "thus says Yahweh" was preceded by a new revelatory experience; rather, the prophet, since his call, is now privy to the divine purpose and declares it from time to time as occasion demands. Having stood within the heavenly council, the prophet knows what God has done and is about to do.

The prophet calls on men to hear, decide, and obey. The wise man summons them to understand and to learn. He does not demand, but seeks to persuade and instruct. Even his moralizing precepts are justified by him on the grounds of reason, custom, and the approval of good men. With the notable exception of Qoheleth (and to some degree, of Job), the wisdom books do not speak simply out of their author's private experience and thought, but articulate the moral standards and beliefs of the community. Yet the good life they commend must be shown to be good. Their authority is that of long social and personal experience and of cultivated discernment. Even when wise men come to opposite conclusions, as in the Joban debate, the method and objective is in principle the same. But Job persists in search of a more satisfying understanding of a situation which his more conventional friends hesitate to probe.

The two theological perspectives differ correspondingly. The prophets' God was the living, active, personal deity who had confronted them in the moment of their call. His name was Yahweh, as other gods like Chemosh of Moab and Marduk of Babylon had personal names to distinguish them among the gods. In prophetic religion and in Israel's 'holy history' Yahweh was incomparable, the

[30] Jer. 1:5, NEB. Cf. Amos 7:14–15; Isa. 6:1, 8.

unique, divine reality. Those who worshiped him could have no other god, for none was like him. This Yahweh had intervened and would continue to intervene in his people's history—from above, as it were. "Behold, I will again do marvelous things with this people, wonderful and marvelous" (Isa. 29:14). The prophets' theology was a kind of vertical theology, a theology of revelation, of salvation, and of judgment within time and history. Time was experienced as the interpenetration, almost the simultaneity, of past, present, and future. Yahweh was doing what he had always been doing in the fulfillment of his purpose. At the same time his every act was new. The coming judgment and blessing were at hand.

Among the wise men, the practitioners of the secular variety did not have (or at least did not show) any theological interest. Theirs was the wisdom of practical affairs, of expediency, in the day-to-day life of the world. There is nothing particularly religious, indeed, about many of the admonitions in Proverbs, such as the warning against greed: "If you find honey, eat only what you need; too much will make you sick." The calculating politicians of Isaiah's day scoffed at his prophetic insights. They asked for the kind of evidence that a realistic statesman could take into account: "Let [Yahweh] make haste, let him speed up his work for us to see it."[31]

On the other hand, the moral instruction given in home and school by the religious group of sages had, from the first, a theological basis. This lay in the conviction, in Israel as in Egypt, that there existed a divinely established order and structure of reality which, above all, was good. Man's well-being and happiness depended on his conformity to this order. The opening chapter of Genesis

---

[31] Prov. 25:16, NEB; Isa. 5:19, NEB; cf. Isa. 30:1–2; 31:1–3.

embodies this idea, culminating as it does in the creation of mankind. Wisdom theology was, at least originally, anthropocentric, as prophetic theology was theocentric. Hence its area of concern comprised God and humankind, rather than Yahweh and his special people Israel. Man is thought of as an individual member of the human race rather than as "the whole family which [Yahweh] brought up from the land of Egypt." God is thought of as the Creator who established the world order in the beginning and who continually sustains it by his providential care. In this aspect wisdom theology can be described as a horizontal theology.[32] Time, though made up of many "times" or moments, was an everlasting and unchanging present, extending over the horizon, as it were, into former and future generations where all had been and would be the same. This idea is expressed most definitely in Qoheleth 1, but Proverbs and Job are equally indifferent to historical time. If the same cannot be said of Sirach, this is because by the second century B.C. the streams of prophetic and wisdom thinking had flowed together and mingled.

When the religious school of wisdom undertakes the intellectual exploration of theological issues as such, its independence of the salvation-history theology is evident. This is especially true of Qoheleth, whose agnostic and fatalistic conclusions are, however, not typical. Hebrew thought is constitutionally averse to, and possibly incapable of, abstraction. Instead, the composer of the poem in Proverbs 8 personifies wisdom pictorially. First, she is portrayed as appealing to men to hear her voice (in the words of the teachers who speak for her). She defines her essence as truth, right(eousness), and the power of discernment. She affirms her value for and in human lives at their most

[32] Cf. J. C. Rylaarsdam, *Revelation in Jewish Wisdom Literature* (1946), p. 55.

successful. Then, in a climactic passage of profound theological import, she identifies herself with God's own wisdom made manifest in the creation of the order of the world, especially as this concerns the sons of men.[33]

In the Book of Job the poet affirms that the riddles of human existence and suffering cannot be resolved by the attempted rationalizations of conventional wisdom, but only through a divine self-revelation that puts them in a wider, indeed, in a cosmic, context. Theophanies to divinely chosen leaders and prophets had been prominent in the religious tradition. In prophetic experience, such a theophany was an intervention in history by Yahweh, in furtherance of his purposive activities. In Job it is the Creator's response to the creature man, the manifestation of all-encompassing divine wisdom to the searcher who has been halted at the frontier of human understanding.

The practical concerns and objectives of the prophets differed from those of the wise men, although again one must beware of comparisons that are not universally applicable. The prophets bore their testimony to the word and will of Yahweh, calling on men to believe and to respond. Whether or not they used the word *covenant*, the postulate of all of them was that Israel stood in a unique relationship to Yahweh and under an unequivocal obligation to serve him alone. The primary targets of their denunciations and exhortations were the men of power in society, the king and his ministers, the priesthood, the professional prophets, the men of wealth and prestige. It was these who determined the rules on which society customarily operated. It was their corruption that led to the moral disintegration of the body politic, for it denied the principles of justice and humanity that were basic to the covenant ethic. Hence, the tone of prophecy is intense and imperative.

[33] On Prov. 8, see above, pp. 83–84.

The same is true of its call for faith in Yahweh's power to preserve and lead his people amid the surging tides of historical events.

The wisdom scholars and teachers moved in another realm of discourse together. They addressed themselves to individuals, offering counsel based on social experience and their own reflections about the nature of the world and of the good life for men. What they taught would be applicable to human relationships anywhere, as is clear from its similarities to the wisdom teaching of other peoples. Wisdom had no national or religious frontiers. Its concern was with knowledge and self-knowledge, and with a way of life conducive to individual well-being and social order. The advice it gave was to be considered and weighed, and to be accepted only if the hearer was persuaded that the advice was good. Young men were trained in the understanding of life's values and in moral discernment, and were encouraged to make prudent judgments for themselves. If profounder philosophical and theological issues were raised, as in Job and Qoheleth, the effort was still to discern the truth beneath appearances and to win consent through argument.

In the matter of literary and rhetorical forms of utterance, again the prophets and the wise men usually went by different ways. The distinctive prophetic form was the oracle, a message delivered on behalf of Yahweh and ostensibly a quotation of the divine speech itself. As Lindblom says, "Because it was a divine word from Yahweh's own mouth the prophetic word was a word with effective power."[34] In the words of the Bible, "Yahweh has sent a word against Jacob, and it will light upon Israel." "I have hewn them by the prophets, I have slain them by the

[34] J. Lindblom, *Prophecy in Ancient Israel* (1962), p. 114.

words of my mouth." "The word which comes from my mouth [shall] prevail."[35]

The principal note in the oracles of the pre-exilic prophets is that of divine judgment, usually accompanied by an accusation stating the sin or crime that calls the judgment forth. Many oracles follow the familiar pattern of the lawsuit, in which the accused is summoned to hear the complaint, his fault is detailed, and the sentence pronounced.[36] Others begin with the mourners' cry of lamentation, *hoy*, "alas for." This word is often translated "woe to," but since what is lamented is the misbehavior rather than the punishment, a better rendering might be "shame on [those who do such things]."

The prophetic oracle frequently is introduced with the messenger formula "Thus speaks Yahweh." Nevertheless it is not this formal authentication which makes the message the divine word, but its substance and inspiration. The actual words in which the message is cast are undoubtedly the prophet's own contribution, as he prepares the message for a particular audience. The corresponding promise or salvation oracle is comparatively rare in the pre-exilic prophets. Most examples of it come from their disciples, speaking in a later time when the predicted doom had fallen and when restoration was now confidently expected because of Yahweh's changeless love for his people. The opening phrases "in that day," "in later days," "at that time" are marks of these later oracles of promise.[37]

The three major wisdom books of the Hebrew Bible are unlike in form as well as in content. Proverbs provides

---

[35] Isa. 9:8, EVV; Hos. 6:5; Isa. 55:11, NEB.

[36] E.g., Mic. 3:9–12. On this section, see R. B. Y. Scott, *The Relevance of the Prophets*, rev. ed. (1968), pp. 107–12; and G. Ernest Wright, "The Lawsuit of God," in *Israel's Prophetic Heritage*, ed. B. H. Anderson and W. Harrelson (1962), chap. 3.

[37] See Amos 9:11–15 (a postexilic addition to the book); Mic. 4:1–4; Zeph. 3:19–20.

materials for instruction in the ideas, methods, and skills of a conservative and partly secular wisdom; these are prefaced by a hortatory moral and religious contribution by the teacher who has edited these materials. Job is a theological and deeply religious inquiry, in the form of a debate between two schools of wisdom. Qoheleth retails the reflections that led one teacher to an agnostic and fatalistic philosophy, balanced by a courageous practical ethic for living. Common to all three is an emphasis on knowledge and rational understanding; indifference to a religion of revelation through supernatural events, sacred history, and cultic observance; and the contrast between two ways of life, those of the wise man and the fool. Their primary concern is with the individual and with his grasp of a meaningful order of life and thought, with corresponding standards of behavior to which he gives his free consent.

The principal literary forms of the wisdom books, the proverbs, precepts, riddles, parables, allegories, hortatory discourses, debates, and soliloquies, have been discussed in earlier chapters. Here are listed some characteristic stylistic features and vocabulary, for comparison with those of prophetic writings.

One of these features is the use of illustrations drawn from observation of the natural world. "If a tree is cut down, there is hope that it will sprout again . . . ; but a man dies, and he disappears" (Job 14:7, 10, NEB). The imagery of the divine speech in Job 38:4–39:30 testifies to the poet's thoughtful observation of the world about him. So with Qoheleth, "All the rivers flow continually to the sea, but the sea does not become full." And Proverbs, "Like clouds and wind without rain is a man who boasts of a gift he [promises but] does not give."[38]

[38] Qoh. 1:7, AB; Prov. 25:14. Cf. Prov. 16:15; 25:23; Qoh. 11:4; Job 22:12–14.

A second stylistic feature is the paternal tone of the teacher's admonitory discourses, "Hear, my son," "My son, attend to my wisdom," "Hear, my son, and be wise, and direct your mind in the way."[39] A third is the use of rhetorical questions in argument or instruction, "How long, you simpletons, will you prefer ignorance?"[40] Another is the exclamatory beatitude form, "Happy is he who," familiar from its use in the Sermon on the Mount and Psalm 1.[41]

Finally, there is the numerical parallelism idiom (x—1, x) already discussed, as in "Three things are never satisfied, four never say 'Enough!' "[42]

The wisdom books have a characteristic vocabulary. The words of this are rarely peculiar to it, but their proportionate frequency is noticeable. The following list will be useful in assessing wisdom influence in other parts of the Old Testament such as the prophetic writings and the Psalms.

'ᵉwil	obstinate fool	hebel	breath, emptiness
'awen	evil, wickedness	hiqshib	pay attention
'omnam	truly	hiwwah	inform
'orah	path	hatta'	sinner
'ashre	happy, fortunate (is)	hush	hasten
		hakam	be wise
bin	understand	hakam	wise
binah	understanding (n.)	hokmah	wisdom
ba'ar	brutish, stupid	haneph	godless
da'ath, de'ah	knowledge	hephes	pleasure; thing, affair
derek	way	haqar	investigate

[39] Prov. 1:8; 5:1; 23:19. Cf. the opening of the Egyptian Instructions.
[40] Prov. 1:22, AB. Cf. 20:6, 9, 24; Job 3:20–23; 4:7; Qoh. 1:10.
[41] Prov. 3:13; 29:18; Job 5:17; Qoh. 10:17.
[42] E.g., Prov. 30:15, 18, 21, 29; Job 5:19. See above, pp. 70–71.

ḥeqer	investigation	nethibah	path
heḥerish	be silent	sod	council; counsel
ḥashab	think, devise	sakal	fool
yir'ah	fear (of Yahweh)	'awelah	wickedness
yada'	know	'iwweth	make crooked
yasar, yisser	admonish, discipline	'amal	toil, trouble
		'esah	advice, counsel
ya'as	give counsel	'aṣel	lazy
hokiaḥ	decide, reprove	'arum	clever, prudent
ho'il	profit, benefit (vb.)	'ormah	cleverness
		pethi	simple, uninstructed
horah	teach, direct		
yashar	upright, straight	ṣaddiq	righteous
yosher	uprightness	qalon	contempt
kazab	lie (n.)	rasha'	wicked
ka'as	trouble, vexation	rib	contend, dispute (vb.)
kesil	insolent, stupid	rib	dispute, accusation (n.)
limmad	teach		
leb, lebab	heart, mind	remiyyah	neglect, deceit
		rason	wish, favor (n.)
la'ag	mock	siaḥ	consider, complain (vb.)
les	insolent, scoffing	siaḥ, siḥah	meditation, complaint
leqa'	learning (n.)		
madon	strife	ta'awah	desire (n.)
musar	training, discipline	tebunah	insight
		tokaḥath	rebuke, blame (n.)
mezimmah	scheme, scheming	takan, tikken	estimate, measure
mashal	proverb, wise saying		
		tam, tamim	blameless, righteous
nabal	vulgar fool		
nebalah	folly	tom	integrity
nabon	discerning	tamak	grasp (vb.)
nakoaḥ	straightforward	tushiyyah	ability, success

Common Elements and Mutual Influence

Prophecy and wisdom each played a large part in the cultural and spiritual life of ancient Israel for centuries.

In spite of their differences in outlook and interests (sometimes leading to friction between their representatives), they shared a common inheritance and social experience. Basically they had much in common and, in addition, influenced each other through association in the same community.

Both groups belonged to the intellectually active and articulate stratum of society. Both dealt in the potent mysteries of language as their principal tool, though the prophets stood in the oral tradition of the ballad singers and charismatic orators, and the wise men in the tradition of writers and teachers. Indeed, as Heaton says, "the content of the prophets' moral teaching is derived from the common stock of ethical thinking to be found throughout the ancient Near East,"[43] and the same could be said of the wisdom teachers. This can be illustrated, for example, from the concern stated in Hammurabi's law code "that the strong might not oppress the weak, that justice might be dealt the orphan and widow," and from Amen-em-ope's forbidding the removal of the neighbor's landmark.[44]

In their attitudes to cultic religion and its ceremonies, too, the sages and the prophets were not far apart. The former (until we come to Sirach) ignore these almost entirely. The latter insist that in Yahweh's sight they are quite secondary to moral obedience. "I hate, I spurn your pilgrim-feasts; I will not delight in your sacred ceremonies . . . [But] let justice roll on like a river, and righteousness like an ever-flowing stream."[45] No better summary of the prophets' view can be found than Proverbs 21:3, "To do

[43] E. W. Heaton, *The Hebrew Kingdoms* (1968), p. 274.
[44] *ANET*, p. 178a; cf. Ex. 22:22; Deut. 27:19; Isa. 1:17; Jer. 7:5–7; Job 31:16. With *ANET*, p. 422b, cf. Deut. 19:14; Isa. 5:8; Prov. 22:28; Job 24:2.
[45] Amos 5:21, 24, NEB. Cf. Isa. 1:10–17; Jer. 7:1–15.

what is right and just is more acceptable to the Lord than sacrifice" (NAB). And again, "By loyalty [*or*, kindness] and integrity, guilt is atoned for."[46] It is possible, of course, that such sayings show prophetic influence on later generations of wise men. The point is that such ideas were readily assimilated, while in other matters the views of the two groups remained distinct.

A corresponding influence in the reverse direction, of wisdom on prophecy, is apparent, particularly in Amos and Isaiah.[47] Fichtner suggests plausibly that Isaiah had been a scribe or a counselor at court before his call to prophesy. This would throw light on his references to writing and scrolls, his occasional use of wisdom vocabulary and literary forms, and also his ready access to the king and other prominent persons in the early period of his prophetic ministry.[48] Even Isaiah's later controversaries with the politicians may reflect a previous familiarity with the decision-making process in international affairs. His own vision of Yahweh as the sovereign Lord of history, whose plan (*'esah*) encompassed the fortunes of foreign peoples as well as of Judah and who even could designate Assyria as "the rod of his anger," fits the same picture.[49]

Isaiah makes use of distinctively wisdom forms such as the riddle, the parable, and the proverbial saying. The initial message given him to deliver, "Hear and hear, but do not understand; see and see, but do not perceive," remains something of a riddle, even with the ironic ex-

---

[46] Prov. 16:6, AB. Cf. Ps. 51:16–17 (Heb. 51:18–19).

[47] See J. Fichtner, "Jesaja unter den Weisen," in his *Gottes Weisheit* (1965): pp. 18–26; S. Terrien, "Amos and Wisdom," in *Israel's Prophetic Heritage*, pp. 108–15; H. W. Wolff, *Amos' geistige Heimat* (1964); J. Lindblom, "Wisdom in the Old Testament Prophets," in *Wisdom in Israel . . .*, *VT Supp.* III (1955), pp. 192–204; B. S. Childs, *Isaiah and the Assyrian Crisis* (1967) pp. 128–36.

[48] See Isa. 7:1–17; 8:1–2, 16; 29:11–12; 30:8.

[49] Isa. 7:4–7; 8:3–8; 10:5–19; 14:24–27; 30:1–5; 31:1–3.

planation provided in the following verse (Isa. 6:9–10). The paired imperative verbs *hear* and *understand*, *see* and *perceive* are characteristic openings of a wisdom address,[50] as distinguished from the more usual prophetic summons, "Hear the word of Yahweh" or "Thus speaks Yahweh."

The Song of the Vineyard in Isaiah 5:1–7 is a parable, mingling metaphor and interpretation. It reaches its powerful climax in a wordplay ($s^e daqah$, $s^{e'}aqah$) of the kind beloved by proverb makers. The antithetical parallelism is much favored in Proverbs, and the rhetorical question used in argument also is characteristic. The word picture of the neglected vineyard recalls that in Proverbs 24:30–34.

A second Isaianic parable, in 28:23–29, has clear marks of the wisdom style, yet, as in the previous instance, the concluding words identify it as a prophetic oracle. Again we have paired words of address in verse 23, rhetorical questions in verses 24, 25, and 28, and in verse 29 the words *'eṣah* and *tushiyyāh* from the characteristic wisdom vocabulary.

Fichtner suggests that Isaiah 1:3a, 3:10b and 11b are proverbial sayings quoted by the prophet, but this is uncertain. The second certainly emphasizes the law of retribution as applied to individuals. The relative frequency of wisdom terms in Isaiah as compared with most other prophets will catch the eye: *know, understand, teaching, reprove, plan, counsel, be quiet, wisdom, discernment, mock, scoffer, wise in his own eyes, show partiality*. Particularly interesting is the fact that the rare words $z^{e'}er$, "a little," and *sig*, "base metal," occur only in Isaiah and in the wisdom books.[51]

Turning to Amos we find similar evidence, from which it has been argued that the slightly earlier prophet influ-

---

[50] Cf. Isa. 1:2 and Prov. 4:1, 10; 23:19; Job 13:6; 34:2.
[51] Isa. 28:10, 13; Job 36:2; Isa. 1:22, 25; Prov. 26:23.

enced Isaiah. It has always seemed strange that the first prophet whose words have been preserved in written form should have spoken with such eloquence and literary mastery, as if he were the heir of a highly developed literary tradition. Wolff has proposed that he indeed did so, but that the tradition was that of wisdom rather than of prophetic oratory. In another connection Gerstenberger has traced back the 'apodictic' form peculiar to many Israelite laws to the same source in the prohibitions and warnings of family or tribal instruction.[52] Both arguments are impressive.

Amos certainly shows affinities with the wisdom tradition in thought and literary forms, while at the same time no other prophet displays more vividly the features of prophecy. There is, first, the really extraordinary point that Israel is condemned by the same moral standard applied impartially to neighboring nations, the almost abstract idea of what is right. "They do not know how to do right" (3:10). This word *nekohah* never appears in the covenant tradition or its laws. It occurs once in Isaiah 30:10, and twice in Proverbs. Proverbs 8:9 is instructive: "[The teachings of Wisdom] are right to the discerning man." Moreover, *good* in Amos is not material well-being, as often. To love good, here, is to enthrone justice (Amos 5:15), as in Proverbs 18:5, "It is not good . . . to deprive the innocent of justice." Another striking point is the correlation of Amos 5:4, 6 and 14, "Seek Yahweh and live," "Seek good and not evil that you may live," with the repeated injunction of Proverbs, "Forsake your ignorance, and find life."[53]

In matters of form the reader of Amos is struck by the use of the *three/four* formula in the oracles of the opening

---

[52] E. Gerstenberger, *Wesen und Herkunft des "Apodiktischen Rechts"* (1965).

[53] Prov. 9:6, AB; cf. 4:4; 7:2; 11:19; 12:28.

chapters. This 'x—1, x' construction is found nowhere else in the Old Testament except in the wisdom books.⁵⁴ The arguments from effect to cause in 3:3–8, with the concluding rhetorical question; the wordplays in 5:5 and 8:1; the sarcastic imperatives in 4:4–5; the riddle in 6:12; the reference to prudent silence in 5:13; the proverbial 'better-this-than-that' form in 6:2; the frequent antitheses, all these belong to the wisdom style. The paired terms *righteousness/justice* (Amos 5:7, 24; 6:12) are here, as in Proverbs 16:8, applied to man's obligations, but elsewhere to Yahweh's acts. Amos' repeated pairing of terms for the poor and needy also recurs in Proverbs and Job, but this is not so distinctive.⁵⁵ Thus Amos, like Isaiah, clearly shows evidence of being influenced by wisdom.

To a lesser degree this is true also of some of the other prophets. Hosea quotes at least two colloquial proverbs, "Like people, like priest" (4:9) and "They sow wind and reap a gale" (8:7). The cause-and-effect figure from common experience appears in 2:21 ff., 10:12 ff., and 14:5–6. Hosea is notable for his gift of visual illustrations, "like morning mist," "like the dew," "like an oven," "like a stubborn heifer," "like swirling chaff," "like smoke from a vent."⁵⁶ Micah, like Amos, identifies *good* with conduct that is right in the eyes of Yahweh (3:2; 6:8). Those who "think up" wickedness (Mic. 2:1) are counterparts of the schemers of Proverbs 16:30. The wisdom term *tushiyyah*, "success," appears in Micah 6:9. Otherwise there are few marks of contacts with wisdom in Micah. The progressive numerical formula in 5:5 (Heb. 5:4) belongs to a later addition to the prophecy.

A favorite phrase in Jeremiah is "to receive instruction,

---

⁵⁴ See above, pp. 70–71.
⁵⁵ Amos 2:6–7; 4:1; 5:12; 8:4, 6; Prov. 14:31; 22:22; 31:9; Job 24:14.
⁵⁶ Hos. 6:4; 4:16; 7:6; 13:3.

discipline" (*laqah musar*), recalling the frequent use of the phrase in Proverbs.[57] In Jeremiah, however, the nuance is different. Yahweh is the teacher, and *musar* refers to repeated punishments in spite of which a stubborn Israel refuses to learn her lesson. *Leb* here is not the perceiving mind, but the resisting will. The parables of the waistcloth and of the potter are not, as in Isaiah, literary forms in which the message is cast, but symbolic experiences of the prophet himself.[58]

Ezekiel's use of allegories has already been noted, and his references to the Tyrian king's claim to possess the wisdom of primal man in the Garden of Eden. Otherwise, except for his use of some proverbial sayings, he shows no sign that the wisdom tradition affected his thought and language.[59]

The wise men of whom Deutero-Isaiah speaks are Babylonian interpreters of omens. The idol worshipers take counsel together in vain. Yahweh alone has an effective plan (*'esah*), and his will (*hephes*) alone can prevail. Men will "see and know . . . consider and understand" only when this sovereign will is recognized.[60] The most striking parallel with wisdom language appears in the rhetorical questions about Yahweh's creative power in Isaiah 40:12–17, 21–26 and in the demands made on Job by the divine voice from the storm (Job 38:4 ff.).

Jonah is an imaginative tale about a prophet, rather than a collection of oracles and narratives presenting his message, as is more usual in the books of the prophets. Indeed, the book's message is found not in Jonah's words, but in God's, in the pointed question to the prophet which

---

[57] Jer. 2:30; 5:3; 7:28, etc.; Prov. 1:3; 8:10; 19:20; 24:32.
[58] Jer. 11:18; 32:33; 5:23; 12:3; 13:1–7; 18:1–4.
[59] Ezek. 17:2–24; 19:2–14; 23:2–35; 27:3–36; 28:2–10; 12–19; 12:22.
[60] Isa. 41:20; 44:25; 45:21; 46:10.

is its climax: "Should not I pity Nineveh, that great city?" The parable of the Good Samaritan ends similarly with a rhetorical question, to draw from the hearer the answer which Jesus wished to drive home.[61] The method is that of the wisdom teacher, but the message of God's boundless mercy is prophetic. The story presents a theological conundrum: If the people of a wicked pagan city like Nineveh were to repent, would God forgive them? Have even the prophets who preached to Israel the righteousness and mercy of Yahweh any conception of how profound that mercy is? A nameless prophet has answered that question in a parable.

The Influence of Prophecy on Wisdom

The reverse process can be dealt with more briefly. Prophecy had a long history; it was to reach its greatest heights in the centuries immediately preceding the fall of Jerusalem in 587 B.C., and in the period of the exile. Wisdom had an equally ancient lineage, but its *religious* development, broadly speaking, followed on the great moments of prophecy. The messages of the prophets preserved in writing had immensely increased their influence in the light of events. The effect on the wisdom teachers was twofold: (1) The specifically Yahwist faith was assimilated by them, resulting in the growth of a new wisdom form of piety, and (2) they began to concern themselves with theological issues such as the nature of wisdom and its relationship to God, revelation, theodicy, the creation of the world, and man.

The new religious note is heard in the introduction to the Book of Proverbs in chapters 1–9; there are also similar insertions and modifications in the following collections

[61] Jon. 4:11; Luke 10:36.

of maxims and adages with their predominantly secular and often utilitarian tone. An example of the remodeling of a proverb is found in Proverbs 15:16–17, where two variants of the same saying appear side by side: "Better is a little with the fear of the Lord than great treasure and trouble with it. Better is a dinner of herbs where love is than a fat ox and hatred with it." "The fear of the Lord" is the indispensable precondition for acquirement of wisdom, according to the editor's theme-motto in 1:7, and it seems probable that he is responsible for this rewording of an originally secular saying.

This spiritualization of wisdom[62] teaching is fully developed in Sirach, where religious meditations, prayers, and hymns are interspersed with proverbs for purposes of instruction. Somewhat similarly there appear in the editorial introduction to Proverbs two poems, 1:20–33 and 8:1–31, in which wisdom is personified. The first of these is metaphorical, introducing wisdom in the guise of a prophetess. On the second, as well, some indications of the literary influence of prophecy can be seen.

In his exploration of the nature of wisdom in the remarkable, independent poem in Job 28 the poet declares that man, who can mine precious metals from the earth, can neither discover wisdom for himself nor purchase it with things of utmost value. Only God knows what wisdom is and where it is to be found, because when he made the world, "then he saw wisdom and appraised it, gave it its setting, knew it through and through"[63] (28:27, NAB).

The theme of Yahweh's wisdom as involved in his creation of the world is taken up again in Job 38–39 and

---

[62] On this development see below, Chap. 8. See also McKane, *Proverbs*, pp. 17 ff.

[63] As a tailpiece to the poem, some later wisdom pietist has added the very different assertion that wisdom is to be equated with religion and morality.

Proverbs 8:22–31.[64] This thought of the divine wisdom as underlying and manifested in the natural order of the world and in history had come to the fore in Deutero-Isaiah:

> Who has gauged the waters in the palm of his hand,
>   or with its span set limits to the heavens?
> Who has held all the soil of the earth in a bushel [measure],
>   or weighed the mountains on a balance
>   and the hills on a pair of scales?
> Who has set limits to the spirit of the Lord?
> What counsellor stood at his side to instruct him?
> With whom did he confer to gain discernment?
> Who taught him how to do justice
>   or gave him lessons in wisdom?[65]

This passage has affinities with Job 28:24–27. At the same time its references to counselors and teachers of wisdom as the customary custodians of wisdom demonstrates that these are prominent in the prophet's experience, so the influence flowed both ways.

Perhaps the most important example of the influence of prophecy on wisdom is the theophany with which the Book of Job reaches its climax. The twin problems of theodicy and of the relation of an individual man to God the Creator are there resolved on a different plane than reasoned debate. Job's discussion with his friends has reached an impasse. God tells Job that he has only clouded the issue by argument in ignorance of truth. Job had struggled in vain with a crisis of understanding. Now he is faced with a decision of belief. "I will ask [the] questions, and you shall answer. Dare you deny that I am just or put me in the wrong that you may be right?" (40:7b–8, NEB).

---

[64] See above, pp. 130–31. Cf. Sir. 1:1–9; 24:1–9; Wis. Sol. 7:22–26; 8:1.
[65] Isa. 40:12–14, NEB. Cf. 41:20; 42:5; 45:12, 18.

The answer could come only through a divine revelation. There is an analogy here with the prophet's call—when a divine reality heretofore dimly apprehended from tradition and in personal experience becomes suddenly the final overwhelming fact with which a man has to do. This is a cataclysmic religious experience, humbling human pretensions and disclosing to a man who he is and who God is.

> I know that you can do all things,
>   and that no purpose of yours can be hindered.
> I have dealt with great things that I do not understand;
>   things too wonderful for me, which I cannot know.
> I had heard of you by word of mouth,
>   but now my eye has seen you (Job 42:2–3, 5, NAB).

God is not "he," but "you."

The Authority of the Prophet and the Authority of the Sage

In a recent work H. H. Schmid poses (but does not answer) some searching questions about the alternative claims of the prophets and the wise men to spiritual authority.

What does it mean for the understanding of the Word of God if the prophets proclaim as a Word of God what elsewhere had already been formulated as wisdom, pertaining to men in general? What does it signify for a theological ethic if the prophets, claiming divine authority, demand from their people exactly what wise understanding also has shown to be right and pregnant with the future? What does it mean theologically that the prophet . . . depends less on the authority of ancient Israelite tradition than on the evidence of his own experience?[66]

[66] H. H. Schmid, *Wesen und Geschichte der Weisheit* (1966), p. 200, n. 286 (my translation).

In other words, is the authentic knowledge of God and of his will to be found more definitely in the inspired rhapsody of the prophet than in the reasoned wisdom of the sage, with its roots in the consensus of good men?

James Barr has pointed out that the idea of revelation through history, and particularly in the *Heilsgeschichte* of Israel, is inadequate as a primary comprehensive category of biblical revelation. Barr agrees that in the Bible "there really is a *Heilsgeschichte*, a series of events set within the plane of human life and in historical sequence, through which God has specially revealed himself." But there are other important elements which cannot reasonably be subsumed under this head, such as personal revelatory experiences of individuals, mythological narratives, and the wisdom literature.[67]

The idea that Yahweh has acted and still acts in historical events, and in so doing makes known his will and his power, is a fundamental assertion of prophecy.[68] But an even more dominant feature in the words of the pre-exilic prophets is their denunciation of current religious falsity and moral corruption. Their God is much more the living, present God who confronts men with critical choices than he is the God of the national religious tradition, however venerable. He is not tied to Israel and her sacred history anymore, once the covenant has been shattered, except through his uncovenanted, but continuing, love and mercy. Prophecy stems from its spokesmen's personal experiences of a powerfully present God, and the inescapable obligation to articulate the meaning of that divine presence

[67] J. Barr, "Revelation through History in the Old Testament and Modern Theology," *Princeton Seminary Bulletin* 56, no. 3 (May 1963): pp. 4–14.

[68] See Amos 2:9–10; 3:1; 5:27; 9:7–8; Isa. 7:3–7; 10:5–19; Jer. 1:10.

for the situation in which they and their people stood. They were radically realistic about the nature and requirements of religion and the essentials of morality.

The wisdom teachers seem less forthright, less urgent. Their primary task was to kindle and instruct the minds and stimulate the consciences of young men who were learning about life, its temptations, its anomalies, and its goals. They apprehended God in terms of a created order, visible in the workings of the world and seeking realization in a moral order of human life and relationships. Their God was present in a structure of meaning that a man could, and should, apprehend. For them, knowledge of God comes through the response of faith and moral obedience, rather than through the testimony of men who have undergone cataclysmic religious experiences. It is there for those who have eyes to see and ears to hear. Day by day it shows itself in the reality of human goodness and wisdom that is not overwhelmed in the welter of human folly and evil.

The respective roles of the prophet and the wise man are, in a sense, related to different aspects of man's experience of time. The prophet is the voice of God in moments of critical decision, recognized or unrecognized. When men are brought to the place where they confront the living God, the space-time framework of ordinary daily experience disappears. Time is not measured in hours or days or years when "deep calls unto deep."

For the wise man the present moment has recognizable, but distant, horizons. He is conscious of a far-reaching human experience that goes back to when God made the world and saw that it was good. Whatever personal perplexities or social upheavals may threaten him, whatever injustices challenge his faith in the order of the world and the goodness of its Creator, he can remain steadfast if he has wisdom. Even Qoheleth, who had no faith (in the traditional sense), remained unmoved because he had thought things through and knew where he stood. On whatever level of understanding, life requires a structure of meaning to support it, a good that can be recognized and grasped.

The basic answers to Schmid's questions may lie in the simple fact that the wisdom books, as well as the books of the prophets, so clearly proved themselves to be valid testimony to the truth of God that they were admitted to the canon of sacred scripture. The canon only ratified formally what men of religion and integrity already knew. Prophecy and wisdom do not contradict one another. Both speak to the human condition, but on different planes, and having approached from different directions. Through the mental and spiritual agony of his individual dilemma, Job won his way to a new, profounder knowledge and understanding of God, man, and the universe. Such knowledge and understanding is no less authoritative than if it had been prefaced with the prophetic formula, "thus speaks Yahweh." The criterion is whether or not the word spoken becomes the truth of God for the life of man.

6
Wisdom in Revolt: *Job*

IN THE HEAT of his argument with the three sages who came to console but remained to reproach him, Job cries out sarcastically, "Truly you are men of knowledge, and yours is perfect wisdom! But I have a mind as well as you. I am not your inferior!"[1] The poem of Job represents a debate within the circle of the wisdom teachers. In his opening speech Eliphaz implies as much when he says that Job, after he has "instructed many," now falters when the blow strikes himself.[2] Job certainly has abandoned the theory of an exact retributive justice—if he ever held it, as his friends still do. His personal agony has proved the inadequacy of the theory and now drives him in search of a deeper understanding. A wisdom rooted in shattering personal experience revolts against scholastic dogma.

Divergent Doctrines of Wisdom

There is no single wisdom doctrine in the Old Testament. Quite various views have been gathered under the umbrella of the wisdom literature, just as various philosophies and theologies are included in the broad fields of

[1] Job 12:2–3, reading *hayyode'im* with Klostermann and Driver-Gray for the meaningless *'am* of MT; and also *tammuth* for *tamuth* with Tur-Sinai.
[2] Job 4:3–5. See M. H. Pope, *Job*, AB (1965), p. 34.

philosophy and theology. Unfortunately the general term *hokmah*, "wisdom," has no particularizing plural, either in Hebrew or English; in order to make the needed distinctions one must speak of the various views or doctrines.

The extent to which these differing doctrines of the wisdom schools were contemporary, successive, or overlapping can be determined only in broad outline, because the literary evidence is incomplete and often ambiguous. Moreover, the writings of the wise men were collected, arranged, rearranged, and supplemented by their coworkers and heirs, as anyone can see for himself by noticing the cautionary footnote appended in its last four verses to the radically unorthodox Book of Qoheleth.[3] The Book of Proverbs is a collection of older and somewhat miscellaneous materials, as edited by the principal author of its hortatory introduction in chapters 1–9. Even so, the extraneous insertions in chapters 6 and 9 show that the book has not reached us quite in the form in which it left his hands.[4]

The earliest distinctive type of wisdom teaching has been called "Old Wisdom."[5] This had two sources: native folk wisdom, and the international wisdom literature (in this case, principally Egyptian). To begin with, 'old wisdom' concerned itself with norms of individual behavior conducive to a good and satisfying life for that person, and to community well-being. This begins with parental in-

[3] Cf. p. 5, n. 7, for the reasons why this name is to be preferred for the work traditionally known as Ecclesiastes.

[4] Textual variants in the LXX, and particularly the different order of sections following 24:22, indicate that the book was still not in its final form as late as the first century B.C. See G. Gerleman, *Studies in the Septuagint III: Proverbs* (1956), and McKane, *Proverbs* (1970), pp. 33–47.

[5] See H. Gese, *Lehre und Wirklichkeit in der alten Weisheit* (1958); G. von Rad, "Josephgeschichte and ältere Chokma," *VT Supp.* I (1953): pp. 120–27; W. McKane, *Prophets and Wise Men* (1965); ——— *Proverbs*, pp. 11, 17 and passim.

struction and develops into more formalized cultural and moral training for a successful career. This kind of wisdom was mundane, empirical, practical, and prudential in subject matter and tone. Its sanctions were chiefly those of success and social approval.

There is, nevertheless, to be recognized in the old wisdom of both Egypt and Israel a deep feeling for an established order that was right and good, underlying human life. A man would disregard this at his peril,[6] for it corresponded to the divine order established by the Creator. As von Rad puts it, "Wisdom thus consisted in knowing that at the bottom of things an order is at work, silently and often in a scarcely noticeable way, making for a balance of events"; and again, "a man comes up against mysterious limits set for him by God."[7] "Be not . . . angry with yourselves because you sold me here," said Joseph, revealing his identity to his startled brothers, "it was not you who sent me here but God; and he has made me . . . ruler over the whole land of Egypt" (Gen. 45:5, 8).

As time went on, this sense of an unseen structure of reality was correlated with the observation that good or bad behavior had appropriate consequences—if not always, at least often enough to establish this as a general rule. In the first instance the consequences were sanctions imposed by the family or society for its own protection. Where these did not apply, and particularly in such matters as the gift of children or early death, lying beyond man's control, blessing or ill fortune were explained as rewards or punishments from God. In some such way, and

---

[6] See above, pp. 115–16. It may be significant that the social structure and way of life under a monarchy are called, in 1 Sam. 10:25, its *mishpat*, or "right ordering."

[7] G. von Rad, *Old Testament Theology* I, Eng. trans. (1962): pp. 428, 433.

with the belief reiterated by prophets and priests that Yahweh was a powerful God demanding obedience to his ethical commandments, there developed a dogma of exact reward and retribution attributable to divine judgments.

Testimony to this conviction that God's moral judgments are directly related to the individual's fortunes or misfortunes appears in the Book of Proverbs, "The Lord does not let the righteous go hungry, but he thwarts the craving of the wicked" (10:3) and "The Lord tears down the house of the proud, but maintains the widow's boundaries" (15:25). This is the stubbornly held conviction of Job's counselors, who maintain it with a rigidity that drives the sufferer to distraction, "Who that was innocent ever perished? or where were the upright cut off? As I have seen, those who plow iniquity and sow trouble, reap the same" (4:7–8); and again "God abases the proud, but he saves the lowly" (22:29). As Rowley says, "It is the way of the doctrinaire theologian to wish to reduce the complexity of experience to the simplicity of a single formula."[8]

Such doctrinaire teaching must have become firmly lodged in the theological wing of the wisdom teachers to have called forth such a passionate rejoinder as the Book of Job. Job, too, is a wise man, but one whose searing personal suffering has brought him down from the clouds of theorizing to the hard ground of reality. The truth that emerges from his physical and mental torment confronts the mechanical oversimplifications of scholastic teaching. Job's concern for justice as integral to the nature of the sovereign God, intensely perceived by such prophets as Amos, Micah, and Isaiah, becomes for him central to the idea of the divine but mysterious order of the world.

Qoheleth, too, was a wise man in revolt against the traditional doctrine of retribution, as this had become

[8] H. H. Rowley, "The Book of Job and its Meaning," *BJRL* 41, no. 1 (Sept. 1958): p. 197.

fixed in a doctrine which illogically applied to the individual life the covenant promises and threats propertly belonging to an ongoing society. His objections were made on different grounds. Qoheleth was an intellectual who searched for wisdom in his own way, and failed to find that the traditional claims made for it were true for him. The only world order he could see was the perpetual cycle of nature and the successive generations of man, an order massively indifferent to the individual man. He did not find that, in his experience, virtue always was rewarded and vice punished. His God was not the Yahweh who had revealed himself for Israel's salvation, but a remote and mysterious Being whose ways no man could know. Qoheleth's wisdom was not that of his heritage; it was his own, painfully discovered. It lay in acceptance of life as men actually experienced it, with its joys and sorrows, but especially with its joys. For life is the only light man has, and life is short and death soon brings darkness.

Thus the authors of Job and Qoheleth are wise men in revolt against the unexamined assumptions of their colleagues. They share many of their colleagues' views and methods of teaching and argument. They speak the same language. Each goes his own way, and the two ways are not the same. The Bible is vastly enriched by inclusion of these two highly individual departures from conventional religious thinking. When considering their contribution we should notice also a minor rebel, Agur, who was not an Israelite, but whose positively agnostic view is quoted in an appendix to the Book of Proverbs (30:1-4).

The Book of Job

The Book of Job is generally acknowledged to be one of the literary masterpieces of human culture. "The Iliad is great because all life is a battle, the Odyssey because all life is a journey, the Book of Job because all life is a riddle."⁹ Its greatness is in its emotional power, in the splendor of its poetic imagery and in its probing of great questions—human suffering and divine justice, life and death, and the possibility of man's knowledge of God. Its wisdom is not the detached intellectualism with which Qoheleth contemplates the human situation. Job's is the wisdom of man's soul, of his experience of the lonely self in an apparently hostile universe, and of the ambiguity and contradictions of existence. It explores man's final values and hierarchy of values, his innate hunger for truth and justice and meaning, his longing for a God he can truly worship with gratitude and awe.

Here speaks a free religious spirit, untrammeled either by orthodox belief or by dogmatic atheism. What manner of being is man, who suffers, he knows not why; who cares more to understand than to escape his suffering? Job knows full well the limitations imposed by his bodily weakness, brief life, and imperfect knowledge; yet he has intimations of something that transcends these. In the name of right and justice and personal integrity he challenges the very world order of which he is a part. From his dung heap he can demand an answer from the Creator of the universe. Is this what the Greeks called *hubris*, the intolerable insolence of a man who would make himself God's equal? Or is it the profoundest kind of religious faith, ranging far beyond the little shibboleths with which most men identify religion, a sublime confidence that to ask ultimate questions of God is not to turn away from him but to draw nearer to him?

The poem takes as its starting point the problem of why a good man should suffer, if God is both omnipotent and just. This is a problem that recurs again and again in the

⁹ An epigram attributed to G. K. Chesterton.

Old and New Testaments. It has appeared in the reflective literature of many peoples ancient and modern, right down to the reworking of the Job story as a modern Broadway play—

> If God is God He is not good,
> If God is good He is not God.[10]

The issue is raised squarely for the biblical Job by the fact that in the past he himself has experienced the goodness of God and has observed the operation of his moral order in the world. But now Job's outer and inner worlds have collapsed in ruin. Why?

Before considering how this question is dealt with in the Book of Job, two related matters must be touched on as background: (1) the theme of the innocent sufferer elsewhere in the Old Testament, and in other ancient Near Eastern literatures, and (2) the literary and critical problems that complicate our interpretation of the book.[11]

The Theme of the Suffering Just Man

The idea that human suffering and misfortune result from the displeasure of the gods was early and widespread in the ancient Near East. From it there developed the perplexity of some who were not conscious of special guilt and felt unjustly dealt with. "The big problem in Babylonian thought was that of justice," says Lambert. "A man

[10] Nickles, in the Prologue to *J. B., A Play in Verse*, by A. MacLeish (Boston: Houghton Mifflin Co., 1957).
[11] The literature on both is enormous. The reader is referred to the bibliographies in M. H. Pope, *Job*, AB (1965); R. Gordis, *The Book of God and Man* (1965); and O. Eissfeldt, *The Old Testament: an Introduction*, trans. P. R. Ackroyd (1965).

served his god faithfully but did not secure health and prosperity in return."[12]

Various explanations were put forward for this anomaly. The first is that suffering is a penalty for some sin of which the sufferer is unaware. In one text the speaker complains, "I have been treated as one who has committed a sin against his god." Another was given a personal name that means "What is my guilt?" In a Babylonian dialogue between a man and his god, the man protests, "The crime which I did I know not."[13] This was one of Job's complaints, "Let me know why thou dost contend against me" (10:2).

A second explanation is offered in a Sumerian work containing a dialogue between a man and his personal advocate among the gods, namely, that suffering is to be expected since sin is universal.[14] "Never has a sinless child been born to his mother" (l. 102). This was counsel given to the sufferer by the Sumerian sages; it is also one of the arguments of Eliphaz to Job, "What is frail man that he should be innocent . . . ? If God puts no trust in his holy ones, and the heavens are not innocent in his sight, how much less so is man!" (Job 15:14–16, NEB).

A third attempt to plumb the mystery is found in a Babylonian work known by its opening line as "I will praise the Lord of Wisdom"; it is sometimes called the Babylonian Job.[15] The document describes how a pious man was forsaken by gods and men and afflicted by disease; finally he is restored and indites this hymn of praise to the god Marduk. In the depth of his misery he wonders

---

[12] *BWL*, p. 10.
[13] *BWL*, pp. 10–11.
[14] See S. N. Kramer, "Man and his God," *VT Supp. III* (1953); pp. 170–82; and in a rev. trans., *ANET Supp.* (1969), pp. 153–55.
[15] See *BWL*, pp. 21–62; R. H. Pfeiffer in *ANET*, pp. 434–37; R. D. Biggs in *ANET Supp.*, pp. 160–64.

if "what is proper to oneself is an offense to one's god. . . . Who knows the will of the gods in heaven?" (Tablet II, ll. 34, 36). That is to say, suffering may come because of unwitting transgressions, deeds or words which a man does not know to be sinful in the eyes of a god. Again we are reminded of one of Job's outcries, "Does it seem good to thee to oppress . . . ? Dost thou see as man sees?" (10:3–4)

Another work known usually as the Babylonian Theodicy[16] resembles Job in being a debate between a sufferer and a friend. The latter accuses the sufferer of blasphemy for saying that his piety has been a useless burden. But he is forced to admit that if men are evil it is because the gods made them so; hence suffering is allotted arbitrarily and without moral reason. All that a man can do is to beg for mercy. So Job again, "Even if I am right, I cannot respond, but must make supplication to my opponent."[17]

Going farther afield to India, we find in the Hindu scriptures a mythical tale with remarkable similarities to the narrative prologue in Job 1–2. The prologue, as will be noted, pictures Job as submissive, rather than defiant as in the following poem. He accepts humbly the blows by which God permits the Satan to test the genuineness of his piety. He refuses his wife's advice to "curse God and die." There are several forms of the Indian story of Hariscandra, a faultless prince who is tested by suffering in order to settle an argument among the gods as to whether any human being is truly righteous.[18] Like Job in the prologue, the hero meets the test, and his divine cham-

---

[16] *BWL*, pp. 63–91; Pfeiffer in *ANET*, pp. 438–40; Biggs in *ANET Supp.*, pp. 165–68.
[17] Job 9:15, as translated by Gordis, *Book of God and Man*, p. 249.
[18] See F. E. Pargiter, *The Mārkandeya Purana, Translated with Notes* (1904), p. xx.

pion's faith in him is vindicated. Thus the suffering of a good man may be probationary and not punitive, to test the genuineness of his piety.

Finally, among the Greek tragedies, the *Prometheus Bound* of Aeschylus treats of the Titan who stole fire from heaven, and as punishment was tied to a rock for endless years while a vulture fed on his liver. Although admonished for his folly and insolence, Prometheus continues to defy the tyrannical power of Zeus. If the original poem of Job ended (as some think it did) with Job's proud oath of innocence,[19] its theme was indeed almost Promethean. The difference is that, for Job, God must be just in order to be God.

Turning to the Old Testament we find in the wisdom books and elsewhere various tentative explanations offered for suffering, and especially the suffering of the innocent.[20] These may be summarized as follows:

1. As *retributive*, the deserved punishment of sin. Travail and pain are taken to be the penalties of man's first disobedience. The catastrophic deluge was provoked by human wickedness. Moses set before Israel the alternatives of blessing or curse as the alternative sanctions of the covenant. Hosea declared that they who sow the wind shall reap the gale, and Ezekiel that each man must bear the penalty of his own sin. It is on this ground that Job's counselors assert that his suffering proves his sinfulness.[21]

2. As *disciplinary*. "He humbled you and made you hungry . . . to teach you that man cannot live on bread alone." "Do not spurn the Lord's correction . . . for those whom he loves the Lord reproves." Both Elihu and Eliphaz

---

[19] 31:35–37. Note 31:40c, "The words of Job are ended."
[20] See H. W. Robinson, *Suffering Human and Divine* (1939); J. A. Sanders, *Suffering as Divine Discipline* (1955).
[21] Gen. 3:16–19; 6:5–7; Deut. 30:15–19; Hos. 7:12–13; Ezek. 18:4; Job 4:7–9; 8:20; 22:4–5.

146 / *The Way of Wisdom*

point out to Job, "Fortunate the man whom God corrects!" and "He saves the afflicted by affliction, opens their ear with tribulation."[22]

3. As *probationary*. When God put Abraham to a fearful test which the patriarch was able to meet because of his obedience and trust, we are told that God said, "Now I know that you fear God, seeing you have not withheld your son, your only son, from me." The forty years of wandering in the wilderness is said to have been required to test Israel's obedience. In Job 1–2 the Satan was allowed to afflict Job to see if his piety was real or only professed with an eye to its rewards. Sirach warns believers to prepare themselves for testing, "for gold is assayed by fire, and the Lord proves men in the furnace of humiliation."[23]

4. As *temporary*, or *only apparent*. One of the psalmists was tempted to say that his devotion had been in vain, when he compared his troubles with the good fortune of the impious. But then he realized that their footing was on slippery ground which might at any moment precipitate them into disaster. All three of Job's interlocutors press him on this ground to desist from his defiance. "The hands that smite will heal," "God will not spurn the blameless man, . . . he will yet fill your mouth with laughter," "The exultation of the wicked is short-lived."[24]

5. As *inevitable*, since all men are sinners. Eliphaz declares to Job, "Misfortune does not come forth from the ground. . . . it is man who gives birth to evil, as surely as the sparks fly upward."[25]

6. As *necessarily mysterious* because the purposes of

[22] Deut. 8:3, NEB; Prov. 3:11–12, NEB; Job 5:17, AB; 36:15, AB.
[23] Gen. 22:1–12; Deut. 8:2; Job 1:6–12; 2:1–10; Sir. 2:1, 5.
[24] Ps. 73; Job 5:18, NEB; 8:20–21, NEB; 20:5, from Gordis's trans. in *Book of God and Man*, p. 265.
[25] Job 5:6–7, Gordis's trans. (cf. JB and NAB), adopting Budde's repointing of the second verb as *hiph'il*.

God are hidden. "Can you find out the deep things of God?" demands Zophar of Job. And when Job finally is humbled by his vision of God at the climax of his great protestation, he acknowledges that he has been uttering things "too wonderful" for him to understand.[26]

7. As *haphazard and morally meaningless.* "One man ... dies crowned with success ... , another dies in bitterness of soul and never tastes prosperity; side by side they are laid in the earth." "The race is not won by the swift, nor the battle by the warrior; still less does bread come to the wise, riches to the intelligent, or favor to the learned. When the time comes, [mischance] overtakes them all."[27]

8. As *vicarious.* Moses "stood in the breach" to turn away Yahweh's destroying wrath from Israel and brought that wrath upon himself. In Isaiah 53 the Servant of Yahweh, "despised, ... tormented and humbled by suffering, ... though he had done no violence and spoken no word of treachery, ... bore the sin of many."[28]

Literary-Critical Problems of the Book of Job

Even a casual reader of the Book of Job soon becomes aware that this is a work in majestic poetry that lays bare the agony of a human soul. More careful scrutiny brings to light certain problems about the literary form in which the work has reached us across the centuries. These are questions of literary type and structure, of sequence and consistency, and, if the reader is working with the Hebrew Bible, of language, text, and translation. Scholars have come to no general agreement about solutions, and this results in many diversities of interpretation.

[26] Job 11:7; 42:3.
[27] Job 21:23, 25–26, NEB; Qoh. 9:11–12, AB.
[28] Ps. 106:23; Deut. 4:21; 9:18 ff.; Isa. 53:3, 9, 12, NEB.

The main divisions of the book in its present form are clear enough:

Chaps. 1–2: Narrative prologue, with alternating scenes on earth and in the court of heaven.
Chaps. 3–31: Three cycles of debate in poetry between Job and his three friends, beginning with Job's initial outburst in chapter 3 and ending with his final statement in self-defense and his oath of innocence, chapters 29–31. The third cycle is in disorder, and chapter 28 is an intruded independent poem.
Chaps. 32–37: The intervention of a newcomer, Elihu, in four speeches supplementary to the debate.
Chaps. 38–42:6: The theophany—two speeches of Yahweh "from the storm," to which Job humbly responds in 40:3–5 and 42:1–6.
Chap. 42:7–17: Narrative epilogue, in which Job is approved and restored by Yahweh.

The main substance of the book is found in the second and fourth poetic sections; but the poem as it stands begins in midair in Chapter 3 unless some such "framework-story" as the prologue is provided to set the stage and introduce the participants in the debate.[29] Similarly, at the end, a corresponding tidying up of the situation seems called for, even though the material compensation of the hero suggests that the epilogue was contributed by a dull mind on which the whole great argument had been lost. As for the Elihu speeches, these are explicitly supplementary to the case against Job as put by the original three wise men: "There was no one to refute Job. . . . Now I, too, will give my views."[30] It is clear that different hands have been at work in the book, and this must be taken into account in its interpretation.

---

[29] See N. H. Tur-Sinai, *The Book of Job* (1957), pp. lvii ff., 30 ff.
[30] 32:12, 17, Gordis's trans.

The first critical problem is that of the relationship of the prose prologue and epilogue to the debate in poetry. They differ markedly in their representations of Job and his situation, as well as in some details. In the prologue, Job is the ideally pious man, patient and submissive when repeated calamities strike him. In the poem he is angry and rebellious, saying things to and about God that would have shocked the pious. The three friends come, in the first case, in order to condole with Job and share his burden; in the second case they grow increasingly hard and critical to the point where he must implore their compassion (19:21). The prologue begins like a once-upon-a-time folktale; it is at once stylized and dramatic. Its picture of Yahweh as a monarch who allows a faithful servant to suffer in order to disprove the calumnies of one of his courtiers is strange. Certainly it belongs to a different world of ideas than the hidden God of the debate and the self-revealing God of the climactic "voice from the storm." The story writer describes Job's misfortunes as a detached, though admiring, observer. But the poet, as Terrien truly says, "writes about himself."[31]

The prologue is written in straightforward, classical Hebrew. The poetry is not. To quote Pope, "The language is ostensibly Hebrew, but with so many peculiarities that some scholars have wondered whether it might not be influenced by some other Semitic dialect."[32] In keeping with this the Deity is referred to as Elohim or Yahweh in the prologue and epilogue, whereas in chapters 3–37 the former is rare and the latter never occurs (with one possible exception). The divine names used instead are El, Eloah, and Shaddai.

The prose and poetry are, therefore, distinct compositions. Various explanations of how they came to be com-

---

[31] S. Terrien, in *IB*, vol. iii, p. 886.
[32] M. H. Pope, *Job* (AB), p. xliii.

bined have been proposed. One possibility is that the poetry of the debate and the theophany, with Job's submission, was inserted into an existing prose form of the story, replacing its central section. Chapter 42:7–9 seems to refer back to a slightly different account of preceding events.

The second major critical problem is the evident disorder in the third cycle of the debate, following chapter 24. In the first two cycles each of Job's opponents had spoken in turn and had been answered by Job. But after the third cycle begins similarly with Eliphaz's speech and Job's rejoinder in chapters 22–24, Bildad's speech is very brief and Zophar's is missing altogether. Yet, following Bildad's speech, three successive speeches are attributed to Job in chapters 26–31, and in them Job asserts some of the very views he has been disputing.[33] Many attempts have been made to reconstitute the original form of the third cycle by rearranging the material of chapters 24–27, but without agreed success. It may be that the cycle was begun but never completed by the original poet. The insertion of the extraneous contributions of Elihu and other supplements is somehow related to the present disorder in the concluding part of the debate. The poem on the inaccessibility of wisdom in chapter 28 is generally held to be an independent piece. Its style is similar to that of the main poem, but the view expressed does not fit into its argument. In fact, it seems to anticipate part of what is said later in the divine speeches.

A third critical problem is that of the intruded speeches of Elihu in chapters 32–37. That these are an intrusion seems clear from their interruption of the sequence of Job's final challenge to God in 31:35–37 and the divine response

---

[33] E.g., 27:7–12. Gordis, *Book of God and Man*, pp. 182–83, explains these as quotations made in order to refute them.

beginning at 38:1. There is also the peculiarity that Elihu appears nowhere else in the book, even in the epilogue where Yahweh rebukes Job's opponents (42:7–9), and his is the only Hebrew name among the disputants. Indeed, the author of the Elihu chapters must have had the debate in front of him in literary form, since he quotes from it in the course of his attempt to strengthen the case against Job. He even anticipates parts of the divine speeches from the storm. In spite of some undoubted excellences, the Elihu material does not reach the level of the main poem. There are also some minor oddities about it; for instance, that Elihu addresses Job by name, which the three original counselors never do.

Finally, the originality of the two speeches by Yahweh also has been questioned, chiefly on the ground that they seem a very indirect answer to Job's problem. Furthermore, they rebuke Job for his presumption; whereas in 42:7 he is commended for having spoken rightly about God. It seems strange that there should be two divine speeches, and that Job should twice submit. Some scholars would combine the speeches into one, and almost all agree that the descriptions of Behemoth and Leviathan are irrelevant additions. But on the main issue there can be no doubt that Pope is right, "Either the book ends in magnificent anticlimax, or we must see the highlight in the divine speeches."[34] There are two speeches because the second makes a different point, as will be seen below.

For the purposes of the following exposition the view is taken that the primary material in the book consists of the poetic debate in two cycles and part of a third (i.e., chapters 3–23), together with the two divine speeches and Job's responses (38:1–40:14; 42:1–6); that this poem replaced an account of the debate in a prose form of the

---

[34] Pope, *Job*, p. lxxiv.

story, of which only the prologue and the epilogue remain; that the Elihu speeches are a later insertion; and that the disordered sections in chapters 25–28 may have originated in part from the author of the principal poem, in part from the author of the Elihu speeches, or from some other. One cannot speak too positively about an original Book of Job, for the story appeared in at least two forms, in prose and in poetry, in what order it is impossible to be sure. We are able, however, to describe the magnificent poetry of the debate and its sequel the theophany as the primary content of the present book.

The Interpretation of Job

THE PROLOGUE, CHAPTERS 1–2

This serves to introduce the participants in the debate, Job and his three friends (and also, incidentally, Job's wife), together with two unseen presences, Yahweh and the Satan. It is a stylized drama in five episodes, three on earth, and two in the heavenly assembly where the spiritual powers are gathered about God's throne. The audience is taken behind the scenes, as it were, to be shown in advance the cause of Job's suffering, which, in this form of the story, is that he is being tested to see if his piety is genuine.

The Satan[35] is here depicted as a kind of traveling inspector of the behavior of mankind, who reports periodically to Yahweh, and is not above acting as an *agent provocateur*. In this case, he suggests, Job is pious because piety pays; the loss of his possessions and his health will

---

[35] The use of the definite article here, as in Zech. 3:1–2, shows that the Satan or accuser is an official title, not a proper name, as it later came to be used for personified evil or the chief devil (cf. Mark 1:13; Rev. 12:9).

show that he is a sham. But Yahweh believes in Job and permits the test.

The atmosphere of these chapters is that of a folktale, characteristically vague about time and place. Job is a wealthy sheikh dwelling somewhere on the fringe of the north Arabian desert. Neither he nor the three wise men who come from afar to condole with him are Jews, a hint of the universality of the problem of unmerited suffering. Having expressed their horror in traditional gestures of mourning, the friends sit with him in silence for seven days, politely waiting for Job to be the first to speak. This pause in the action covers the transition from the introductory narrative to the poetic debate. Perhaps there is also the subtle suggestion that what follows corresponds to the conflict that raged in Job's own mind during the silence, as the full implications of his situation forced themselves upon him.

At first sight, the idea of a God who would permit an innocent man to suffer in order to prove himself right in an argument (to put it baldly) is revolting. But there is more to it than that. The writer in his own way is asserting (1) that a man's suffering is no proof that he is a sinner in God's sight; (2) that suffering does not come through God's intention, but from demonic forces at work in human experience—forces to which God has imposed limits; (3) disinterested piety and moral integrity are facts no less real, though less common, than the fact of suffering, and equally call for explanation.

THE PASSIONATE OUTBURST OF JOB, CHAPTER 3

Preceding the opening of the debate, Job's outburst, giving vent to his pent-up anguish and despair, bursts like a tornado on the awesome silence that had preceded it. If such be life, he would prefer death or nonexistence. "Perish the day when I was born! . . . Why is life given to men who find it so bitter? . . . Why should a man be born to wander blindly, hedged in by God on every side?"³⁶

This is no abstract academic discussion. The one who wrote these lines speaks from his own remembered agony. Life on such terms is intolerable, birth a tragedy, and death a deliverance. Job's misery is not the misery of a hurt animal. His pain is compounded by the fact that he is a religious man and a thinker. The mystery of pain becomes for him the riddle of God's ways with a human being who is *capax Dei*, and who has honestly sought to serve God. It is the riddle of eternal justice and truth, and of the very nature of God.

THE DEBATE PROPER, CHAPTERS 4–25 (–27?)

This is a forensic argument after the fashion of an Israelite court case, cast in poetic form.³⁷ Accusers and accused restate their respective positions with increasing vehemence, making little or no attempt to meet the arguments of their opponents.

The Charges against Job. Eliphaz begins with grave courtesy. Job has been a tower of strength to others, yet falters when he himself becomes the victim. "It touches you and you are unmanned. Is your religion no comfort to you? Does your blameless life give you no hope?" (4:5–6, NEB).

The rewards of righteousness and the punishment of sins are plain for all to see.³⁸ Only God is perfectly good. "Can a mortal be pure before his Maker? . . . Even His angels He charges with folly. How much more so those who dwell

---

³⁶ Job 3:3, 20, 23, NEB.

³⁷ Alternatively, Tur-Sinai, *Book of Job*, p. lvii: "The Book of Job contains a problem-poem which attempts to solve a religious-philosophical problem by debate. This literary form is based on the genre of the debating-contest." On the latter, see above, pp. 39, 55.

³⁸ Eliphaz, 4:7–9; Bildad, 8:11–22; Zophar, 11:14–20.

in clay houses?"[39] Hence man's experience inevitably includes suffering (5:7). It is unthinkable that God would pervert justice (8:3). Even if justice be delayed, it will not be denied, in the end (5:17–18; 20:5).

Not only is Job guilty, as all men are; his present suffering proves it. In pretending to be blameless he is hypocritical; the sin he hides from men, and even from himself, he cannot hide from God (22:4–14). Why should God permit him to suffer unjustly, as if by his virtue he would be doing God a favor? (22:2–3). Finally, and here the charge comes closer to the mark, Job's wild accusations against God are proof enough of his sinful pride, "You are undermining the sense of reverence. . . . It is your guilt that teaches your mouth. . . . Why do your eyes flash with ire, that you let loose your anger against God?"[40]

Job's Arguments. These state the case from a different perspective. The theory of recompense according to behavior may operate as a general rule, but it cannot be applied mechanically. The individual is not just a statistical average of all men. His person and his circumstances are peculiar to himself. So far as Job can see, there is no necessary connection between his conduct and his unusual misfortunes. If the incidence of suffering is as random and as disproportionate as it seems, how can it be deserved? But "no man can win his case against God" (9:2, NEB).

What kind of a Being, then, is God, who will not let a man know why he must suffer? (10:2). What kind of a creature is man, whose mind yearns for meaning and whose soul cries out for justice, as his lungs gasp for air? "I shout for help, but there is no redress," cries Job. "He has blocked my way so I cannot pass" (19:7–8, AB). How can God be just if he cares nothing for the anguish of the

[39] 4:17–19, Gordis' trans. Cf. 15:14–16.
[40] 15:4–5, 12–13, Gordis' trans.

innocent? (10:3, 8). Is man only the plaything of an amoral, irrational tyrant whom he can neither understand nor resist? "If the appeal is to force, see how strong he is; if to justice, who can compel him to give me a hearing" (9:19, NEB). As Franz Kafka wrote, "It is an extremely painful thing to be ruled by laws that one does not know."[41]

Furthermore, declares Job, man is unfairly handicapped. His knowledge is finite and his life is brief (14:1–2; 7–12). His capacity to endure pain is not unlimited. "Is my strength the strength of stones, or is my flesh made of bronze?" (6:12, Gordis). He has been condemned unheard and punished without mercy: "I know you will not release me. I am already found guilty" (9:28–29, AB).

Three Certainties. In this impasse, the sufferer clings to three certainties that save him from complete despair. The first is that he himself has, in the past, known God's goodness as a fact of experience. "By his light I walked through darkness" (29:3), before the light went out. "Your hands molded and made me, and then turned to destroy me. . . . Life and love you granted me, . . . yet these things you hid in your mind" (10:8, 12–13, AB). His thoughts go "back to the old days, to the time when God was watching over me" (29:2, NEB). Job cannot repudiate that past experience as an illusion. God had been his friend. This makes all the more dreadful his dilemma—why has his friend become a stranger and an enemy? "I was at ease, but he set upon me and mauled me" (16:12, NEB).

The second certainty to which the hero clings is that he must not betray his own integrity and "speak falsely for God." The conviction is overwhelming that he must be true to his own conscience if he is to be true to God and to expect justice from him. He must not default in

---

[41] Franz Kafka, *Parables* (1947), p. 119.

order to escape from his present torment. "He may slay me, . . . [but] I will defend my conduct to his face" (13:15, AB). The friends see this only as proud defiance. That God should pervert justice is impossible, because God is God (8:3). They are denying what Job is sure lies at the heart of all morality and all true religion—the value in God's eyes of a man's pure love of truth.

The third assurance that helps to hold Job steady is his faith that, if only he could pierce the cloud that hides God from him, he would find that God has been on his side all along. "If only I knew how to find him . . . I would state my case before him. . . . Would he exert his great power to browbeat me? No; God himself would never bring a charge against me" (23:3, 4, 6, NEB).

Job's Search for a Solution. Job's speeches show how his mind is groping for a solution. The doubts he expresses are radical. Is God only the name of a blind force behind all things? Is the unseen world like a dry gully from whose rocky walls man's cry echoes ever more faintly until all is silent again? "As a falling mountain-side is swept away . . . as water wears away stones . . . so thou hast wiped out the hope of frail man" (14:18–19, NEB). Is the Creator all-powerful, and nothing more? Indifferent to the sight of suffering and unconcerned with what men call justice? One who "removes mountains and they know it not, . . . [who] alone stretches out the heavens, . . . [but] passes by me and I do not see Him?" Is man not made in God's image after all? Or is the gulf between them so vast that the unlikeness cancels out the likeness? "God is not a man like me, whom I could answer when we came to trial together." Is what man calls evil, good, and vice versa? "Does it seem good to thee to oppress, . . . to favor the designs of the wicked?"[42]

---

[42] 9:5, 8, 11, 32, Gordis's trans.; 10:3.

Job's mind ranges in great exploring sweeps of thought, plunging and soaring. Are these pessimistic ideas the only possibilities? Could it be that the appearance of God's indifference or enmity is deceptive, that God is really just, but unseen there behind the curtain? Is there a hidden justice, a hidden mercy, and a hidden wisdom which are the reality of God? After a man dies and goes down to Sheol, is it conceivable that he should still be alive enough to await consciously the day when God will justify him? "If a man dies, can he live again?"[43] However, Job is not playing with the possibility of resurrection from Sheol. He hopes that even there he may know the moment when the charge against him has been dismissed.[44] For he is sure now that he has a witness and an advocate in the court of heaven (16:19). This champion and vindicator will secure him a hearing. In the end, since God must be just or he cannot be God, justice will be done. This is more than a hopeful surmise. It is a leap of faith. "I know for myself that my champion lives; at last he will rise from the ground [*i.e.*, to speak], . . . [Though] not in my flesh, I shall see God . . . on my side [*or* for myself], with my own eyes behold him, estranged no more."[45]

THE PERORATION, CHAPTERS 29–31

In an eloquent peroration Job looks back longingly to the days before affliction struck him and laments his pres-

---

[43] 14:14a, NEB. Literally, "If a man dies, will he be alive?" In most translations the adverb *again* is supplied, and the line is taken as a rhetorical question synonymous in meaning with 12a, "So mortal man lies down, never to rise" (NEB).

[44] In Isa. 14:9–10, 16–17 the denizens of Sheol are represented as pale ghosts still retaining consciousness and memory.

[45] 19:25–27. At this crucial point the Hebrew text has been damaged in transmission beyond repair. The above translation omits what is quite unintelligible but gives the overall meaning with reasonable certainty.

ent rejection by those who had been his friends, including God. Finally and proudly he asserts his innocence, challenging God to state his accusations openly and meet him face to face in court. "Behold my signature, let Shaddai answer me. Let my opponent write a document. I would wear it on my shoulder,[46] I would bind it on like a crown . . . I would approach him like a prince." (31:35–37, AB).

This peroration is not a summation of Job's previous arguments addressed to his three interlocutors, but leads up to the formal challenge, which in turn calls forth the divine voice from the tempest. With good reason Fohrer divides the main poem into two parts: (1) the dispute between Job and his three friends and (2) the exchange between Job and God.[47]

THE TWO SPEECHES OF YAHWEH,
CHAPTERS 38–39 AND 40:6–14

The silence of heaven is broken at last.[48] Job quickly discovers that God can ask questions too, and they put his own questions in a new light.

In the first speech of Yahweh, Job is overwhelmed by the wisdom and power seen in the panorama of God's creative works:

[46] Like a symbol of rank worn on the shoulder; possibly a brooch or decorative clasp fastening the distinctive robes of a prince or high officer. Cf. Isa. 9:6 EVV; 22:22; 1 Kings 22:10, 30.
[47] G. Fohrer, (Sellin-Fohrer) *Introduction to the Old Testament*, trans. D. E. Green (1968), pp. 326 ff.
[48] Scholars are divided about the omission from the second speech of the lengthy descriptions of Behemoth and Leviathan in 40:15–41:34, as not original. The author agrees with those who omit them. Whether the creatures are interpreted as the hippopotamus and the crocodile or as mythological monsters, their introduction here interrupts the sequence between Yahweh's challenge in 40:6–14 and Job's response in 42:1, adds nothing relevant to the challenge, and leads to a lame rather than a climactic conclusion.

> Who is this whose ignorant words
> cloud my design in darkness? . . .
> Where were you when I laid the earth's foundations? . . .
> Who stretched his measuring-line over it?
> On what do its supporting pillars rest?
> Who set its corner-stone in place,
> when the morning stars sang together
> and all the sons of God shouted aloud? . . .
> Have you descended to the springs of the sea
> or walked in the unfathomable deep? . . .
> Which is the way to the home of light
> and where does darkness dwell? . . .
> Who has cut channels for the downpour
> and cleared a passage for the thunderstorm? . . .
> Can you bind the cluster of the Pleiades
> or loose Orion's belt? . . .
> Did you proclaim the rules that govern the heavens,
> or determine the laws of nature on earth?
> Do you know when the mountain goats are born? . . .
> Does the wild ox consent to serve you? . . .
> Did you give the horse his strength? . . .
> Does your skill teach the hawk to use its pinions
> and spread its wings toward the south? . . .

Then the Lord said to Job: "Is it for a man who disputes with the Almighty to be stubborn? Should he that argues with God answer back?" And Job answered the Lord, "What reply can I give thee, I who carry no weight? I put my finger to my lips."[49]

Job is not vindicated, except that his demand to confront God is met. He is simply asked, who is he to find fault with the Creator whose whole creation proclaims his wisdom, power, and beneficence? Job's defiant shouts are silenced. He is stopped in his tracks. He no longer struts like a prince. But he does not repent!

[49] 38:2, 4, 5b–7, 16, 19, 25, 31, 33:1a, 9a, 19a, 26; 40:1–4, NEB.

This seems to be an anticlimax. None of Job's agonized questions have been answered. He has simply been reminded that no man can argue on equal terms with God, that he is a fool to deduce from his limited experience that the whole universe is unjustly governed. The superb eloquence of the divine speech seems to miss the point of what the debate has been about. Nothing at all is said about justice or about human suffering. Indeed man does not appear at all in the sweeping survey of creation's wonders.

But there follows a second divine speech, much shorter, less eloquent, but even more significant. This time Yahweh speaks as the one who bears the burden of the moral government of mankind, the God of history and the judge of human actions. "Will you deny My justice, put Me in the wrong so that you may be in the right? Have you an arm like God; can you thunder with a voice like His?"[50]

Only God can understand the dimensions of justice, for he must administer it. Has Job, or any man, the wisdom to know what justice must encompass in universal terms? Has Job really been concerned with justice, or only with justifying himself? In his innocence, or relative innocence, he has been right in defending himself against the unfair insinuations of the three counselors; but in doing so he has no right to condemn God, whose perspective is, to say the least, somewhat wider. Will he now, in fact, accept the conditions of his creaturehood, or does he presume he has the wisdom to mount God's throne and judge all men with a more authentic justice?

Deck yourself out, if you can, in pride and dignity, array yourself in [my] pomp and splendor; unleash the fury of your wrath, look upon the proud man and humble him; look upon every proud man and bring him low, throw down the wicked

---

[50] 40:8-9, Gordis' trans.

where they stand; . . . Then I in my turn will acknowledge that your right hand can save you.⁵¹

Has Job been saying to God, by implication, Let me have a try at administering the universe justly? Is he really prepared to say that he knows what justice must mean in its total context? And Job replies, in effect, Come to think of it, I don't believe I am!

THE PROSE EPILOGUE, CHAPTER 42:7–17

This is the counterpart of the prologue, except for the fact that the Satan is unaccountably missing. The idea that Job's suffering was permitted in order to test the genuineness of his piety is simply dropped. Job is again recognized by Yahweh as his faithful servant who offers burnt offerings and intercedes for others. Nowhere in the poem has he been pictured in this way. More remarkably, (1) Job is here commended for what he has been saying about God, and the three counselors conversely are condemned, and (2) Job is now to be doubly rewarded with material blessings, a result confirming the friends' arguments which Job in the poem has so emphatically denied.

There are other incongruities. Job's brothers and sisters and former acquaintances come to comfort him only now, after he has been restored to favor and fortune. The seven sons and three daughters he had lost are replaced in full maturity as suddenly as, in the prologue, they had died in a tornado. One can only surmise that variant forms of the folktale of Job, the suffering just man, underlie these inconsistencies, just as they do the marked contrasts between the Job of the prologue and of the main poem.

What is the conclusion of the matter, as we lay down the Book of Job? We must bear in mind, first, to distin-

⁵¹ 40:10–12, 14, NEB.

guish between (1) the views expressed by Job, the central character in the poem; (2) the views of the poet himself who speaks through his hero, through the struggle between Job and his friends, and finally in the Voice from the storm; and (3) the meaning and impact of the entire work in its present form (except for the interpolations).

The problem of the suffering of the innocent, from which the discussion takes off, is answered in the book as a whole in three ways, on three levels. In the prologue and epilogue the good man is being tested by suffering to see if his professed religion is genuine, and he will be compensated for his sufferings. In the dialogue, followed by the divine words from the storm, the message is that human suffering, especially the suffering of the godly, cannot be explained in terms of human knowledge and wisdom, but only in a vastly wider context. That context is the mystery of an all-encompassing goodness and almighty power which man can come to know and learn to trust. This knowledge of God is the wisdom of the soul. It is not the same thing as intellectual knowledge, but it is knowledge none the less. It is an awarenes of a transcendent One, a seeing, a knowing, and being known. Mystery remains, for man's capacity to understand is finite. For Job to be innocent of transgression is not enough. Without a trust that accepts the finiteness of his knowledge and the limitations on his freedom, without the humility befitting the smallness of his apprehension, no man is really good.

The third answer may be taken as the effect of the book as a whole on its readers. This is conveyed by suggestion rather than explicitly, and it has to do with the springs of life. Man cannot live by doctrinaire formulations of theology or find rest to his spirit through speculation on matters that literally are beyond his ken. These are but the ideas and speculations of men as finite as himself. In circumstances of personal trial and tragedy they will prove to be a quicksand beneath his feet. Each man is cast into the buffeting waves of life where he must swim or go down. God does not come to him like a life preserver tossed from a ship's deck. A man will drown unless he believes that God intends him to swim.

The tension between doubt and trust, between fear and faith, is of the very essence of religion. The good man may suffer like anyone else; but what will matter more to him than his suffering, his dedication to truth and meaning, to justice and self-giving love, is that these are precious most of all to God. The Book of Job tells us that the keystone of all genuine morality and all true religion is personal integrity, not proud but humble, committed utterly to truth and love and goodness in the faith that these are what sustain the universe.

God's approval is the only sure reward of those who trust him, whether or not they realize his presence. Beside this, all lesser reliefs and rewards are insignificant. At the margin of finite human knowledge and experience there is, and must be, mystery. But it is a divine mystery, luminous with goodness and wisdom, and strong with the power of everlasting mercy.

7
Wisdom in Revolt:
Agur and Qoheleth

TWO OTHER REVOLTS against dominant wisdom doctrine moved in an opposite direction from Job. The first is the problematical little piece in Proverbs 30:1–4 entitled the Sayings of Agur ben Yaqeh. This denies the possibility of man's knowledge of God, and is answered in verses 5–6 by a believer in revelation.[1] The second is the strangely moving skeptical work known as Ecclesiastes or Qoheleth.[2] Both speak from within the wisdom tradition, as Job and his friends do, but represent a very different reaction from his to the religiously conservative and dogmatic wisdom school.

The inclusion here of the first-named may be objected to on the ground that Agur was a non-Israelite and that his words are cited only to be refuted. Yet such views must have had some currency in Israel for a refutation to have been thought necessary. A more important difficulty is that

---

[1] McKane (*Proverbs* [1970], p. 643) takes exception to the present writer's description of 30:1–6 as a dialogue (Scott, *Proverbs-Ecclesiastes* AB [1965], pp. 775–77). Even if not formally a dialogue, this juxtaposition of Agur's agnostic views with those of an orthodox rejoinder is, in effect, a dispute between opposing schools of wisdom.

[2] The title Qoheleth is to be preferred for the reasons stated in n. 7, p. 5 above.

the text and translation of verses 1–4 are problematical at several points, leaving in doubt the precise nature of Agur's heresy. Obviously a correct interpretation depends on what the biblical text is understood to say. The translation given here is defended in the notes following.

(THE SAYINGS OF AGUR)

(v. 1) The words of Agur ben Yaqeh, of Massa',
        The portentous saying of the man who has no God:
        "I have no God, but I can [face this *or* survive].
(v. 2) Surely I must be more brute than man,
            and devoid of human understanding!
(v. 3) I have not learned 'wisdom,'
            nor have I knowledge of [any] holy Being."

(A SUPPORTING QUOTATION)

(v. 4) Who has ascended the sky and assumed dominion?
        Who has gathered up the wind in his cupped hands?
        Who has wrapped the waters in his robe?
        Who has fixed the limits of the world?
        What is his name, and what is his son's name?
            —as if you knew!

(A REJOINDER)

(v. 5) All that God says has stood the test;
            he is a shield to those who take refuge with him.
(v. 6) Do not add to his words, lest he correct you
            and you be exposed as a liar.

Several intriguing questions are posed by this short piece, so unlike the content of the rest of Proverbs. Who was Agur, and why are his words described as "portentous" (lit., "oracular")? Why does the above rendering translate[3]

---

[3] As do NEB, NAB, AT, AB, Gemser, McKane, and others.

the words in verse 1 which in KJV and RSV are transliterated as proper names? Is Agur denying the existence of God, or saying simply that he has no knowledge of him? Why does the long verse 4 sound like an echo of Job 38 or Isaiah 40:12 ff.? What is the relationship of this verse to what precedes it? Does its opening line envisage man's ascending the heights of heaven to return with divine knowledge, as the traditional vocalization of MT suggests? Or does it refer to God, like the other rhetorical questions here?

The title of the piece is clear enough. Agur evidently was a famous sage of Massa', one of the "peoples of the east" with whose wisdom that of Solomon was compared.[4] He was from the kingdom of Massa',[5] mentioned in Assyrian and early north Arabian inscriptions and located near Tayma, about 250 miles Southeast of Aqaba.[6] In Genesis 25:14 Massa' is listed among the sons of Ishmael, the desert tribes of northwest Arabia.

The second problem is more difficult to solve. Some plausible alternative must be found for the meaningless "The man says to Ithi-el, to Ithi-el and Ucal" of RSV (cf. KJV, JB). Neither the Septuagint nor Vulgate take these as proper names, but rather as verbs or verbal clauses.[7] Modern scholars who follow their lead have made various proposals: "I am wearied, O God, and spent" (AT, cf. NEB); "I am not God, that I should prevail" (NAB); "There is no God, and I can [not know anything]" (AB); "There is no God, and I am exhausted" (McKane); "I am

---

[4] 1 Kings 4:30 (Heb. 5:10); cf. Job 1:3. This is not meant to suggest that Agur and Solomon were contemporaries.
[5] Reading "the Massa-ite" for *hammassa'*, "the doom oracle." Cf. "Lemuel, king of Massa'" in 31:1.
[6] See F. V. Winnett and W. L. Reed, *Ancient Records from North Arabia* (1970), pp. 101–02.
[7] Targ. takes them to be proper names. Syr., Aqu., and Theod. retain only Ithiel.

not God, that I should have power" (Torrey); "I have struggled with God and triumphed" (Gemser).[8]

The first of these explanations of "to Ithi-el" is ruled out by the fact that it addresses the deity of whom, in verse 3, the poet expressly denies any knowledge, and a similar objection applies to Gemser's proposal. The others assume that the line is in Aramaic, which is unlikely in a passage otherwise expressed in Hebrew. None of these objections applies to the rendering "I have no God" (lit., "there is not to me a god") suggested above.

The self-depreciation in verses 2–3 is ironical or sarcastic.[9] Agur mocks his opponents who seem to think him subhuman because his wisdom does not rest on belief in God.

The series of demanding rhetorical questions in verse 4 recalls, both in form and substance, the questioning of Job by the divine voice from the tempest, even to the scornful "as if you knew!"[10] Tur-Sinai's remark is illuminating, that what we have here is "a remnant of an ancient Wisdom poem . . . , intelligible only in a context such as that of the Book of Job."[11] This fragment, it seems, is quoted by Agur in support of his claim that no one can know God or who he is, "What is his name, and what is his son's name?— as if you knew!"[12] The apparent reference to a man's ascending to heaven and coming down again results from an interpretative vocalizing of the consonantal text. With different vocalization it can be read, "and assumed do-

[8] C. C. Torrey, "Proverbs, chapter xxx," *JBL* 73 (1954), pp. 93–103; B. Gemser, *Sprüche Salomos*, 2nd ed. (1963), p. 102 (my trans.).

[9] See E. M. Good, *Irony in the Old Testament* (1965), pp. 26, 214–15.

[10] Cf. Job 38–39, esp. 38:5, 8, 25, 36–37; 39:5.

[11] N. H. Tur-Sinai, *The Book of Job* (1957), pp. lix–lx.

[12] "His name . . . his son's name" is simply poetic parallelism, like "What is man . . . and the son of man?" in Ps. 8:4 EVV, and does not necessarily imply polytheistic imagery.

minion," which makes this question, like the others, refer to God.

In verses 5–6 a believer responds that Agur has misused the quotation and added to God's words. This confirms the supposition that the speaker in verse 4 is God, in a fragment from an alternative form of the divine speech in Job 38–39 which the hearer recognizes. For him, the knowledge of God is to be based on a devout relationship with God, not on rationalistic arguments. The life of faith produces its own evidence which is no less valid because it is outside the experience of the unbeliever. As we have seen, one of Job's difficulties was that he was unable to reconcile what seemed to be the present hostility and injustice of God with his own past experience of God's goodness, a reality he was unable to deny.

Detached Note on 30:1

The word $n^{e\prime}um$ translated here as "portentous declaration" is common in the prophetic formula "oracle of Yahweh" (e.g., Jer. 23:4, 11, 12), but is used also in conjunction with the identification of the human spokesman, by name or otherwise, as in Numbers 24:3, 15 and 2 Samuel 23:1. In these instances the word *haggeber* is followed by a descriptive relative clause. It is probable that the same is true in Prov. 30:1, with the letters of the relative clause concealed in the first $l^{e\prime}ithi\prime el$. It is suggested that the original reading was $lo\prime\,{}^{\prime}itto\,\prime el$, "with whom God is not," that is, "who has no God." Vulgate reads *vir cum quo est deus*, omitting the negative particle. For "be with" meaning "have," see Genesis 39:6; Jeremiah 8:8; Proverbs 8:18; 11:2. Agur's own words begin with the second $l^{e\prime}ithi\prime el$, so that this is to be read as first person, $lo\prime\,\prime itti\,\prime el$, "I have no God." The word $w^{e\prime}ukal$ is the Qal Impf. of *yakol*, "I am able," used without complementary verb as in Isa. 1:13; Ps. 101:5. In verse 4 *wayyired* (from *radah*, "rule") is to be read in place of the same consonants pointed in MT *wayyerad* (from *yarad*, "descend").

Qoheleth

The Book of Qoheleth, like the Words of Agur, sets forth a view diametrically opposed to the doctrine that Yahweh, a personal God, had chosen Israel to be a people peculiar to himself and had made known to her his will. Both Agur and Qoheleth affirm that man cannot attain to the knowledge of God by wisdom or through revelation. The agnosticism of the former is that of a foreigner and is countered at once by a positive statement of belief, and further is encapsulated in a work, Proverbs, whose motto is that reverence for Yahweh is the first principle of wisdom. Qoheleth's philosophy has no such qualifications except for one or two marginal comments and a final cautionary footnote. And, unlike the Song of Songs, this book cannot be allegorized to make it say metaphorically something different from what it says literally. The divergence is too fundamental.

The author is no atheist. Indeed he affirms God's existence and power as the presuppositions of his agnostic and fatalistic philosophy. He even counsels discriminating participation in the religious rites of the community, "in order to learn." But what God is in himself remains mysterious. What he expects of men is unknown. Man can only use his powers of observation, seek understanding through reflecting upon experience, and acquiesce in what cannot be altered. All the effort he pours out seems to make no difference and to have no permanent results. The same fate overtakes man and beast, the righteous and the

Wisdom in Revolt: Agur and Qoheleth / 171

wicked. All human values are cancelled out by a man's inevitable and rapidly approaching death.

Such pessimistic and fatalistic conclusions contrast so sharply with the positive affirmations of the rest of the Bible, both Old and New Testaments, that apologists have been hard put to justify on theological grounds the inclusion of this book in a Holy Scripture. Their principal argument has followed the line of the earliest Christian commentator on the book, Gregory Thaumaturgus (died A.D. 170), namely, that its purpose was to show that all the affairs and pursuits of man are vain and useless, in order to lead us to the contemplation of heavenly things.[13] If so, one can only remark that this seems a remarkable example of the indirect method.

The facts are a little different. The real explanation is historical. While the sequence of events which led eventually to the gathering of the books of the Old Testament into a fixed and sacred canon is largely obscure, one thing is certain. This literature, in its parts and finally as a whole, had approved itself in the religious life of the community before being officially defined as uniquely sacred and authoritative. We have a glimpse of the latest stages of the process in the debate among the rabbinic authorities toward the end of the first century of the Christian era as to whether or not Qoheleth should be included in Holy Scripture. The reasons for questioning it were manifest. But traditional usage was upheld on the grounds that "its beginning is religious teaching and its end is religious teaching."[14]

The book must have by this time secured its place

---

[13] Quoted in G. A. Barton, *The Book of Ecclesiastes*, ICC (1908), p. 20.
[14] Lit., "words of Torah." *Talm. Bab.*, Shabbath 30b. Cf. *Mishnah*, Eduyoth 5:3; Yadaim 3:5. The school of Shammai opposed the inclusion of Qoheleth.

among the esteemed wisdom writings. Its editorial postscript in 12:9–11 shows that its author had been a celebrated sage whose readers found that his words were like goads prodding their minds but also like nails firmly driven home. There had always been radical thinkers among the wise men, who were unwilling to accept the bland assurances of the orthodox. The Book of Job is sufficient evidence of that. Just as in Egypt and Mesopotamia, there were, in Israelite wisdom, two divergent tendencies: the one, represented chiefly by Proverbs, was conservative, optimistic, and life-affirming; the other, skeptical of traditional beliefs, found expression in Job and Qoheleth.[15] When eventually the third part of the Hebrew canon, the more miscellaneous "Writings," was added to the central core of the Torah and the prophets, both types of wisdom literature were included.

The daring originality of Qoheleth's views was glossed over to some extent by the addition of a few orthodox annotations such as 11:9c, "Yet know that for all these things God will call you to account."[16] At the end an editorial colophon sums up the caution which the reader ought to keep in mind, "Reverence God, and observe his laws. This applies to everything. For God will judge every deed according to its hidden intention, whether good or evil" (12:13–14, AB). Beyond question, the fact that the author in chapters 1 and 2 assumes the role of Solomon the philosopher-king (though without naming him!) helped to quiet doubts about the book. That this was a purely literary role is clear from the biographical footnote in 12:9–11; there the author is described as a wisdom teacher —*haqqoheleth*, "the teacher." It had become a literary

---

[15] See above, pp. 20–21, 26, 40–41.
[16] See also 3:17–18.

convention to ascribe wisdom books to Solomon,[17] on the basis of 1 Kings 4:32 (EVV).

The Book of Qoheleth undoubtedly appealed to thoughtful Jewish laymen at a time when the windows of Judaism were opening on a wider world than the provincial community of postexilic Jerusalem, and new ideas were abroad. It seems to have been written shortly before or soon after the conquests of Alexander had vastly reinforced the influence of Greek culture, which was already spreading in the Mediterranean world. The days of the great prophets lay far in the past. While, doubtless, there were among the priests sincere and pious men, the priesthood of Jerusalem had become professionalized and the temple cult a formal and traditional institution. One anonymous minor prophet, Malachi ("my messenger"), of the Persian period had condemned the priests for their bored indifference to their obligations. As we have already noted, the wisdom teachers had little to say about cultic matters; what they do say would hardly be acceptable to the priestly establishment: "By loyalty and faithfulness iniquity is atoned for."[18]

In the editorial title of the book the word *Qoheleth* is used as a proper name: "The words of Qoheleth, the son of David." But in 12:8 (and also in 7:27 in LXX) it is a common noun with the definite article, "the qoheleth." Elsewhere in the book it can be read in either way. The form is that of the active participle feminine of the verb *q-h-l*, from which is derived the noun *qahal* meaning "assembly, congregation." The participial form may be explained as an occupational designation which could have become a proper name, like Sophereth, "member of the

---

[17] Cf. Prov. 1:1; 10:1; 25:1; Song of Songs 1:1 and Wisdom of Solomon, a work composed in Greek in the first century B.C.
[18] Mal. 1:6–2:17; Prov. 16:6.

scribal profession."[19] In the context of the wisdom schools, however, and particularly in the light of Qoheleth's activities described in 12:9, it seems clear that the *qahal* here means "an assembly of pupils," and that *qoheleth* means "teacher."[20] The pupils would address him as "Teacher," and thus his personal name has been lost.

The Form and Structure of Qoheleth's Book

The Words of Qoheleth do not form a clearly structured book, as is to be expected in what appears to be a posthumous collection of "the teacher's" literary remains. Broadly speaking, the first six chapters set forth his philosophy and the last six chapters his ethical conclusions and counsel. Framing the whole discussion in 1:2 and 12:8 is the famous aphorism, "Vanity of vanities, all is vanity."[21] This succinct summation of Qoheleth's philosophy is expanded in various aspects as he proceeds. It is accompanied by supporting arguments and illustrations, and is followed by counsel on attitudes and behavior appropriate to such an outlook on life.

More specifically, the contents of the book may be categorized as follows:

A (1) Philosophical statements related to the general thesis, (including the poem on predetermined "times" in 3:1–8).
   (2) Supporting evidence drawn from general observation.

---

[19] Neh. 7:57. Cf. the English surnames Penman, Scribner.
[20] Because in the NT *ekklesia* corresponds to the OT *qahal*, Luther took the assembly to mean a congregation gathered for worship and translated *haqqoheleth* by "der Prediger"—whence the incongruous subtitle "the Preacher" of EVV.
[21] On the meaning of the aphorism, see below, p. 178.

Wisdom in Revolt: Agur and Qoheleth / 175

    (3) Supporting evidence drawn from Qoheleth's personal experience.
    (4) Supporting evidence from common adages quoted as generally acknowledged truth, or modified to express new insights.
B (1) Direct admonitions and precepts, with supporting arguments and illustrations.
    (2) Indirect admonitions through the use of proverbs, illustrations and comments (including the metaphorical poem in 12:1–7).

With these categories and forms in mind, the somewhat loose structure of the book may be outlined in this way:

1:2: The thesis. All that man sees, knows and does is vain, empty, ephemeral (A: 1).

1:3–11: Effort is useless, nothing is changed, nothing is new (A: 1, 2).

1:12–18: The search for wisdom is frustrating (A: 1, 3).

2:1–11: The search for pleasure brings no lasting satisfaction (A: 1, 3).

2:12–17: The superiority of wisdom over folly is cancelled by the common fate of all men (A: 1, 3).

2:18–23: Toil and achievement are finally futile (A: 1, 3).

2:24–26: The only good is present enjoyment in living, which comes as God decides (A: 1, 2, 3).

3:1–8: Everything must happen at its appropriate time (A: 1).

3:9–15: God determines what happens; man can neither change his fate nor understand it (A: 1, 3).

3:16–4:3: Injustice and oppression show that men are no more than animals (A: 1, 3).

4:4–8: Toil and ambition are fruitless (A: 1, 3, 4).

4:9–12: Companionship emphasizes, even as it mitigates, man's helplessness (B: 2).

4:13–16: Power and prominence are ephemeral (A: 1, 3).

5:1–7 (Heb. 4:17–5:6): Be circumspect in religious observances (B: 1).

5:8–9 (Heb. 5:7–8): Do not yield to indignation at injustice, but reflect on its outcome (B: 1).

5:10–6:9 (Heb. 5:9–6:9): Struggle for wealth is futile; such happiness as God permits is to be relished; wealth, honor, and long life are worthless without contentment (A: 1, 2, 3; B: 2).

6:10–12: Human life is fated and incomprehensible (A: 1, 2).

7:1–22: See life in perspective, and behave with moderation (B: 1, 2).

7:23–8:1: Wisdom is indefinable except in contrast with folly; all women and most men are fools (A: 1, 3).

8:2–9: Do not challenge irresistible powers (A: 1, 2, 3; B: 1).

8:10–9:12: Men are not rewarded according to their moral behavior but suffer a common fate; God's ways are inscrutable; happiness is incidental and to be enjoyed gratefully (A: 1, 2, 3, 4; B: 1).

9:13–10:1: Wisdom is valueless unless applied, and can be counteracted by folly (A: 3, 4; B: 2).

10:2–11:6: Miscellaneous reflections and admonitions (A: 2, 3; B: 1, 2).

11:7–10: The positive worth of life and youth (B: 1, 2).

12:1–8: An admonition to reflect, supported by a metaphorical poem on the swift approach of death (B: 1, 2).

12:9–11: Biographical footnotes by the editor and anthologist.

12:12–14: Cautionary colophon by an orthodox scribe.

The Philosophy of Qoheleth

The bare outline of the contents of the book brings into stark relief the contrast of Qoheleth's negativism with the religious affirmations of the other books of the Bible. It makes it all the more strange that this work should have been included among the sacred writings of ancient Israel. The reason for the difference should have become clear: this is essentially a philosophical work, motivated by a search for understanding of human experience through the application of man's reason to observable data. The special data of a religion of revelation are excluded as unverifiable. The teacher's one major assumption is the existence of God and the inscrutability of his power. He concludes that a rational explanation of life as viewed from the human standpoint is impossible. Man's chief good is the positive enjoyment of such moments of happiness—uncovenanted, unexplained, and temporary—as God may permit him to have. One's youth is to be specially prized as the time when life is at the full and its enjoyment least hampered by care or weakness. For life passes quickly, and, as one grows older, the lengthening shadows presage the approach of night.

The philosophical character of Qoheleth's work, together with some linguistic indications of its date about the fourth or third century B.C., have led scholars to suspect the influence on his thought of Greek philosophical teachings. Heraclitus's view that all things are in perpetual flux seems echoed in his opening reflections on the restless cyclical motions of the natural world and the passing of the human generations (1:4–11). "Whatever has been is what will be, and whatever has been done is what will be done" (1:9, AB) recalls the Stoic theory of world cycles endlessly repeated. "Everything has its season and . . . proper time" (3:1, AB) sounds like the Stoic doctrine that man should live according to nature. The later saying of Marcus Aurelius that "worldly things are but as smoke, as very nothingness" so closely resembles Qoheleth's dictum that "all is an empty breath" as to suggest the influence on him of an earlier Stoicism. The hedonist element in Epicureanism might be ultimately responsible for the conclusion that "there is nothing better for a man to do than to eat and drink and enjoy himself in return for his labors" (2:24, NEB).

The similarities at these points are undeniable. But there is no evidence of more far-reaching and decisive Greek philosophical influence. The most that can be said is that Qoheleth was probably stimulated by the air of free inquiry in the Hellenistic age and may have picked up some snatches of Greek philosophy in the talk of the Phoenician port cities. He does not speak like a resident of a provincial town. Yet his deepest roots are (1) in the skepticism native to one strain of the Near Eastern wisdom tradition,[22] and (2) in certain deeply ingrained convictions of Hebrew religion, such as the real existence of the one God, his creation of the world and man, his sovereign power over events, and the awesome mystery of his Being.

In his opening sentence, and again in his final word, Qoheleth summarizes his philosophy in epigrammatic form, "A breath of breaths! A breath of breaths![23] Everything is a breath!" The word *hebel* is figurative of something real and recognizable but without substance or permanence, hence empty, futile, profitless, impossible to grasp. Its meaning is clarified in the recurrent synonym "a grasping at [*or* chasing of] the wind." The theme sentence may be paraphrased: Everything is empty and utterly futile, like the thinnest of vapors. Fleeting as a breath, it amounts to nothing. All a man's experience, his desires and his hopes, his efforts and his accomplishments, even his righteousness and his wisdom, are transient and without result. They change nothing and they add nothing. "What has a man

[22] See pp. 20-21, 26, 40-41, 172 above.
[23] For this idiomatic superlative, cf. "holy of holies," Song of Songs.

to show for all his trouble and effort during his brief lifetime?" (1:3, AB).

The teacher then passes on to observe that "there is nothing new under the sun," that is, in the phenomenal world. He observes the natural forces in constant movement—the sun rises and sets, the wind circles, the rivers flow continually to the sea—but nothing is changed. So with the human generations which pass in endless succession, toiling and weary beyond comprehension or expression. Everything that happens has happened before and has been forgotten. What, then, is the surplus or profit (*yithron*) that could give meaning to so colossal an outpouring of energy and effort? (1:3–11).

Seeking an answer to this question the author imagines himself in the role of Solomon, wisest and most powerful of kings. Since "a king . . . can do as he pleases" he would be free of the limitations which inhibit ordinary men in their search for understanding. But even under the best conceivable conditions wisdom is unable to discover the *yithron*. There seems to be refractory element in the world as it can be observed and thought about, and also something missing, "a crookedness not to be straightened, a void not to be filled."[24] Even the attempt to understand the process of thinking is self-defeating, "For with more wisdom comes more worry, and he who adds to his knowledge adds to his pain" (1:18, AB).

The author then describes an experiment, such as would theoretically have been possible for an absolute monarch like Solomon, with the object of determining if pleasure is to be identified with the good. But power, possessions, and the freedom of self-indulgence prove to have as little positive and enduring value as does the self-conscious cul-

[24] 1:15, as trans. by R. Gordis, *Koheleth: the Man and his World*, 3d ed. (1968), p. 148.

tivation of wisdom. All that results is momentary pleasure that is not worth the effort (2:1–11). The same conclusion is reached in an attempt to identify the advantage (*yithron* again!) of wisdom over folly; it is only temporary, for death obliterates both equally, and wisdom leaves no lasting memory. The fruits of a lifetime of skill and toil must be left to a successor who may turn out to be a fool. "So," says Qoheleth, "I came to hate life, . . . [and] to detest all that I had achieved. . . . Once more I fell into despair" (2:17–18, 20, AB).

Having failed to find permanent value in toil, pleasure, or even the search for wisdom, the teacher turns to another problem. Why must things happen as they do and not in some other way, and when they happen and not at some other time? His first thought is that for everything there is an appropriate occasion:

> A time to be born and a time to die,
> A time to plant and a time to uproot,
> A time to kill and a time to heal, . . .
> A time to weep and a time to laugh, . . .
> A time to be silent and a time to speak, . . .
> A time for war and a time for peace (3:1–8, AB).

The awareness that there are suitable times for silence and for speech, for example, is an old theme of the wisdom tradition, "A shrewd man holds his tongue," but "What is better than a well-timed word!"[25] So it is with the whole series of contraries, each fitted to its suitable place and occasion. The various actions named are carried out apparently at man's volition—all but the first. The times of his birth and death are not his to decide, and this gives the clue to Qoheleth's meaning. Just as surely as birth and death, so all other events and human actions take place when and as God deems them fitting. In verse 11 this is

[25] Prov. 10:19, AB; 15:23, McKane.

stated specifically, "God makes each event right [lit., beautiful] for its time" (AB). What happens to man is predetermined by God, and man is in no position to argue with omnipotence. "Whatever is, was long ago given its name" (6:10, NAB); that is, it was decided upon. "Whatever God does remains forever—to it one cannot add and from it one cannot subtract" (3:14, Gordis).

Man, however, is left in the dark about what God is doing and has been doing from first to last. He sees only that aspect of omnipotence which determines the conditions of his own existence. Here, unfortunately, the translation and meaning of a crucial verse are uncertain, as the different renderings of 3:11c indicate:

He has put eternity into man's mind, yet so that he cannot find out what God has done from beginning to end (RSV).

He has given men a sense of time past and future, but no comprehension of God's work from beginning to end (NEB).

He has put the timeless into their hearts, without man's ever discovering, from beginning to end, the work which God has done (NAB).

Yet he has put in their minds an enigma, so that man cannot discover what it is that God has been doing, from beginning to end (AB).

He has also implanted ignorance in their mind, so that mankind cannot discover the work which God has done from beginning to end (AT).

Though he has permitted man to consider time in its wholeness, man cannot comprehend the work of God from beginning to end (JB).

He has also placed the love of the world in men's hearts, except that they may not discover the work God has done from beginning to end (Gordis).

The problematic word is *ha'olam*. This has the primary meaning "that which is hidden," and, by extension, "that which will endure into the unknown future" (as in *'ad 'olam*, "forever"). In late usage the word can mean also "the world" as man experiences it. The meaning of the sentence, then, is either that man is made aware that time and "times" continue forever, by God's appointment; or that their meaning is hidden from man because of his invincible ignorance or forgetfulness. The latter explanation accords better with the following clause in 3:11b; what lies behind the irresistible determinism of man's fate is, by God's will, beyond man's comprehension.

One possible result of the belief that everything happens inexorably by God's decision is a feeling of moral impotence. Apparently nothing can be done about relieving human misery or about the cruelty and oppression of those who hold power in human societies (4:1-3). Moral indignation like that of the prophets accomplishes nothing, in Qoheleth's opinion. One can only reflect that every man who exercises power over his fellows is responsible to his superior, in a hierarchy of authorities culminating with the supreme power of God (5:8 EVV). "All is God's doing. Man cannot discover what it is that is going on in this world. . . . Just and wise men and what they do are in God's power; whether he will favor them or not, no one knows" (8:17; 9:1, AB).

The author thus emphatically rejects the theological dogma that retribution inevitably overtakes wickedness, and that goodness receives its reward in prosperity and happiness. His own experience does not confirm this. The righteous and the wicked, the wise man and the fool, meet the same doom in death. "I have seen it all during my transitory existence—the innocent perishing in spite of his innocence, and the wicked man who lives long in spite of his wickedness" (7:15, AB; cf. 8:14). He can only conjecture that, since morality pertains not to animals but to men, God is showing men that they are no better than the beasts. "The fate of men and the fate of animals is the same; as one dies, so dies the other. . . . Man has no superiority over the beasts, for all are a breath that vanishes" (3:19, AB).

As life is negated by universal death, so all human values are cancelled out by their opposites. "The more wisdom, the more grief, and increasing one's knowledge means increasing one's pain" (1:18, Gordis). A famous man is soon forgotten (4:13–16). Wealth accumulated in a lifetime of toil and anxious care may be lost in one unlucky venture, leaving its owner as naked as when he was born (5:13–16 [Heb. 5:12–15]). "One mistake can undo many things done well" (9:18, NEB). Arbitrary power in human hands can be destructive of social order (10:5–7). Every kind of excellence is subject to misfortune. There is a worm in every apple. "The race is not won by the swift, nor the battle by the valiant; the wise is not sure of a livelihood, nor the shrewd of wealth, nor the expert of winning favor. When the appointed time comes, mischance overtakes them all" (9:11). Death is the final and universal negation of human values, "How alike in death are the wise man and the fool!"[26]

Such utterly pessimistic conclusions, if they stood by themselves, would be destructive not only of human values but of the will to live. They run counter to the whole tone and substance of the rest of Hebrew religious literature. H. Wheeler Robinson has commented, "It was fitting enough that such an un-Hebraic philosophy of life should reach its climax in an eloquent and sombre picture of death. The book has indeed the smell of the tomb about

[26] 2:16, AB. Cf. 3:18–21; 6:6; 8:8; 9:3; 12:1.

it."[27] Yet that is not the total impression made by Qoheleth on most readers. There is more to his teaching than that. Wisdom, as we have seen, is basically counsel about how life should be lived; and it is here that Qoheleth makes his positive contribution. Far from suggesting rejection of life, let alone self-destruction, he is truly Hebraic in affirming life in spite of its anomalies and limitations. He himself is better than the stark philosophy to which he has come by unaided reason. Because he is after all a *Hebrew* wise man, his soul affirms what his reasoning had led him to doubt and deny. "Sweet is the light of day, and it is good to see the sunshine with one's eyes! If a man live many years, let him be happy in them all!" (11:7–8, AB alt.).

The Ethical Wisdom of Qoheleth

One may well wonder how this teacher was able to pass over from his agnostic and pessimistic philosophy to an affirmative ethic. He tells us, indeed, that at first he was driven to despair. After the failure of his experiment with pleasure and of his attempt to identify rationally the superiority of wisdom over folly, he says, "So I came to hate life, because it depressed me that all men's activities under the sun are only a breath and a clutching at the wind" (2:17, AB alt.). As he witnessed the tears and groans of the oppressed and helpless, he thought they would be better off dead (4:1–2). Man cannot remold the world according to his preference (1:15; 7:13). He cannot determine the course of his life, for this has already been done by God (8:6b–8). He cannot ensure his success and happiness by his own planning and efforts, driven by desire (2:22–23; 4:4; 6:7). What will happen to him is in God's hands and no one knows what are God's plans (8:16–17).

[27] H. Wheeler Robinson, *Inspiration and Revelation in the Old Testament* (1946), p. 258.

But, after all, why should a man think he is wise enough and good enough to be autonomous and omnicompetent? Within the limits of his knowledge, ability, circumstances, and his brief life-span, he does have relative freedom. At least he can choose to be a wise man rather than a fool. He can learn to live within the prescribed bounds and to accept the uncertainties of the unknown future; for who would dare to predetermine the course of his own life? Above all, he can enjoy his good fortune if and when it comes. He can relish the satisfactions and joys of life even while he knows he cannot count on them. The good to be experienced is more than enough to make life worth living, so that he will not choose to die. Here the teacher strikes a positive note most emphatically in his counsel to young men to revel in the days of their vigor (11:9). His philosophy has not cut the nerve of life.

In the first place, his pupils must learn to think for themselves. They must be ready to face the facts about life's uncertainties and perplexities and to accept their own finiteness. Common or inherited beliefs which will not stand up under examination must be abandoned as untrue. All too often virtue is not rewarded and vice punished, as conventional morality would have it. Nor is it true that the pursuit of pleasure or wealth as goals, or even dedication to wisdom and virtue, will add up to lasting satisfaction in life. Happiness comes unawares to those who are prepared for it; one must watch for it and not miss it when it comes.

Secondly, a man must learn to accept the inevitable and to live with what cannot be changed. The world as it is, and as it seems to work, is something *given*; if, from man's standpoint, it seems to be "bent," nothing he can do will straighten it (1:15). Man has no choice but to accept the world into which he was born. Time rolls on, apparently heedless of the passing generations. The "times" when things happen are appointed and cannot be evaded. There is no release from the ranks of battle, no escaping the common fate. What God is about is his affair, and he has not admitted man to the secrets of creation and providence. Human attempts to transcend the limits of mortal existence through struggle or through wisdom are doomed to failure. Therefore it is the part of wisdom to accept life with serenity and courage, and so to find its hidden treasure.

For there are compensations. The very fact of being alive, especially when young, is a fundamental and joyous good. The capacity to relish the joys of life and love and the activity of mind and body is a fundamental virtue. One should accept gratefully such happiness as is granted, when it comes. He who does not savor the present joy will live to regret that it has passed unnoticed. A restless dissatisfaction with the present that is forever straining toward tomorrow will rob a man of this precious jewel. "Better a joy at hand than a longing for distant pleasures" (6:9, Gordis).

So then, eat your bread with cheerfulness and drink your wine with a glad heart, since already God has approved what you do. At all times let your clothing be white, and perfumed oil on your head not be lacking. Enjoy life with the woman you love all the fleeting days that God grants you under the sun, for that is your rightful portion. . . . Everything your hand finds to do, do with your full strength; for there is no doing or thinking, knowledge or wisdom, in Sheol whither you are bound. (9:7–10, AB).

Life can be sweet and should be relished, for old age comes soon, and then the dark.

The good of life is the living of it. The profit of effort is in the struggle, not in some residue of achievement and success. The fruit of wisdom is not in the solution of mysteries, but in knowing how to live best under life's difficulties and uncertainties. Man is no more the master of his life than he is of the day of his death. He can find contentment and serenity only in coming to terms with the given conditions of his existence.

This is essentially a religious ethic, though it is a far cry from an ethic of obedience to the commandments of a personal God. Like the other wisdom teachers of the Hebrew Bible, Qoheleth has little to say about the cultic and community aspects of religion. What he does say is that respectful, yet discriminating, openness to learn from religious observances means far more than thoughtless participation in them for conventional reasons (5:1–7 [Heb. 4:6–5:6]). At the same time, if a man does join in a cultic act such as making a religious vow, he should not make this a mockery by neglecting its fulfillment. "Better not vow at all than vow and fail to pay" (5:5, NEB). A wise man will not be disdainful in the presence of the great mystery with which religion is concerned. Even though he cannot accept uncritically all that traditional religion affirms, and will speak and act with reserve, he will know that God is great beyond human understanding. To accept life as God has given it, and to respond positively to that gift of life is his form of faith.

The Significance of Qoheleth

Qoheleth's rationalism may seem to result, as indeed it does, in a minimal declaration of religious faith. It is not this which has sustained the Jewish people through all their vicissitudes from the days of Moses until now. It requires more than this to give substance to the Christian's hopes and make him certain of realities he does not see.[28]

[28] See Ep. Heb. 11:1, NEB.

Yet both Judaism and Christianity have accorded this book a place in their sacred scriptures, to whose teaching and spirit it seems in many ways so alien. Both traditions would be poorer without it.

Who was Qoheleth, and when and under what circumstances did he speak and write? From the biographical footnote in 12:9–11 we learn that he was a celebrated and stimulating wisdom teacher, an industrious and profound scholar, and a literary craftsman. From his advice to his pupils to make the most of their days of youthful vigor, we may infer that he himself was approaching the twilight which heralds oncoming night. He speaks as a member of a cultural elite in a stratified and stable society, under the rule of a distant king. He gives no hint of having witnessed war or social upheaval.[29]

The situation envisaged suggests that of Judea under the later Persian empire in the fourth century B.C., or in the early years of Ptolemaic rule which followed after a brief period of confusion. The apparent evidence of some acquaintanceship with Greek philosophic thought points to the same period. So does the linguistic evidence; the Hebrew in which the book is written is definitely postclassical. It is contaminated by Aramaisms and Phoenicianisms; two Persian words are used, but no certainly Greek words or grammatical constructions.

This is a fascinating work of Hebrew wisdom. If it seems out of place in the Bible, let us consider its value as a counterweight to the smug self-righteousness of unexamined religious belief. On the writer's premises his conclusions are not easily proved wrong. His is a mood into which most believers fall at times. By forcing us to be honest with ourselves and with God, by making us look straight at the darkness of our ignorance and the unknown beyond, Qohe-

---

[29] Unless the latter is referred to in 4:13–16 and 10:6–7.

leth compels us to take a stand, to say what we believe, and why. A religious belief that will not bear examination is not worth having; it is no faith at all. A religious man who has never battled with pessimism and doubt has a very shallow religion.

Qoheleth's intellectual honesty and relentless reasoning, even when these lead to unexpected and unwelcome conclusions, are a moral tonic. If, given his philosophical convictions, he was able to attain serenity of mind and happiness in affirming life, the believing Jew or Christian can expect no less of his religious faith.

8
Wisdom Piety

WHEN THE Jewish community was reconstituted and the temple worship restored at Jerusalem after the exile, great changes had taken place as a result of the upheaval. Israel was no longer a territorial nation under its own king, but a people, of which only a part lived in its ancient homeland. Judea was now a small territory in the immediate vicinity of Jerusalem. It was, politically speaking, a temple-state incorporated into the Persian empire, permitted local self-government by the high priest and his council under the supervision of a Persian-appointed governor. The latter might be a Jew, like Nehemiah, or a non-Jew, like the Bagohi of the Elephantine papyri. The temple was no longer a dynastic shrine, or even a national temple in the former sense. Jerusalem and its temple had become, rather, the religious capital of this people scattered in many lands, the symbolic focus of their traditions and of their faith and hope.

In preexilic times the temple cult had been accessible to all—at least in theory. This was no longer true, simply because of distance, though many pious men made the long pilgrimage when opportunity offered. Yet Jews everywhere now had two religious possessions in common: (1) a written scripture which could be copied and transported abroad, and (2) the institution of the synagogue. Synagogues were local assemblies for prayer and for the reading and exposition of the sacred scrolls and were located wherever a sufficient number of Jews were resident. In a sense they served as surrogates for temple worship, providing for the continuance of its nonsacrificial elements. The written Torah, accompanied by the records of ancient prophecy, was heard as Yahweh's living voice to his people. Hence the scribes who became experts in the study and interpretation of the holy books inherited much of the regulative authority in matters of belief and religious obligation that had been in former times the prerogative of the priests.

One consequence of this, and of the fact that the synagogue was a smaller and more intimate place of religious assembly, was increased participation by laymen under the guidance of the learned. There developed a new kind of personal piety centered on the Torah. The three streams of priestly, prophetic, and wisdom types of religion and theological thought were mingled in what Tournay has called "a symbiosis" of piety and the older wisdom tradition.[1]

One of the marks of this symbiosis was the identification of Yahweh, God of Israel, with "God" in the more generalized sense common to the writings of international wisdom. As we have seen, wisdom thought presupposed belief in a divinely established world order as the basis for the right ordering of human life.[2] Wisdom had thus been, from the first, religious in a broad sense, in spite of its preoccupation with empirical rules for the achievement of success and social approval. An example of this nonspecific use of the word *God* is preserved in what may be the oldest stratum of Proverbs, "The glory of God lies in what he

[1] R. Tournay, "En marge d'une traduction des Psaumes," *RB* 63 (1956): 503.
[2] See above, pp. 115–16, 138.

conceals, The glory of kings in what they bring to light."[3] In the Book of Job the proper name *Yahweh* appears only in the prose prologue and epilogue which frame the poetry;[4] the poetry itself uses instead the words *El, Eloah, Shaddai,* and rarely *Elohim.* The older usage is resumed in Qoheleth, where the personal name of God is deliberately avoided.

The confluence of the wisdom tradition with later orthodox piety is evident in Proverbs 1–9, in certain of the Psalms, in Sirach, the Wisdom of Solomon, and to a lesser degree in other works that are found in the English Apocrypha. (The last-named and Proverbs 1–9 have already been touched on in previous chapters.)

The Wisdom Psalms

The reader of the Psalms who is familiar with the literary forms, characteristic diction, and favorite themes of wisdom writings will recognize signs of these from time to time. In some instances, such as Psalms 1 and 37, a poem appears to be a unified composition by a writer who expresses himself in this way. In a larger number the wisdom element shows its presence only in certain verses, and is combined with other features such as prayer, praise, and historical recital which have a different background in the religious tradition. In Psalm 32, for example, only verses 1–2, 8–10 (EVV) have the marks of a wisdom writer; the remainder of the composition is derived from the liturgical forms of penitential prayer and congregational rejoicing. The concluding line of the royal messianic Psalm 2 and the last verse of Psalm 111 are in the wisdom idiom, in each case contrasting with what precedes.[5]

[3] Prov. 25:2, AB.
[4] Except for 12:9 where some mss. read *Eloah,* and in editorial connecting sentences at 38:1; 40:1, 6.
[5] An additional wisdom feature in Ps. 111 is its acrostic form.

The desigination "Wisdom Psalms" has been widely used, but no two scholars seem to agree as to which ones should be included in this category. Murphy has attempted to establish specific criteria of style and content.[6] He concludes that Psalms 1, 32, 34, 37, 49, 112, and 128 can properly be classified in this way, while others (25, 31, 39, 40A, 62, 78, 92, 94, 111, 119, and 127) show wisdom influence. Other scholars have proposed the inclusion of Psalms 19B, 73, 90, 91, 105, 106, and 133. The four on which there is widest agreement are Psalms 1, 37, 49, and 112. Examination of these four will illustrate both their affinities with the thought and language of the wisdom books and some special characteristics of what can be called "wisdom piety."

Psalm 1 is a good example with which to begin. Its purpose is hortatory and didactic, to commend and justify the choice of a devout life rather than a wicked or worldly one. All Jews belong either to "the company of the righteous" (v. 5) or to that other company. There is no middle way. This sharp division between the righteous and the wicked, the pious and the impious, has already appeared in the later strata of Proverbs, corresponding to the older division of all men into wise men and fools.[7] The old law of appropriate divine reward or retribution is still in effect. The two types of men are characterized by the psalmist in similes: the righteous man is truly alive, like a fruit tree planted beside a flowing stream; the wicked man is as dead and useless as wind-blown chaff. The Psalm opens with the exclamatory benediction *'ashre*, "blessed, fortunate is," which is found outside the Psalter chiefly in Proverbs. The word *leṣ*, "scoffer" is quite common in

---

[6] R. E. Murphy, "The Classification 'Wisdom Psalms,'" *VT Supp. IX* (1963): pp. 156–67; cf. S. Mowinckel, "Psalms and Wisdom," in *VT Supp. III* (1955), pp. 205–24.

[7] Prov. 2:20–22; 10:1, 3, 8; 14:1, etc.

Proverbs but occurs only here in the Psalms.[8] Other examples of wisdom vocabulary will be recognized from the list in Chapter 5.

A new note is struck in verse 2, where the Law of Yahweh (undoubtedly the written Torah) is declared to be the focal point of the good man's life and the subject of his constant meditation. The word *hagah*, "meditate," means literally to "murmur," as when something is being read or discussed in an undertone. This verb and its cognate nouns reappear in other wisdom passages in the Psalms.[9] Finally, Yahweh "knows" the members of these two companies moving in opposite directions, and who will meet opposite fates when he comes to judge them.[10] Of this the poet is confident.

Psalm 37 differs from Psalm 1 in structure and length, but its wisdom features are even more noticeable. Its form is that of a series of precepts and proverbs making use largely of wisdom vocabulary and commending the life of piety. The reader is apt to be puzzled by the apparent lack of continuity in thought until he discovers that the continuity is in form rather than content; the composition is an acrostic, its alternate lines beginning with successive letters of the Hebrew alphabet. This device also results in a certain discontinuity of thought where it is used in Proverbs 31, the poem in praise of the capable housewife.

The hortatory tone of Psalm 37 resembles that of the ten discourses in Proverbs 1–9. Verse 16 is a proverb of comparative values, echoing Proverbs 15:16 both in form and content. Verse 21 is a descriptive or characterizing proverb and verses 23–24 are a religious axiom, in both cases recalling favorite themes in Proverbs. The personal witness of experience to the rewards of righteousness, in

---

[8] Elsewhere, significantly enough, only in Isa. 29:20.
[9] Pss. 37:30; 49:3 (Heb. 49:4); 19:14 (Heb. 19:15).
[10] Cf. Ps. 139:1–4; Job 23:10; Wis. Sol. 1:6; 2:24.

verse 25, echoes the claims of Job's counselors and similar affirmations in Proverbs.[11]

Once more, as in Psalm 1, the righteous and the wicked are sharply contrasted, in their fate as in their behavior. The former's wisdom and justice are the fruits of his reverence for the divine law (vv. 30–31). The content of the comprehensive term *righteous* is here spelled out, first by the introduction of approximate synonyms, humble, blameless, upright, peaceable, divinely approved.[12] The negative imperative verbs in successive maxims warn against resentment, anger, envy, states of mind that are incompatible with the serenity of faith. Right and wrong actions are touched on only in general terms: "Turn away from evil, and do good" (v. 27).[13] And finally, the positive content of personal religious faith is brought out in the exhortations to trust in Yahweh, to find delight in him, to commit one's way (or daily life) to his direction, to be silent (i.e., uncomplaining), to cultivate the patience of faith and hope. The words used here occur in Job, but are not otherwise distinctive of wisdom usage.

Unlike the foregoing examples, Psalm 49 definitely identifies itself as a wisdom utterance, a *mashal*.[14] It is concerned with a problem or riddle (*ḥidah*) and is addressed to all sorts and conditions of men. The problem is not, as often elsewhere, Why do the wicked prosper?[15] but, Why should the rich and powerful be permitted to make good men afraid? The first answer is that rich men and poor men, wise men and fools, face the same universal fate, and in death are equal. All perish like the beasts — which

---

[11] Cf. Job 4:8; 20:4–5; Prov. 4:3–9; 13:20–21.
[12] Vv. 11, 18, 22, 37.
[13] "To turn away from evil" (*sur meraʿ*) is a stock phrase of the wisdom writers; see Job 1:1, 8; 2:3; Prov. 3:7; 13:19; 14:16, etc. Cf. Ps. 34:14 (EVV).
[14] See above, pp. 53–54.
[15] Cf. Jer. 12:1; Job 21:7; Ps. 73:3–14.

to Qoheleth was one of life's most painful anomalies.[16] To this thought the psalmist devotes most of his attention. But in verse 15 (EVV) he makes, almost in passing, a more profound suggestion—that the God he has learned to trust will "ransom" him from the power of Sheol (that is, death personified), and will "take" him as Enoch and Elijah were "taken." The choice of the word *padah*, "ransom," instead of a more general word for deliverance is probably deliberate; for this is what the rich man's wealth is not great enough to do (v. 7, EVV). The meaning here is not "deliver from death" by restoration to health or safety.[17] The psalmist has already made it clear that he, like all men, must die. He knows only that the God he has come to trust will not at the last abandon him to be mastered by death and the underworld.

Unlike Qoheleth, this Psalm shows man's reason at work within the bounds of faith. Among connecting links with the wisdom tradition are the opening call for attention addressed to all men, the technical wisdom terms used in verses 3–4 (EVV), the contrasting of wise men with fools and brutes in verse 10, the rhetorical question in verses 5–6, and the admonitory maxim in verses 16 ff. The whole psalm might have been composed with Proverbs 11:7a as its text, "When the wicked dies, his hope perishes."[18]

Murphy states briefly his reasons for classifying Psalm 112 as a wisdom psalm; it is "characterized by the *'ashre* formula, the *rasha'/ṣaddiq* contrast, and its description of the rewards offered to the just make it an implicit admonition."[19] Additional terms from the wisdom vocabulary may be noted, *delight, upright, heart (mind), desire,* as well as the phrase *to fear Yahweh.* Furthermore, the composition

---

[16] Qoh. 2:16; 3:19.

[17] As in Ps. 33:19 (*hiṣṣil*); Ps. 89:48, EVV (*malleṭ*); Ps. 116:8 (*hilleṣ*).

[18] Perhaps significantly, the converse is substituted by the LXX, "At the death of a just man, hope does not perish."

[19] Murphy, "Classification 'Wisdom Psalms,'" pp. 163–64.

is an alphabetic acrostic of single lines;[20] this does not disturb the continuity so obviously as in Psalm 37, because all except the last three lines are devoted to the same topic —the righteous man and his rewards.

The theme and tone of the Psalm are much like those of Psalm 1. Each begins with the expression of approval, "Blessed, fortunate is." Both comment on the devout man's delight in studying the Torah ("his commandments"), and stress the righteous/wicked antithesis. There are links here also with Psalm 37 in the reference to the generosity of the good man, and with Psalm 49 in the mention of his confidence that overcomes fear.

Criteria for Distinguishing Wisdom Psalms

The examination of these four Psalms establishes two kinds of criteria for recognizing wisdom influence in the Psalter: (1) formal and (2) thematic. The most important formal feature is that these Psalms are not addressed to Yahweh in prayer or praise but to men, and especially to the less instructed and less devout. The tone is in varying degrees hortatory, didactic, testifying, and reflective. A second formal feature is the use of some wisdom vocabulary and turns of phrase, and the adoption of wisdom stylistic forms such as proverbs, precepts, similes, illustrations from nature, rhetorical questions, and the teacher's call for attention (as in 49:1, EVV). Some of these, of course, are not peculiar to wisdom speech, but belong to the wider tradition of rhetoric. The alphabetic acrostic form with its artificiality may have originated as a mnemonic aid in teaching.

The themes that have come to light in these four Psalms

---

[20] Half-lines in Hebrew. The introductory "Hallelujah" is outside the scheme.

are: (1) the antithetical ways of life of the righteous and the wicked; (2) the appropriate rewards and retribution in store for each respectively; (3) the qualities and behavior of the righteous as evoking admiration and imitation; (4) the study of the written Torah as the focus of pious meditation and as a source of delight; (5) the worth of righteousness expressed in terms of life and vitality; (6) affirmation of and exhortation to personal trust in Yahweh; (7) the search for understanding of problems of faith.

Since it is generally agreed that these four Psalms are representative of wisdom piety, we may proceed to examine other Psalms which, in whole or in part, exhibit similar characteristics. It has already been noted that in some Psalms only certain sections do so. In other cases the wisdom element is slight and incidental only, and may be due to editorial annotation.[21]

The greatest measure of affinity with the quartet of Psalms discussed above is found in the following:

Psalm 32: A hortatory testimonial by a devout wise man, incorporating in verses 3–7 a psalm of individual thanksgiving.

Psalm 34: An acrostic poem in two sections, of which the first (vv. 1–10, EVV) is a prayer of individual thanksgiving, partly in wisdom language, and the second (vv. 11–22) is an instructional discourse.

Psalm 127: Two expanded proverbs with the didactic tone of religious wisdom, recalling Proverbs 16:3, 9 and 17:6.

Psalm 128: A short declaration of the rewards of piety, concluded by a priestly benediction. Cf. Ps. 1.

Psalm 133: The virtue of familial concord is commended in visual imagery, with the exclamatory "how good and pleasant" (referring to the virtue)[22] substituted for the commoner "happy is he who" (referring to the virtuous).

[21] E.g., the last line of Ps. 2 and the final verse of Ps. 111.
[22] See Prov. 15:23.

A third group of Psalms may be brought into the wisdom category because of their primary concern with meditation on the Torah. This, as we have seen, was the focus of attention of the devout among the sages. These Psalms are of two types: The first is the praise of the law and of the religion centered around it, as in Psalms 19B (vv. 7–14, EVV),[23] and 119. The former opens with a series of six almost synonymous couplets in the rather unusual three/two meter and ends with the poet's humble prayer for the acceptance of his words and meditations. The subject is the precious fruits of the study of the Law.

Psalm 119 is the longest 'chapter' in the Bible and also the most elaborate of the alphabetic acrostic psalms. It comprises twenty-two stanzas of eight lines apiece, each of the eight beginning with the same initial letter. Having imposed on himself so rigid a structure, the poet is unable to develop any sequence of thought. There is much repetition, especially of the synonyms for the Torah, "statutes," "commandments," "instructions," "precepts," "ordinances." Nevertheless the deep religious devotion of the writer is evident throughout. Beginning, like Psalm 1, with congratulation of the pious student of scripture, the psalm is basically a prolonged prayer of thanksgiving, supplication, and devotion. In places there are echoes of the Individual Complaint form, with its cry for divine intervention.[24] The wisdom features are the acrostic form and the use of wisdom vocabulary. At least twenty-one words from the list of wisdom terms in chapter 5 occur, many of them

---

[23] This is clearly a distinct composition from 19A (vv. 1–6, EVV), in form, style, and content. The two have been combined in the process of making up a collection of psalms, just as Ps. 108 combines Ps. 57:7–11, EVV, with Ps. 60:6–12. Conversely, Pss. 42 and 43 form a single psalm.

[24] See vv. 21–23, 69–70, 81–88, 145–52. Cf. Pss. 3, 6, 7, etc.

repeatedly. This confirms the linkage of Torah piety with the wisdom tradition in its scribal form.

Related in some ways to the foregoing, but probably reflecting an earlier stage in the growth of this form of piety, is another group of Psalms which direct their attention to Yahweh's "mighty deeds" in Israel's past—Psalms 78, 105, and 106. Possibly, but not certainly, these Psalms were composed for recital at cultic festivals.

The purpose of the writer of Psalm 78 is religious instruction and admonition. He begins with a call for attention, "Give ear, my people, to my teaching; listen to the words I will speak." This sentence is modeled on the customary opening of the sage's address, with the usual "my son(s)" altered to "my people." He speaks of his message as a *mashal* ("significant utterance") and *hidoth* ("riddles," or "wonderful things").[25] The intention is to encourage faith and obedience to the commandments by recalling Yahweh's mighty acts of old. The epic story is followed from the Exodus deliverance to the covenant choice of David as king and the erection of Solomon's temple. It is not merely an historical narrative in verse. Rather, it is a homily on Israel's persistent rebellion in spite of Yahweh's goodness to her and the punishments her rebellion provoked. Wisdom terminology is restricted to the introductory verses and to the conclusion, serving as a kind of envelope, and justifying, at least in a broad sense, the classification of this as a wisdom psalm.

In Psalms 105 and 106 the subject and intention of the writers are much the same as in 78, though now the tone is that of praise rather than admonition and the formal marks of wisdom are slight. For this reason they can hardly be classified with Psalm 78, in spite of the common element of recital.

There is thus a total of twelve psalms that can be clas-

---

[25] Cf. the opening verse of the wisdom Psalm 49.

sified definitely as wisdom Psalms, namely, 1, 19B, 32, 34, 37, 49, 78, 112, 119, 127, 128, and 133. A few others incorporate short sections of wisdom material,[26] whether by the original intention of the writers or by some vagary of the editorial process. Almost all hymnbooks and prayer collections are composite, and the Psalter in its present form has behind it a long history of the making of shorter collections.

In addition to the examples already noted, four other psalms have the form of alphabetic acrostics, 9 and 10,[27] 25, 111, and 145. The last two of these at least can hardly by any stretching of the term be considered wisdom poems, although Psalm 111 has a single verse of that type appended to it. Like the similar tags at the end of Psalms 2 and 144, this is perhaps an indication of editorial participation by the sages. Still others in which some evidence of wisdom thought may be detected are Psalms 14, 15, 24A, 40, 53, 73, 90, 92, and 104. The wisdom contribution to the Psalter is substantial but should not be exaggerated.

The Wisdom of Sirach (ben Sira')

Sirach, or to give the book its Hebrew name, ben Sira',[28] may be regarded as a latter-day Book of Proverbs. Like

---

[26] Pss. 10:3–11; 41:1–3, EVV; 94:12 ff.

[27] Psalms 9 and 10 were originally one psalm, as they remain in LXX and Vulg. The acrostic is not quite complete in this case, probably owing to corruption in transmission of the Hebrew text.

[28] The title of the book in LXX is Sirach or the Wisdom of Sirach. The Greek translation is the oldest form of the complete text to have survived. In the original Hebrew text, large parts of which have been recovered in recent years, and in the Talmud, the author's name is given as Jeshua' ben Sira'. In the present discussion "ben Sira'" refers to the author, "Sirach" to his book. The title Ecclesiasticus came into English usage from the Latin versions which were made from the Greek. See above, Chap. 1, n. 7.

the older work, it is primarily a collection of wisdom materials for the religious and moral instruction of youth, derived from tradition and supplemented with theological and devotional contributions from the teacher himself. Whereas the editor of Proverbs incorporated earlier collections of precepts and proverbs, making some additions to these, ben Sira' reformulated the older sayings in his own words, added many new ones, and developed others into miniature essays. The religious element is more emphasized and is more inclusive.

This teacher sees himself as an heir of the prophets as well as of the sages. His interests extend to the cult and its priesthood, and to the 'salvation history' of Israel as a chosen people. Prayers, hymns, devotional meditations, and theological reflections are interspersed with the proverbs and exhortations. There are also some biographical passages. On the basis of these and of the preface contributed by the author's grandson and translator, the work and its author can be given a firm historical setting in Jerusalem about 190–170 B.C.

The preface informs us that the work was composed in Hebrew by a certain Jeshua' (Greek, "Jesus"), an erudite scholar of the scriptures, and that it was translated into Greek after the grandson's emigration to Egypt in the 38th year of Ptolemy VII Euergetes, 132 B.C. How much earlier than that date the original work was completed is not stated. From its length and the indications that it was composed in two or more stages we can infer that it was written over a considerable period of time during the first third of the second century B.C. The author's patronymic, ben Sira' (Greek, "son of Sirach") has become for obvious reasons the customary designation of the writer rather than his given name; it may refer to a more remote progenitor than his own parent, as suggested by the variant forms in 50:27. The latter verse identifies Jeshua' as a

Jerusalemite. We learn from the epilogue in 51:13–30 (although the grandson does not mention this) that Jeshua' was both a scholar and a teacher of the lore and piety of wisdom who gathered pupils about him in his own school.[29]

This accords with the predominantly admonitory content of the book. More than once the writer refers in passing to his own education. As a youth he had dedicated himself in prayer to the quest for wisdom, and had submitted himself to the "yoke," or discipline, of instruction which he now commends (51:26). Three times he mentions his foreign travels.[30] In eloquent words he extols the incomparable privilege of becoming a scholar in the divine Torah and the ancient tradition of wisdom—

> who devotes himself to studying the law of the Most High, who investigates all the wisdom of the past, and spends his time studying the prophecies! He preserves the sayings of famous men and penetrates the intricacies of parables. He investigates the hidden meaning of proverbs, and knows his way among riddles. The great avail themselves of his services, and he is seen in the presence of rulers. He travels in foreign countries and learns at first hand the good or evil of man's lot. (39:1–4, NEB)

The grandson's translation of ben Sira's work found its way into the Greek Bible of the early Christian church. The original Hebrew text, on the other hand, was not granted canonical status by the Palestinian rabbis. As a result it had disappeared from general knowledge until the end of the nineteenth century, when medieval copies of large parts of it were recovered from the storeroom of a synagogue in Old Cairo. The authenticity of these was accepted by some scholars and disputed by others, until

---

[29] *beth midrashi*, "my house of learning" (51:23).
[30] 34:10–12; 39:4; 51:13.

204 / *The Way of Wisdom*

in 1952 some small fragments came to light at Qumran, in 1956 part of Chapter 51, and in 1964 almost four additional chapters at Masada in a scroll which can be dated palaeographically to the first century B.C.[31]

The Greek translation remains the standard form of the text, since it is the oldest complete version. This has been preserved in two recensions of unequal length, the longer of which includes various insertions, mostly in the first half of the book. The longer form was translated in KJV. RSV and NEB follow the shorter form found in the oldest and best manuscripts,[32] and relegate to footnotes the supplementary material of the longer version. (To avoid confusion the chapter and verse numbering of KJV has been retained.) The NAB translation is based on the Hebrew text so far as this has been preserved—corrected and interpreted in the light of the ancient versions.

The Wisdom of Sirach resembles the Book of Proverbs in two of its principal features: (1) the provision of extensive moral and religious instruction in proverbs, maxims, and moral exhortations, and (2) the exploration of the idea of wisdom, both as a way of life and as a divine reality at work in the created world and in human life. Sirach goes beyond Proverbs in asserting the special association of the divine wisdom with Israel, through the gift of the Torah. It emphasizes the life of piety as the true way to understanding. The whole rich heritage of Jewish faith is drawn upon, in prophecy, worship, salvation history, and theology. Prayers and devotional meditations are

---

[31] See A. A. di Lella, *The Hebrew Text of Sirach* (1966); F. M. Cross, Jr., *The Ancient Library of Qumran* (1958), pp. 14–15, 34; J. A. Sanders, *The Psalms Scroll of Qumran Cave II* (1965), pp. 79–85; Y. Yadin, *The Ben Sira Scroll from Masada* (1965).

[32] In both Greek recensions the section 30:25–33:13a has been accidentally displaced to follow 36:16a. The original order has been preserved in the Hebrew, Latin, and Syriac versions.

interspersed with proverbs and precepts, and the book reaches its climax in a threefold song of praise. The author is clearly a man of authentic piety and an acute theologian, as well as a teacher of religion and morals.

The book as a whole is not a unitary composition. The arrangement of its contents indicates that, to a first volume (1:1–24:29) with its own discernable structure and completeness, two extensive supplements (that might be called second and third volumes) were added in 24:30–39:11 and 39:12–50:24.[33] The whole is brought to a formal conclusion with the colophon or signature in 50:27–29. Two appendixes, an individual Psalm of thanksgiving, and an acrostic epilogue inviting his pupils to follow in the teacher's steps are added in chapter 51.[34]

The first volume or division begins and ends with important theological meditations on the nature and divine origin of wisdom (1:1–20 and 24:1–29). Between these "bookends" (so to speak) is found the largest of three groups of proverbs, maxims, and brief admonitory discourses. This in turn is marked off at intervals by digressions, three poems where the idea of wisdom is pictorially personified (4:11–19; 6:18–31; 14:20–15:8), a meditation on the works and mercy of God (16:26–18:14), and a prayer (22:27–23:6).

The second division or volume continues with a long series of counsels in 25:1–38:23, interrupted only twice; once in 33:7–15 by a meditation and once in 36:1–17 by a psalm of supplication. This section is concluded with a long essay contrasting the privileged career of a scholar with other occupations (38:24–39:15).

At the beginning of the third division in 39:12 the

[33] Note the similar fashion in which the author's resumption of his writing is indicated in 24:30–34 and 39:12–16.

[34] I.e., of the Greek, and English versions dependent on the Greek. Between these two appendixes the Hebrew version inserts a second hymn of praise.

hearers are summoned to praise the Creator and Sovereign Lord, whose ways bring blessing to the righteous and retribution to the wicked. This is clearly introductory to the noble hymn of praise in 42:15–43:33. For some reason, probably accidental, a series of short wisdom essays has been intruded between the introduction and the hymn itself, culminating in a gloomy comment on the ways of wayward daughters and of women in general. The hymn is followed in chapters 40–49 by the justly famous recital of the names and deeds of the heroes of faith from Adam to Nehemiah.[35] Finally, in chapter 50, this panegyric on famous men of old is followed by a striking and historically important (because apparently firsthand!) description of the temple service as conducted in the Jerusalem temple on the Day of Atonement by the high priest Simon.[36]

The forms and content of the proverbs and precepts which bulk so large in Sirach deserve special notice. A noteworthy example of the way in which the author uses the Book of Proverbs is found in the opening chapter, 1:11–20. This might be called "variations on the theme-motto of Proverbs 1:7, 'The fear of the Lord is the beginning of knowledge.'" This tendency to expansiveness is characteristic of Sirach, in comparison with the earlier work. Another good example is the parallel in Sirach 1:30 to Proverbs 16:18. The older teacher had already expanded the terse (colloquial?) saying, "Pride . . . before disaster!" by adding a second line "and arrogance precedes a fall," to form a "Solomonic" couplet.[37] Sirach expands the two lines to six, "Never be arrogant, for fear you fall and bring disgrace on yourself; the Lord will reveal your secrets and

[35] The somewhat similar recital in Ep. Heb. 11 may have been inspired by this.

[36] Simon II, ca. 200 B.C. On his connection with "Simon the Righteous" cf. R. H. Pfeiffer, *History of New Testament Times* (1949), pp. 365–67.

[37] See above, pp. 53, 59, 66 ff.

humble you before the assembly, because it was not the fear of the Lord that prompted you, but your heart was full of hypocrisy" (Sir. 1:30, NEB).

Another way in which Sirach enlarges upon a single topic is in its grouping together of related sayings and precepts which in Proverbs are scattered haphazardly through the book. The subject of a son's obligations to his parents, for example, is broached in various ways in Sirach 3:2–16 and seldom again. In Proverbs no less than twenty verse couplets touch on this matter, almost all of them isolated amid heterogeneous materials.

In the third place Sirach makes much greater use of the small essay than does Proverbs.[38] In 12:10–18 the maxim "Never trust your enemy" becomes the text for a disquisition on the reasons for such a warning. The *carpe diem* philosophy of Qoheleth is presented in Sirach 14:11–19. In 23:7–27 a lecture against swearing and vulgar talk is followed by one on sexual immorality. Moderation in eating and drinking is linked with advice on proper behavior at a banquet in 31:12–32:2. There are also longer essays, on acceptable worship (35:1–20), on the superiority of the scribal profession (38:24–39:11), on the blessings of wisdom (14:20–15:8), on the works and mercy of God (16:24–18:14). The theological statements on the divine nature and origin of wisdom which open and close the first division of the book in chapters 1 and 24 may be added here, though 1:1–20 is a rhapsody rather than an essay. Above all there are the noble "Praise of the Fathers" in chapters 44–49, and the vivid word painting of the temple service in chapter 51.

In spite of his expansive tendency the writer also makes

---

[38] Examples are Prov. 5:15–20; 6:1–5, 6–11, 12–15; 23:29–35; 24:30–34; 27:23–27. The poem on the capable housewife in chap. 31 might be included, but its acrostic structure distinguishes it from the rest.

use of the older and shorter proverbial forms. The "like mother, like daughter" pattern appears in 10:2, "Like the ruler of the city, so are its inhabitants," and the simple simile in 11:30. A pictorial adage is given a rather obvious application, "Handle pitch and it will make you dirty; keep company with an arrogant man and you will grow like him" (13:1, NEB). The rhetorical question of analogy is illustrated by 13:18, (NEB), "What peace can there be between a hyena and a dog? What peace between rich man and pauper?" Or again, "How can a jug be friends with a kettle?" (13:2, NEB).

The better-this-than-that pattern occurs repeatedly, sometimes in the form x is better than either y or z.[39] The exclamatory "happy is he who" is matched by the corresponding reproach "woe to" (or "Shame on").[40] The writer sometimes makes use of the progressive numerical form (x—1, x) as in 26:5; "Of three things my heart is afraid, and of a fourth I am frightened."[41]

Sirach also has his own distinctive forms of proverbs. The sayings commonly occur in groups of three, sometimes beginning with the same word or phrase.[42] The catechetical structure of 10:19 is unusual. In 37:11 nine alternative applications are given of the dictum of 37:7b, "Some give counsel in their own interest." Maxims, precepts, and warnings directly addressed to the hearers in the second person greatly predominate over the figurative adages and sage observations in the third person, more characteristic of the 'Solomonic' proverbs. Although the content of Sirach's instruction covers much of the same ground as that of

[39] 16:3; 29:22; 30:14–17; 33:21; cf. 40:18–26; Prov. 27:3. Note, "this is better than many of that" in 37:14; cf. Prov. 26:16.
[40] 14:1–2; 25:8–9; 26:1; 28:19 ff.; and cf. 2:12–14.
[41] Cf. 23:16; 25:7; 26:28; 50:25, and see above, pp. 70–71.
[42] E.g., 2:7–18; 3:26–28; 6:14–16; 19:13–15; and cf. 25:1–2.

Proverbs and there are verbal echoes of the older book, only two or three direct quotations are made from it. One is the famous saying, "The fear of the Lord is the beginning of wisdom,"[43] and another the widely disseminated adage, "He who digs a pit will fall into it."[44] It almost seems that ben Sira' deliberately avoids direct quotation, perhaps because he thinks of himself as speaking with inspired authority, "I will again pour out teaching like prophecy" (24:33).

At the same time, in a good many cases, a saying in Sirach is the same in substance as one in Proverbs and similar, though not identical, in wording. "The sign of a happy heart is a cheerful face," says Sirach; "A merry heart makes a cheerful face" is the way Proverbs puts it. Again, "Whoever winks his eye plans evil deeds" (Sirach) is very close to "He who winks the eye causes trouble" (Proverbs).[45]

A much more numerous group of sayings are essentially the same in substance but are differently expressed; for instance, "If a rich man staggers, he is held up by his friends; a poor man falls and his friends disown him as well" (Sir. 13:21, NEB). Cf. Proverbs 14:20, NEB. "A poor man is odious even to his friend; the rich have friends in plenty."[46]

---

[43] Sir. 1:14 ff.; cf. Prov. 1:7; 9:10; and also Ps. 111:10 and Job 28:28.
[44] Sir. 27:26a; cf. Prov. 26:27; Qoh. 10:8; Ps. 7:15 EVV; 'Onchsheshonqy 22:5. With Sir. 28:8b, cf. Prov. 15:18a.
[45] Sir. 13:26a; Prov. 15:13a, both NEB; cf. Prov. 17:22; 18:14, Sir. 27:22a; Prov. 10:10a. Other examples are Sir. 7:3 (Prov. 22:8a); Sir. 10:27 (Prov. 12:9); Sir. 13:20 (Prov. 29:27); Sir. 27:16 (Prov. 11:13; 20:19); Sir. 28:17 (Prov. 25:15b).
[46] Cf. Prov. 18:23; 19:7. See also Sir. 4:3 (Prov. 3:27–28); Sir. 4:5–6 (Prov. 24:11–12); Sir. 8:13 (Prov. 22:26–27); Sir. 18:32–33 (Prov. 21:17); Sir. 20:6–7 (Prov. 15:23; 17:27–28); Sir. 22:15 (Prov. 27:3); Sir. 21:20 (Qoh. 7:6), etc.

The broad spectrum of virtues commended and vices reprobated differs little from that of Proverbs. On the one hand the pupils are encouraged to develop self-control, patience, diligence, steadfastness, prudence in speech and action, foresight, straightforwardness, and liberality. They should show moral courage when this is called for, piety toward parents, concern for the needy, and discrimination in the choice of friends. On the other hand, they are warned against pride, arrogance, greed, passionate anger, hypocrisy, stubbornness, envy or disdain of others, self-indulgence, careless or irreverent talk, gossip, lying, laziness, dishonesty, and sexual irregularities.

The teacher offers counsel on behavior in a great variety of life situations, on domestic harmony and the discipline of children, on avoiding needless strife, on beneficial and risky associations, on true and false friends, on relationships with women, on caution in borrowing and lending, on keeping confidences, on the dangers of excess in food and drink, on manners at a banquet, on the folly of superstition, and the uses of reason. He makes sage observations about the perils of wealth, the blessings of good health, the anomalies of experience; about the misery of a homeless man, the wisdom of old age, and the things that test a man's strength of character.

The positively religious note is struck not only in the prayers and hymns and devotional meditations, but also in observations mingled with the teachings on morals. A man must learn to trust God whatever the trials that come to test him (2:4–11), for "as his majesty is, so also is his mercy" (2:18). Not a man's own anxious toil but the goodness of God can bring prosperity (11:10–28). He must know the difference between acceptable and unacceptable worship (34:18–35:17). Above all he must humble himself in obedience before God, for "he who keeps the Law makes many offerings[47] . . . , and he who gives alms sacrifices a thank-offering" (35:1–2).

This last quotation illustrates the new emphasis on the letter and spirit of the Torah as the focus of religious devotion that we have observed in the Psalms. It shows also that ben Sira', although in chapter 50 he glories in the splendor of temple worship, shared the prophets' view that cult sacrifices are worthless in the sight of God except as sincere expressions of moral obedience.[48] "The Most High," he says, "is not propitiated for sins by a multitude of sacrifices" (34:19). "The prayer of the humble pierces the clouds" (35:17) and "almsgiving atones for sin" (3:30).

But the law of retribution stands. "Every one will receive in accordance with his deeds" (16:14), because he is free to choose between good and evil, life and death. "When [God] made man in the beginning, he left him free to make his own decisions."[49] Man's freedom, however, is not absolute, for God in his sovereign freedom molds a man's life as a potter molds clay, The way of obedience is not servitude but joy to the religious man. He is entitled to his share of happiness, for death comes soon.[50]

The identification of the highest wisdom with the essential teachings of the Torah is made explicit in 24:1–19, where wisdom's divine origin is portrayed against the background of Proverbs 8:22–31 and Deuteronomy 4:6. Wisdom is the divine Word uttered on the day of creation:

---

[47] Cf. 1:26; 19:20; 21:11; 32:14–17; 32:24–33:3.
[48] Cf. Amos 5:21–25; Isa. 1:10–17; Mic. 6:8; Jer. 7:21–23.
[49] Sir. 15:14, NEB. Lit., "in the power of his *yeser* ["inclination, tendency"]."
[50] Sir. 15:11–20; 33:13; 15:6; 14:11–19. Cf. Qoh. 3:12–13; 11:7–12:1.

I came forth from the mouth of the Most High, and covered the earth like a mist. I dwelt in high places, and my throne was in a pillar of cloud. Alone I have made the circuit of the vault of heaven and have walked in the depths of the abyss . . . From eternity, in the beginning, he created me, And for eternity I shall not cease to exist. (24:3–5, 9, RSV)

As in Proverbs 8, Wisdom came to every people and nation. Yet it was in Israel alone that she took root and became embodied in the Law of Moses.[51] Thus the idea of Wisdom, which on one level is a quality of human life to be attained through training and the gift of God,[52] and on a second level is personified almost as a goddess offering herself to mankind,[53] is here represented as an emanation from God himself. She is God's Word, spoken in the divine assembly in the presence of the heavenly host. Here the streams of gnomic wisdom, prophetic word, covenant faith, and personal religious devotion converge and coalesce in wisdom piety.

The Wisdom of Solomon (the Book of Wisdom)

The work now to be considered differs in important respects from its predecessors in the wisdom literary tradition. It was evidently composed in, and primarily for, the large expatriate Jewish community at Alexandria in the first century B.C. It is the only one of the wisdom books to have been composed in Greek. Its author was an unknown Hellenistic Jew, familiar with the manner of argument of Greek philosophical thought, yet steeped in and proud of his ancestral faith.

---

[51] Sir. 24:6–12, 23.
[52] Sir. 6:18–37; 14:20–15:8.
[53] Sir. 4:11–19; 24:19–22; Prov. 8:1–21.

Instead of a compendium of instruction for pupils in a school, like Proverbs and Sirach, this work is an extended treatise addressed to a wider audience, both Jewish and Gentile. Its author has the twofold objective of steadying the faith of his fellow Jews living amid the distractions and temptations of Hellenistic culture, and of making a case for the Jewish concept of wisdom in the face of Greek intellectualism and continuing ancient paganism.

This outward-facing posture of the writer distinguishes him from the authors of the other wisdom works we have examined. He does not focus attention on the Torah as commandment and creed, or on the cultivation of moral and spiritual response through studying it. His primary concern is with the *idea* of wisdom in its theological, philosophical, and historical aspects. He is to be classed with the wisdom pietists only as a philosopher who sought to expound and defend their faith on reasonable grounds, in order to preserve it from erosion in an alien culture.

The book purports to be a manifesto addressed by King Solomon to his fellow monarchs throughout the world. This literary device is even more artificial here than in the case of Qoheleth, since the author writes in Greek and makes use of Greek rhetorical forms and philosophical terminology. It is curious that each of the four biblical books to which Solomon's name has become attached in tradition fastens on different features of the narratives of his reign in 1 Kings 1–11: Proverbs on his fame as a composer of wise sayings and songs, Qoheleth on his wealth and magnificence, the Song of Songs on his uxoriousness, and this work on his prayer for the gift of wisdom and the reported desire of all the kings of the earth to learn from him. Wisdom 9 is a free paraphrase of Solomon's prayer for wisdom in the dream at Gibeon. There are indications that the prayer is thought of as continuing through parts at least of the remaining ten chapters.[54]

The work falls into three parts: chapters 1–5, 6–9, and 10–19. Part three does not rise to the level of parts one and two, either as literature or in quality and profundity of thought; it shows, however, enough marks of continuity to make it likely that it is from the same hand. Possibly some time had elapsed after parts one and two had been completed before the author was able to resume his task, less successfully than in his earlier work.

Although part one begins with an address to "rulers," it is in fact prefatory to part two where they are again summoned with the words, "Listen, *therefore*, O kings!" (6:1). The audience in view in chapters 1–5 is the Jewish community, some of whom are faithful to their religion, while others are Jews in little more than name. The ideas and terms used here are Hebraic and scriptural—righteousness, uprightness, sincerity of heart, spirit of the Lord, the ungodly, covenant, holiness, God the Creator, the secret purposes of God, his chosen, grace and mercy, etc. Such scriptural allusions as that to death as the fruit of the devil's envy (2:24), and to the assumption of Enoch (4:10), would have been lost on Gentiles. Moreover, the views of "the ungodly" in chapter 2 clearly have some reference to Qoheleth's ideas, of which the pious wise men could not approve.[55] This reflects the division existing within the Alexandrian Jewish community between the godly wise and the worldly wise, the righteous and the wicked of the wisdom Psalms.

[54] 1 Kings 4:34, EVV; 3:6–9. Cf. Wis. Sol. 10:20; 11:10; 11:17–12:25; 14:3–6; 15:1–3, 14, 18; 16:2 ff.; 17:1; 18:1 ff., 19:2 ff.
[55] With v. 1, cf. Qoh. 2:15–16; 4:8; 9:4–6, 10; with v. 2, Qoh. 3:19; with v. 4, Qoh. 2:16; with v. 5, Qoh. 3:2; with v. 6, Qoh. 11:9–10; with vv. 7–9, Qoh. 5:18 EVV; 8:15; 9:7; with v. 9, Qoh. 3:22.

The author launches at once into the two related themes of part one, (1) that religious belief and morality (righteousness) are indispensable to sound reasoning about life (1:1–11) and (2) that a wisdom based on religion is life-creating and gives hope of immortality, while human reason by itself is perverted by sin, and folly is actually lethal (1:12–5:23). It "invites death" (1:12). Consequently those who are of the devil's party will experience as punishment the death their corrupt thoughts deserve (2:24, 3:10). But, "The souls of the just are in God's hand, and torment shall not touch them. In the eyes of foolish men they seemed to be dead. . . . But they are at peace . . . they have a sure hope of immortality" (3:1–4, NEB).

In more detail the argument is developed as follows. In 1:1–5 sincere faith and simple trust in God are contrasted with perverted reason, with which the divine wisdom cannot associate. For wisdom is a "philanthropic" spirit working for man's good, a divine force which permeates the world and holds all things together (1:6–7). It cannot disregard the disintegrating and destructive opposition of evil. The product of evil is death, which was not God's original intention for man (1:12–15). "For God did not make death, and takes no pleasure in the destruction of any living thing; he created all things that they might have being" (1:14, NEB). "Righteousness is immortal. But ungodly men by their words and deeds summoned death" (1:15–16, RSV).

At this point the author outlines the unsound reasoning of the impious. Since man is born by chance, since his life is short and full of trouble and his death inescapable and final, he should enjoy himself as much as possible while life lasts (2:1–9). This is essentially what Qoheleth said. But, whereas Qoheleth considered oppression and injustice to be anomalies of human existence which man is helpless to remedy, here the ungodly are pictured as deliberately engaging in oppression, on the principle that might is right (2:10–11). They are particularly hostile to the good man "because he is inconvenient to us" and "a living condemnation of all our ideas" (2:12, RSV; 2:14, NEB). Their hostility is carried to the point of outrage. The believer is to be met with insult and torture, in a cynical experiment to test the truth of his claim that God will deliver him (2:12–20).

According to the doctrine of retribution, the ungodly would have considered their case proved. The psalmist had said, "With long life I will satisfy him," but now the righteous man was to suffer a shameful death. Sirach had reiterated that "Every man will receive in accordance with his deeds" and had counseled his pupils to "call no man happy before his death," when the tale of his life would be totaled up.[56]

The author of the Wisdom of Solomon had a more daring solution: "The souls of the righteous are in the hand of God." "God created man for immortality, and made him the image of his own eternal self." Man's soul, or spirit, is no longer to be thought of simply as the aliveness of his physical body. This marks a departure from the long-held Hebrew view that man in his essence is an animated body rather than (as in Greek thought) an incarnate soul. The clue is found in the declaration in Genesis 1:26–27 that man was created in the image and likeness of his Creator. Hence, like his Creator, he is not subject to death unless he "invites" it by his alienation from God. The righteous sufferers have not been punished by dying. Instead "they have a sure hope of immortality . . . because God has tested them and found them worthy to be his."[57]

In contrast, the unbelieving wicked "will be punished

[56] Ps. 91:16; Sir. 16:14; 11:28.
[57] Wis. Sol. 3:1; 2:23 (NEB); 3:4–5 (NEB).

according to their reasonings," (i.e., as they have reasoned about the fate of the righteous) and they will meet death with consternation.[58] In their last moments they will realize that the good man they have despised will survive them, while they themselves are about to be dispersed like smoke before the wind, because their lives have been worthless (5:1–14). There is no suggestion of everlasting punishment to correspond with the continuing bliss of the righteous in the presence of God. They will become no more than dishonored corpses. Even the hoped-for immortality through offspring will be denied them.[59] But the good man, in addition to everlasting bliss, will have this kind of immortality on earth as well. Even if childless he will be remembered for his virtue. Though he die young, his life, like the antediluvian Enoch's, will be measured by its quality rather than by its length.[60]

At this point the writer, in part two of the book, like St. Paul turns to the Gentiles. He directly assumes the role of Solomon the philosopher-king, and addresses himself to all earthly rulers as one of them. The polemic against faithless Jews is dropped. The author's emphasis changes from righteousness as a necessary constituent of wisdom to wisdom itself. The objective now becomes that of building bridges between the Hebrew concept of wisdom and Greek philosophical thought.

Four reasons are given in chapter 6 why those who bear the responsibility of government should learn from the Hebrew wisdom tradition, here personified in Solomon. The first (vv. 1–11) is that all sovereignty is a delegated sovereignty, so that kings and judges are responsible to the sovereign Lord of all. If they fail to rule and judge

---

[58] Wis. Sol. 3:10–13a, 16–19; 4:18–19; and 4:20–5:14; 5:17–23.
[59] Wis. Sol. 4:18–20; 3:16–19.
[60] Wis. Sol. 3:1 ff.; 5:15–16; 4:7–15; cf. Gen. 5:21–24.

according to his law and justice, they will be strictly called to account. Let them then learn wisdom from the wisest of human rulers. Theirs is a sacred task and they must discharge it with true understanding. For, secondly, such understanding is readily available. "Wisdom is bright and unfading, and she is easily seen by those who love her" (6:12, AT).

The third reason is that wisdom alone can give permanence to sovereignty (vv. 17–21). Those who "delight in thrones and scepters" must honor wisdom if they would continue to reign. Solomon makes this point by employing a Greek logical device known as a *sorites* or chain syllogism which progresses through a series of logical links until, as if it were a necklace, the last link is joined to the first.[61] In the present example the first and last terms do not correspond exactly; it seems that an initial line, "The desire for wisdom is the beginning of wisdom" has been omitted. The sequence of verses 19–20 appears unclear also until one sees that "a kingdom" here means "kingship,"[62] and that "near to God" denotes likeness rather than proximity.[63]

The fourth reason why all rulers should embrace Solomon's wisdom, namely, that "a prudent king [is] the stability of his people,"[64] appears in the exposition of the nature and origin of wisdom (6:12–25). 'Solomon' leads up to this by describing how he himself became wise. There had been nothing supernatural about his birth (7:1–6). When he had seen that wisdom was supreme over all other values, this had been granted him in answer to his prayer, together with "all good things and . . .

---

[61] See Plato *Symposium* 210 ff.
[62] Or, as in NEB, "kingly stature."
[63] So J. Fichtner, *Weisheit Salomos* (1938), p. 27.
[64] 6:24, NAB. Observe that this verse is in the form of a proverbial couplet, rare in this book.

uncounted wealth." But these rewards were insignificant compared to the supreme benefit of "friendship with God" (vv. 7, 11–14). His only wish now is that his thoughts and words should be worthy of his theme. God had given him encyclopedic knowledge of the nature and operation of the phenomena which it had been the object of the Greek natural philosophers to understand. For Wisdom had been the "artificer" of all things when God created the world.[65]

In 7:22b–8:1 the author launches into an exposition in philosophic terms of the nature of wisdom itself. He begins by enumerating twenty-one attributes or qualities of the divine wisdom, as, in the Hymn to Zeus of Cleanthes the Stoic, God is "known by many names."[66] Wisdom is personified, "In her is a spirit that is intelligent and holy, unique in its kind[67] yet made up of many parts, subtle, free-moving . . . and permeating all intelligent, pure and delicate spirits" (7:22–23, NEB).

What is the relationship of this Wisdom of God to God himself? Five metaphors are used in the attempt to convey what the writer has in mind: "Like a fine mist she rises from the power of God, a pure effluence from the glory of the Almighty. . . . She is the brightness that streams from everlasting light, the flawless mirror of the active power of God and the image of his goodness" (7:25–26, NEB).

What is Wisdom's relationship to the world and to man? "She is but one, yet can do everything; herself unchanging, she makes all things new; age after age she enters into

---

[65] 7:15–22a; cf. 8:6; and Prov. 8:22–31.
[66] *Hastings Encyc. Relig. and Ethics* (1913) art. "Cleanthes," vol. iii, p. 688.
[67] *monogenes*, "unique in kind." This epithet is applied in John 1:14 to the incarnate Word, where in KJV it is misleadingly translated "only-begotten." The Johannine expression is undoubtedly influenced by the use of the term in this passage.

holy souls and makes them God's friends and prophets" (7:27, NEB). "She reaches mightily from one end of the earth to the other, and she orders all things well" (8:1, RSV).

In 8:2 ff. "Solomon" proceeds to recount how, in his youth, he became enamored of Wisdom for her excellence, and also on account of her special gifts to those who have the responsibility of rule. These gifts are glory and honor, the ability to judge rightly, ability and courage, immortality and undying fame. Once more he speaks of Wisdom's intimate association with God. She lives with him and is loved by him. She shares God's knowledge, acts as the executive of his works and, as a creative artist, is responsible for everything that exists.[68] She is the author in man of the four cardinal virtues, moderation and prudence, justice and fortitude (8:7, NAB). From her the wise man gains his perspective on past and future, his skill in solving problems, and his ability to interpret omens (8:8).

Greatly desiring such wisdom, Solomon had recognized that it was not sufficient to be nobly born and well endowed by nature in order to obtain her. Only when his longing found utterance in prayer was wisdom granted to him (8:17–21). In 8:19–20 NEB the words "a noble soul fell to my lot; or rather, I myself was noble, and I entered into an unblemished body" are remarkable for expressing a view very similar to the Platonic doctrine of the preexistence of the soul, which at birth became imprisoned in a material body.[69] The influence of the Platonic thought is unmistakable, yet the writer stumbles in attempting to express himself, as if he were uneasy with it. In his earlier discussion he had made use of the Platonic doctrine of the immortality of the soul. Here he may be trying to say, in current philosophical language,

[68] *hairetis*, "executive," lit., "one who decides." *technitis*, "creative artist," lit., "artificer."
[69] See *Phaedrus* 238 ff., *Timaeus* 41D ff.

no more than that to be undefiled in soul and body was not enough.

The prayer for wisdom to which all this has been leading up follows in chapter 9. As already pointed out, this is a free paraphrase of King Solomon's petition in 1 Kings 3:6–9. The king appeals to God for the gift of wisdom, which is also the creative word of God (vv. 1–4). Having been chosen to rule God's people, he finds himself incapable, without this endowment, of so high a task (vv. 5–8). Only the divine wisdom which was present when God made the world can empower and guide him (vv. 9–12). For "the reasoning of man is feeble, and our plans are fallible" (v. 14, NEB). "The corruptible body burdens the soul" (v. 15a, NAB). Once more, the thought and language are Platonic.[70] In its final verses 16–18 the language of the prayer reverts to that of Hebrew wisdom.

The meat of the Wisdom of Solomon is in part one, with its discussion of righteousness and immorality, and in part two which deals with the nature and divine origin of wisdom. In part three (apparently added later) the topics are wisdom in action, as illustrated in Israel's salvation history, and the folly of idolaters. The writer fails to rise to the same heights as in the earlier parts of his book, though here and there are flashes of the old insight and genius. The effort to build bridges to the Gentile community by the use of Greek ideas and terms is given up. Instead, the lessons of Israel's history are presented as a counterblast to Gentile paganism. The errors of idolatry are pointed out in no uncertain terms. There is no further mention of individual souls and their alternative destinies. In chapter 10 wisdom means the providential activity of God; after 11:1 the distinction is dropped and the doer of mighty works is simply God.

The most notable section of part three is the denuncia-

---

[70] See *Phaedo* 81c.

tion of the folly of idolatry in chapters 13, 14, and 15:7–19. Men who worshiped natural elements and heavenly bodies failed to perceive the Creator's hand in the greatness and beauty of created things (13:1–9). More reprehensible were those who gave the name of gods to images and statues, the works of men's hands (13:10–14:11; 15:7–13). The origin of idol worship is traced to the making of memorials of the dead and of statues of distant monarchs to whom reverence was paid. The skill and emulation of artists contributed to the spread of these customs (14:12–21), which resulted in all sorts of moral and religious perversion (14:22–31). The most despicable idolaters of all were the Egyptians, who worshiped not only material images but animals (15:14–19). This contempt for the religious practices of their ancestors and themselves would hardly commend the author to his contemporary Egyptian neighbors, heirs of a great and famous civilization.

The three literary products of wisdom pietism considered in this chapter differ considerably. In the wisdom Psalms, the tone is one of personal devotion, expressed in prayer and praise and in meditation on the Torah. In Sirach the theme is religious and oral instruction in a wisdom tradition now fully merged with the faith and thought of postexilic Judaism. Parts one and two of the Wisdom of Solomon explore further the implications of the deathless quality of fellowship with God, on which the writer of Psalm 73 had built his hope. The ultimate fates of good men and evil men are seen as determined by their relationship to righteousness, and the essential nature of wisdom itself is explored for the first time in philosophic terms.

These three works of wisdom piety, in combination, transcend the contributions which either traditional piety or traditional wisdom could have made alone.

EPILOGUE
The Role of Wisdom

IN THE FOREGOING discussion the role of wisdom in the life and thought of ancient Israel has been considered primarily from the historical standpoint. The wisdom literature of the Old Testament has been examined in its setting in the ancient Near Eastern world. Until quite recent years this topic has been unduly neglected in biblical studies, with the single exception of the Book of Job. Yet it is of real importance in the study and understanding of the religion and life of ancient Israel, and of their legacy in the Old Testament.

But what does all this matter to men of the present day, except perhaps to those of church and synagogue who have a special interest in the historical origins of their religion? Has 'wisdom' any word to say to the average layman? Are not the ethical rules it propounds, and the theological understanding and speculations it incorporates, too conditioned by the ancient setting and limited outlook of their origin to be of any positive value in the almost totally different conditions of life in the modern world? As for the great majority whose interest in the Hebrew-Christian scriptures is slight or nonexistent, what bearing on their multiple perplexities and concerns has this discussion of a single strand in ancient religious and ethical thought?

These are fair questions. No scholar who is not completely immured within the four walls of his study can be unaware of them and fail to feel their force. He must admit to a gnawing sense of responsibility to face them, and, if not to give immediate and satisfying answers, at least to indicate the direction in which such answers may be sought. He shares the puzzlement and frustrations of thinking men and women and the inchoate rebelliousness of whole peoples, because of the gap between what human life is like, and what it might be if the best interests of all, not of some only, were paramount. He knows there is no escaping the clamant demands for action by turning back the pages to a largely forgotten past.

The issues of today are different in magnitude and complexity. Radical changes in the forms and workings of modern societies are necessary and long overdue, to make them truly humane and free. Our social conventions are not laws of the universe. Our political and legal structures are very imperfect embodiments of the manifest truths they claim as their foundation. The diverse and intricate economic structures of the nations fail at many points, often disastrously, to utilize effectively and for the general good the earth's resources, man's labor, and the material wealth which together they produce. Reliance on instruments of war have not brought security, but the reverse. Perhaps worst of all is the sight of human resources wasted, human potential unrealized, and human values submerged and forgotten.

Has an ancient wisdom anything to say in face of all this and any help to offer? Not, certainly, if what is asked is instant relevance and quick solutions. There are no such things. People who think in these terms and identify their immediate opponents with the final enemy are fools, both in the biblical and the modern sense.

The first point to be made is that it is not common sense to begin the search for modern solutions by wiping the slate clean of the accumulated wisdom of thoughtful observers of the human scene in the last 5,000 years. Possibly the supreme evidence of human stupidity is our propensity to make the same mistakes over and over again. "Peoples and governments never have learned anything from history," said Hegel. Ancient Israel's wisdom is at the very least one significant component of man's knowledge of himself. With such knowledge he must begin if he is to envisage realistically the social goals toward which he strives.

The second point is that our problems, in the last analysis, are human problems. The turmoil of our times and the agony it produces arise in the life situations of actual people and communities. The threatening difficulties we face—violence within and between groups and classes and societies, control of the instruments of mass destruction, racial and religious animosities, deterioration of the life necessities of pure air and water, reckless consumption of the earth's resources, proliferation of human beings beyond the capacity of the earth to support them, the yawning gap between rich and poor within and between nations, the ancient hatreds and irrational prejudices which divide men and are manipulated for their own ends by the unscrupulous—all these at their base are human problems. They can never be solved unless this is fully recognized. The long-standing Arab-Israeli conflict is a case in point—two peoples in desperate contention for a homeland they can call their own.

Therefore, it is not irrelevant to ask how men ought to think and behave to one another, and what is the ground for this 'oughtness.' Questions of belief and of what is worthy of belief are ultimately decisive. They determine which way men go and, to a large degree, what happens in this world. Institutions are man-made. If they fail to serve adequately the needs and aspirations of men they can be changed by men, and should be changed with a wisdom that can see beyond the immediate scene to a more distant prospect. There have been wise men before now whose leadership was foresighted in this way. They have deserved well of humanity. It is not impossible that they may have successors. Openness to an ancient wisdom could have some part in their development.

No one can gainsay the fact that a morality suitable and effective in a remote and small-scale society is not readily transferable to the multifarious complexities of twentieth-century living. Yet there is a compensating value for the clarification of principles in the smallness of scale of the ancient context. Injustice was seen as embodied in unjust men who were visible to all, rather than in some distant government, impersonal corporation, or abstract system. Greed and hypocrisy, anger and cruelty, and the tyranny of power, plain stupidity and self-interest, could be observed directly by their victims and the victims' neighbors. So could manifestations of loyalty, integrity, friendship, compassion, self-control, tolerance and the patient endurance which knows that obstacles will emerge one after another between a man and his goal, yet never ceases to struggle. Any glimpse of life that will help us to see clearly the principles at stake is relevant for us. Indeed it may be the most important factor of all.

The third point is inherent in the second. Since the issues we confront are fundamentally human and moral issues, these must be brought to the surface and exhibited for what they are. In the Hebrew-Christian classical tradition this was done supremely by the prophets and wise men of Israel and by Jesus of Nazareth, who cried out like a prophet and taught like a sage. Even though the wisdom writers and teachers of the Old Testament do not seem to speak with a single voice, when their words are sifted it will be seen that in essentials, such as the following points, they are agreed:

(1) The world as God made it to be man's home is an orderly world, as when in the beginning God said "Let there be light" in dark and formless chaos. The world has structure, and that structure is meaningful and good. Rationality and order are of a piece. It is man's perversity which has blurred that given order and reintroduced the chaos in his social and personal living, by ignoring the meaning and rejecting the good.

(2) The basic moral issues are justice and mutuality, truth, the concordance of profession and practice, and the principles underlying the organization and exercise of power among men. Society is seen as a man writ large. Hence the disorder of society is rooted in the disorder of the individual's mind and purpose, because it is of the same kind as that which he displays in the small community where he is known for what he is.

(3) Personal commitment to worthy moral goals is a turning away from chaos toward an order that again is meaningful and good. This is a matter of training as well as of choice. No man can choose responsibly before his mind and conscience have been awakened to see what are the alternatives. He can and will learn from his own mistakes, for the choice must be his own. Yet he may save himself and others much pain and trouble if he does not make mistakes needlessly, through ignorance of the pitfalls he will encounter. His training cannot be restricted to the knowledge of things external to himself, for he himself is part of his own problem. He must be shown the reality of values which it might be slow and costly for him to discover unaided. He needs a set of standards by which to measure his own character and conduct and those of others, even though in so doing he may come to criticize those standards as themselves imperfect, and attempt to

formulate and test new standards that will be at once more radical and more authentic.

(4) Whether or not the man in search of wisdom accepts the traditional idea of God as the undergirding of his philosophy of life, he must know that there is some reality of order and goodness and ultimate meaning to which he owes allegiance. He is obligated by what he knows and what he sees. He cannot surrender to his fears and his hostilities, to his instinctive drives of self-interest and self-aggrandizement, without denying this perception of the reality beyond himself. To do so would be to deny his own integrity as a person and the necessity of rational and moral meaning in a human social order. From the standpoint of religion, Qoheleth may be said to have held this view of respectful agnosticism.

(5) Qoheleth's colleagues and successors took a more positive position. The mysterious world order with which man's life is so obviously out of tune was to them expressive of the mind and will of God, the creator and sustainer of all that is. They thought of him as personal because he appeared to deal with men as persons. The beginning and foundation of human and humane wisdom was "the fear of the Lord," a basic reverence toward this ultimate source of meaning and direction in human life and thought. Their belief was not an inherited superstitious credulity, but a confidence in something worthy to be believed. Their God provided a universal moral standard, and at the same time a ground for that hope without which a man cannot have (in Tillich's phrase) "the courage to be."

Such wisdom does not deny, but welcomes, the insights of other religions and philosophies, for it knows, modestly, that no one can perceive all truth. The teachings of other wise men who have expressed differently their understanding of reality and God are not excluded, and indeed they and the Hebrew-Christian wisdom tradition have much in common. In its insights and its positive affirmations this Hebraic wisdom need not fear comparison with other forms of spiritual and moral guidance.

To all spokesmen of wisdom man is not merely the animal which in one aspect he is. He is other and more than a political entity, a warrior willing or unwilling, an economic integer. He is a person who feels and thinks and can believe. His life values are not to be measured in the marketplace. He is a being who can learn to live well and worthily, and find in living a more than ephemeral happiness. He may choose to live for something beyond himself which is greater and better and, as Job found, more true and wonderful and gracious than anything he had imagined.

Herein is wisdom. What the scriptures have to tell us concerning wisdom is germane to life.

INDEX OF SUBJECTS

Acrostics, 86, 192, 194, 197–99, 201
Aesop, 37, 60
Agur, 18, 140, 165–70
Ahiqar, 40, 45, 91, 93
Ahithophel, 90, 105
Allegories, 54, 81, 84
Amarna letters, 35
Amen-em-ope, 23–24, 29–30, 33, 45, 57, 61
Amos, 125-27
Assyrians, 35, 40

Babylonian wisdom literature, 34–35, 143–44
Babylonian wise men, 111, 128
Baruch, Book of, 20
Baruch, scribe, 16, 23
Ben Sira'. *See* Sirach

Chaldaeans, 44, 96
Cherub, 100
Cleanthes, Stoic, 219
Cosmic order, 21, 33, 115–16, 138, 191
Counsels of Wisdom, 39, 95
Court counselors, 90, 105–09, 124
Cultic religion, 123–24

Daniel, Book of, 86, 95–96, 112–13
  additions to, 20
  wisdom in, 96, 112–13
David, 104–05
Deutero-Isaiah, 111, 128, 131
Deuteronomic history, 2, 101–02, 111
Deuteronomy, Book of, 110–11
Discourses, Ten, 54, 57–58, 112, 121, 194
Disputation fables, 37
Dreams, interpretation of, 87, 96

Ecclesiastes. *See* Qoheleth
Ecclesiasticus. *See* Sirach
Edomite wisdom, 25, 47
Egyptian and Hebrew wisdom, 32–34
Egyptian "Instructions," 26–31, 57, 94
Egyptian wisdom literature, 26–34, 92–93, 138
Elihu, 148, 150–52

Esther, Book of, 20, 86, 91
Exile, 16, 35, 110–11
  return from, 17, 20, 112–13, 190
Ezekiel, 111, 128
Ezra, 17, 20, 103, 112

Fables, 37–38, 81, 97
Folk wisdom, 12, 18, 63–70, 137
Fool, characteristics of, 9, 210
  words of, 48
Former Prophets, 102, 110

Gad, prophet, 105
Gilgamesh, 41, 98
Golden rule, 95
Greek philosophy, 177–78, 216–17, 219, 220
Gregory Thaumaturgus, 171

Hammurabi, 123
Hariscandra, 144–45
Hebrew style, 72–75
Hezekiah, 15, 110
Hosea, 127

Idolatry, 222
Illustrations, 79–80, 120
Imagery, 73–74, 120
Immortality, 215–16, 220
Isaiah, 124–25

J epic, 106–07
Jeremiah, 127–28
Job, Book of, 10–11, 21, 32–33, 110, 117, 120, 130, 139, 147–52, 162–64, 192
  counselors of, 136, 139, 146
  epilogue, 148–50, 162–63
  the man, 10–11, 136, 141, 154, 163
  prologue, 149–50, 152–53, 163
  reasoning of, 155–59
  speeches of Yahweh, 148, 151, 159–62
  third cycle, 148, 150
Jonah, Book of, 79, 128–29
Joseph, story of, 14, 86–88, 90, 138
Josiah, 110
Judgment after death, 46, 217
Judith, Book of, 92
Justice of God, 41–44, 46, 139, 142–43, 161

Index of Subjects / 231

Knowledge, 3, 8, 34, 118
Knowledge of God, 163, 166–68

Luther, 174

Ma'at, 26, 33, 46, 63
Malachi, 173
Marcus Aurelius, 177
Massa', 166–67
Mesopotamian wisdom, 34–45
Metaphors, 38, 77–78, 84–85
Mishnah, 171
Myths, 96–98

Nathan, 105–06
Nehemiah, 190

Old Testament canon, 20, 171–72, 203
  narratives, 74–75, 85–91
  sources of, 1
  theme of, 1–2
Old Wisdom, 137–38
'Onchsheshonqy, 91, 209
Onomastica, 14, 34, 36

Parables, 77–80, 97, 125, 128–29
Paradigmatic tales, 85–96
Parallelism, 64–66, 73
Parental instruction, 8, 49–50, 137–38
Personification, 54, 212, 219
Phoenician wisdom, 25, 47
Platonism, 218, 220–21
Precepts, 52
Problem literature, 40–41, 154
Prohibitions, 50, 195
Prometheus, 145
Prophets, 2, 102, 104–05, 108–09, 111–15, 117–18, 133–34
  oracles of, 55, 118–19
  theology of, 114–15, 117–18
  and wise men, 83, 102, 109, 111–19, 122–29, 132–35
Proverbs, Book of, 52–53, 120, 137
  common, 58–63, 67
  duplicate, 68–69
  literary, 64–66
  numerical, 55, 70–71, 121, 126–27, 208
  patterns of, 59–63, 194, 208
Providence, 88–90

Qoheleth, Book of, 2, 4, 11, 53, 120, 134–35, 165, 170–76, 188–89
  ethics of, 184–87
  philosophy of, 11, 33, 176–84
  radicalism of, 18, 112, 137, 139–40, 170–71, 176–77, 188–89
Qoheleth, the teacher, 112, 139–40, 188

Rechabites, 50
Retribution, doctrine of, 10–11, 46, 63, 91, 125, 136, 139–40
Rhetorical questions, 121, 128–29, 158, 168–69
Riddles, 38, 55, 78, 124–25, 127
Ridicule, 85
Ruth, Book of, 20, 79, 86

Samuel, 104
Satan, the, 152, 162
Saul, 74, 104
Schools, 8, 16–17, 44–45, 50, 52–53, 112, 138, 202–03
Scribes, court, 14–15, 107
  professional, 16, 24, 173–74
  of Torah, 109, 191, 202–03
  of temple, 109
Septuagint, 19, 137, 196, 201
Similes, 75–77
Simon II, high priest, 206
Sirach (Ben Sira'), Book of, 4–5, 21, 59, 103, 112, 130, 201–12
Solomon, reign of, 13–15, 106–07, 213
Solomon's wisdom, 4, 6, 13–15, 95, 106–07, 167, 213, 217
Solomnic proverbs, 53, 59, 66, 206
Succession history, 88–91, 105, 107
Suffering of innocent, 32, 41–44, 141–47, 154–56, 162–64
Sumerian wisdom, 36–38, 41–42, 142–43
Synagogues, 191

Talmud, 112, 171
Theology of wisdom, 21, 33, 97–100, 114–17, 129–31, 134–35, 138–39, 191–92, 204–05, 207, 212, 215, 219–21
Time, 115–16, 134, 180–82
Tobit, Book of, 20, 93–95
Torah, Books of, 17, 109, 190–91
Torah piety, 17, 191, 194–95, 197, 199–200, 211, 212
Tree of knowledge, 98

Wisdom
  in creation, 130–31, 159–60

of God, 111, 117
literature, 2, 19–22, 120–21, 137, 199
meaning of, 3, 5–11, 21–22, 103, 136–37, 184, 212, 219–20, 225–29,
piety, 192–93, 204–05, 210–12, 225–29
psalms, 192–201
revealed, 96, 112, 131–32
of kings, 217–18
secular and religious, 18, 113, 115, 129–30, 137–38, 214
of Solomon, (Book of Wisdom), 4, 18–21, 112, 173, 212–22

spiritualizing of, 130, 190–92, 202–04, 210, 222
style and vocabulary, 53–56, 72–73, 121–22, 124–26, 193–200
universality of, 118
teachers
  authority of, 4, 22, 114, 132–35, 191, 209
  methods of, 4, 22, 48–49, 52–53, 56–59, 66–67, 80–81, 85–86, 118, 134, 210–11
tradition, 3–4, 12–18, 21, 112–13, 137–38, 226
Wise man, characteristics of, 9–10, 195, 210
Wise women, 105–06

INDEX OF AUTHORS

Albright, W. F., 35, 47
Alt, A., 14, 34, 50

Barr, J., 133
Barton, G. A., 171
Baumgartner, W., 23
Biggs, R. D., 42–43, 143–44
deBoer, P. A. H., 22

Childs, B. S., 124
Cowley, A., 40
Crenshaw, J. L., 88, 91
Cross, F. M., Jr., 204

Dahood, M. J., 47, 82

Eissfeldt, O., 142

Fichtner, J., 102, 124–25, 218
Fohrer, G., 159
Frankfort, H., 26

Gardiner, A. H., 34
Gemser, B., 166, 168
Gerleman, G., 137
Gerstenberger, E., 50, 126
Gese, H., 2, 137
Glanville, S. R. K., 27
Good, E. M., 168
Gordis, R., x, 67, 142, 144, 146, 148–50, 155–57, 161, 179, 181, 183, 186
Gordon, E. I., 37–38, 45, 61
Gray, J., 82
Gressmann, H., 24

Heaton, E. W., 124
Hermisson, H.-J., 69
Herrmann, S., 34
Holladay, J. S., Jr., 82, 108

Johnson, A. R., 53

Kayatz, C., 58
Kramer, S. N., 36–37, 39, 41–42, 45, 98, 143

Lambert, W. G., 24–25, 35–46, 142–44, 149–50
Lamdin, T. O., 35
di Lella, A., 204
Lewis, C. S., 72
Lindblom, J., 118, 124

MacLeish, A., 142
McKane, W., x, 54, 58, 62, 65, 82, 84, 130, 137, 165–67, 180
McKenzie, J. L., 98
Mowinckel, S., 193
Murphy, R. E., 193, 196

Noth, M., 14, 25, 111
Nougayrol, J., 45

Pargiter, F. E., 144
Pfeiffer, R. H., 25, 143–44, 207
Pope, M. H., 136, 142, 149, 151

Quiller-Couch, A., 74

von Rad, G., xi, 14, 34, 54, 87–90, 137

Rankin, O. S., 23
Reed, W. L., 167
Richtner, W., 50, 56
Robinson, H. W., 145, 183–84
Rosenthal, L. A., 91
Ross, J. S., 102
Rost, L., 89
Roth, W. M. H., 70
Rowley, H. H., 139
Rylaarsdam, J. C., 116

Sanders, J. A., 145, 204
Schaeffer, C. F. A., 47
Schmid, H. H., 26, 36, 63, 132
Scott, R. B. Y., 14, 24, 57, 119, 165

Talmon, S., 91
Terrien, S., 102, 124, 149
Thomas, D. W., 14
Torrey, C. C., 168
Tournay, R., 191
Tur-Sinai, N. H., 148, 154, 168

de Vaux, R., 16

Whybray, R. N., 31, 57–58, 88–91
Williams, R. J., 23, 81
Wilson, J. A., 27
Winnett, F. V., 167
Wolff, H. W., 50, 102, 124, 126
Wright, G. E., 47, 119

Yadin, Y., 204

INDEX OF BIBLICAL REFERENCES

Genesis
 chaps. 1-11, 96
 1:26–27, 216
 chap. 3, 97, 100
 3:1–7, 5
 3:16–19, 145
 3:22–24, 98–99, 100
 5:21–24, 217
 6:5–7, 145
 8:22, 36
 9:24–27, 15
 10:9, 12, 53, 64, 76
 14:19, 84
 18:23–25, 67
 22:14, 64
 24:64–65, 74
 25:23, 15
 29:1, 25
 31:24, 29, 99
 41:8, 39, 5, 25
 42:23, 54
 45:4–5, 87
 45:25–28, 74
 49:2–27, 15

Exodus
 7:11, 25
 12:26–27, 49
 13:14, 8
 15:1, 15
 17:16, 15
 18:21, 9
 19:5–6, 2
 20:4–12, 6
 35:31–34, 7–8, 48

Numbers
 10:35–36, 15
 21:8, 55
 21:14–30, 1, 15
 22:21–35, 97
 23:7–10, 18–24, 15, 54
 24:3–9, 15–24, 15, 169

Deuteronomy
 chaps. 1–4, 111
 1:13, 9
 1:9, 99
 4:5–8, 111, 211
 4:21, 147
 9:18, 147
 16:18, 7
 19:14, 68, 123
 25:1, 67
 26:1–9, 4
 27:17, 68
 27:19, 123
 30:15–19, 145
 32:1–43, 15, 84
 33:8–12, 4, 89

Joshua
 6:26, 15
 10:12–13, 15

Judges
5:2–31, 8, 15
6:3, 25
9:7–15, 37
14:10–18, 38, 71
15:16, 15
19:23, 48

Ruth
4:11, 76

1 Samuel
3:1–21, 104
9:1–10:16, 61, 64, 104–05
15:17–23, 28, 104
16:1–13, 104
18:7, 15
19:20–24, 105
21:1–9, 75
22:5, 105
24:13, 3, 12, 64
29:5, 15

2 Samuel
1:18–27, 1, 15
8:16–18, 13, 103, 105
12:1–14, 79, 105
12:24–25, 89
13:1–14, 3, 106
13:22, 109
14:1–23, 7, 12, 22, 79, 106
15:31–34, 12, 105
16:15–17:14, 5, 7, 12, 105
17:23, 49
19:35, 99
20:15–26, 5, 7, 12–13, 64, 106
23:1–7, 15, 169
24:10–13, 105

1 Kings
chaps. 1–2, 88–89
chaps. 1–11, 6
1:6, 50
2:1–6, 6
3:5–14, 6, 9, 14, 99, 214, 221
3:16–28, 5–6
4:1–6, 13, 103
4:19–34, 4–6, 13, 25, 33, 167, 173
5:6, 7
5:7, 12, 6
8:12–13, 15
9:27, 7
10:1–13, 14
11:29–31, 106
14:29, 1
20:11, 12, 59, 64
20:35–42, 79
22:10, 159
22:39, 1, 7

2 Kings
18:37, 103
20:20, 1
22:8–23:3, 8, 109
24:12, 16
25:19, 8

2 Chronicles
15:3, 4
chaps. 29–32, 15

Ezra
7:11–26, 5, 17, 103

Nehemiah
7:57, 174
8:1–9:3, 17–18
9:38, 17

Esther
1:13, 25
4:14, 91
7:9–10, 30

Job
chaps. 1–2, 86–87, 144, 148, 152–53
1:1, 195
1:3, 25, 167
1:8, 195
2:11–13, 25, 73
chaps. 3–31, 148
chaps. 3–23, 121, 151, 153–54
chaps. 4–25 (–27), 154–58
4:3–9, 10, 42, 63, 74, 121, 136, 145, 154
4:17–19, 155
5:7–8, 42, 155
5:13, 6
5:17–19, 121, 155
6:12, 156
6:24, 48
8:3–10, 10, 155, 157
8:11–22, 145, 154
9:5–11, 32, 157
9:15–29, 144, 156
10:2–8, 99, 143–44, 156–57
11:7, 147, 154

11:14–20, 154
12:2–9, 10, 136, 192
13:6, 125
13:15, 157
14:1–19, 120, 156–58
15:4–5, 155
15:12–18, 8, 143, 155
16:12–20, 54, 156, 158
19:21, 149
19:25–27, 158
20:4–5, 155
21:7, 195
21:23–26, 147
22:2–14, 120, 145, 155
23:3–6, 157
23:10, 194
24:2, 123
chaps. 25–31, 150, 152
26:14, 73, 127
27:1, 54
chap. 28, 5, 130, 150
28:14–28, 9, 81, 130–31, 209
chaps. 29–31, 81, 158–59
29:2–3, 10, 156
30:1–6, 10, 33, 165–66, 169–70
31:16, 123
31:35–40, 145, 150, 159
chaps. 32–37, 148, 150
32:12, 17, 148
33:23, 54
36:2, 125
38:1–42:6, 34, 130, 148, 151, 159, 160–61
38:4–39:30, 120
38:36, 7
39:17, 7
40:6–14, 131, 159, 161
40:15–41:34, 159
42:1–6, 147, 159
42:7–9, 151
42:7–17, 148, 162

Psalms
1, 18, 67, 192–94, 199, 201
2, 192, 198
3–7, 199
7:14–16, 30, 91, 209
9–10, 201
19, 193–94, 199, 201
25, 15, 193
31, 193
32, 192–93, 198, 201
33:19, 196
34, 193, 195, 198, 201
37, 192–95, 201

39–40, 193
40:1–3, 201
42–43, 199
49, 193–96, 201
51:16–17, 124
57:7–11, 199
60:6–12, 199
62, 193
73, 193, 195, 222
78, 193, 200–01
89:48, 196
90, 48, 193
91, 193, 216
92, 15, 193
94:12, 210
101:5, 170
106, 147, 193, 200
107:27, 7
108, 199
111, 9, 192–93, 198, 209
112, 193, 196–97, 201
116:8, 196
119, 18, 193, 199–201
127, 60, 73, 193, 198, 201
128, 193, 198, 201
133, 193, 198, 201
139:1–4, 194
144:15, 201
148, 34

Proverbs
chaps. 1–9, 9, 18, 53–54, 58, 66, 112, 129, 194
1:1, 4
1:2–7, 48, 49, 52–55
1:7, 9, 83, 130, 209
1:8–19, 8, 49, 58, 121
1:20–33, 9, 54, 58, 83, 121, 130
chap. 2, 5, 10, 52, 56, 58, 193
3:1–7, 10, 52, 56, 58, 195
3:13–34, 48, 82, 84, 121, 209
4:1–10, 49, 58, 82, 125–26
4:18–24, 40, 58, 73
5:1, 58, 121
5:15–20, 207
6:1–11, 9, 40, 68, 85, 207
6:12–20, 49, 58–59, 207
7:1, 26, 58, 83
7:22–8:1, 219
chaps. 8–9, 54
chap. 8, 21, 58, 83, 84, 116–17, 130
8:1–21, 126, 212
8:22–31, 5, 18, 83–84, 131, 211, 219

9:1-6, 13-18, 58, 83, 126
9:10, 9, 83, 209
chaps. 10-31, 9
10:1-22:16, 53, 63
10:1-14, 4, 10, 14, 30, 33, 53, 63, 67, 68, 193, 209
10:15-32, 10, 33, 67-68, 85
11:1-12, 33, 67, 69, 196
11:13-20, 10, 51, 68, 126, 209
12:1-14, 67, 68, 69, 209
12:21-28, 10, 30, 48, 62, 67, 126
13:1-7, 33, 40, 49, 50, 67, 68, 85
13:9-24, 10, 40, 50, 67-69
14:1-18, 9, 10, 48, 67, 69, 193, 195
14:20-35, 10, 51, 67, 127, 209
15:2-13, 10, 48-50, 59, 76, 209
15:16-33, 9, 10, 51, 61, 68, 76, 85, 130, 209
16:1-11, 10, 18, 20, 30, 33, 40, 65-66, 124, 127, 173
16:12-16, 40, 51, 66, 67, 120
16:18-26, 51, 60, 65, 69, 73
16:30-33, 10, 65, 127
17:14-22, 30, 48, 61, 69, 209
17:27-28, 10, 33, 209
18:5-8, 30, 68, 69, 126
18:11-18, 68, 69, 209
18:22-23, 52, 59, 86, 209
19:1-14, 30, 51, 52, 86
19:16-28, 10, 30, 49, 53, 56, 69
20:2-12, 30, 51, 62, 65, 121
20:13-17, 10, 56, 66, 67
20:19-24, 10, 121, 209
21:3, 20, 28, 123
21:9, 68, 76
21:17-31, 7, 10, 76, 209
22:3-8, 10, 52, 63, 68, 69, 209
22:15-21, 49, 52, 53, 56
22:17-24:22, 9, 33, 45, 53, 55, 57
22:22-28, 30, 68, 123, 127, 209
23:4-14, 30, 40, 57, 68
23:19-35, 49, 56, 121, 125, 207
24:6-20, 68, 209
24:23-34, 52-56, 69
24:27-34, 30, 68, 85, 125, 207
chaps. 25-19, 53, 63
25:1, 4, 8, 12, 14, 33, 53, 110
25:2-15, 51, 76, 120, 192, 209
25:16-23, 56, 71, 78, 120
25:24-27, 56, 60, 68, 76
chap. 26, 61
26:1-11, 9, 30, 60, 68
26:14-22, 68, 70, 85, 208
26:23-27, 30, 62, 91, 125, 209
27:1-3, 9, 10, 62, 208-09
27:7-12, 40, 45, 48, 68, 70
27:15-27, 51, 62, 71, 207
28:10-25, 10, 51, 52, 62, 69
29:5-27, 9, 50, 60, 121, 209
chaps. 30-31, 52, 70
30:1-4, 48, 55, 140, 165, 169-70
30:5-14, 18, 59, 70
30:15-31, 53, 55, 70, 81, 121
31:1-9, 39, 54, 57, 127, 167
31:10-31, 86, 207

Qoheleth
chap. 1, 116
1:2, 174-75, 178
1:3-11, 120-21, 175, 177, 179
1:12-18, 11, 59, 175, 179, 183-85
2:1-11, 11, 175, 180, 214
2:12-17, 11, 175, 183, 196, 214
2:18-23, 175, 180, 184
2:24-26, 11, 175, 178
3:1-8, 36, 175, 177, 180, 214
3:9-15, 11, 175, 180-82, 214
3:16-4:3, 175
3:18-22, 183, 196, 214
4:1-6, 59, 78, 175, 184, 214
4:9-16, 175-76, 183, 188
5:1-12, 39, 59, 62, 76, 176, 182, 187
5:13-18, 183, 214
6:6-9, 183-84, 186
6:10-12, 11, 59, 60, 176, 181
7:1-15, 11, 59, 70, 74, 182, 184
7:23-8:1, 11, 176
8:2-9, 30, 176, 183-84
8:10-17, 11, 176, 182, 184, 214
9:1-6, 11, 183, 214
9:7-12, 31, 119, 147, 183, 186, 214
9:13-18, 7, 176, 183
chap. 10, 59
10:1-7, 48, 61, 70, 176, 183
10:8-17, 30, 48, 61, 78, 121, 209
11:1-4, 18, 30, 59, 120
11:7-10, 52, 172, 176, 184-85, 211, 214
12:1-7, 82, 175-76, 183, 211
12:8, 174, 176

12:9–11, 18, 48, 52, 95, 172, 174, 176, 188
12:12–14, 18, 52, 172, 176

Song of Songs
1:1, 173
1:15, 73

Isaiah
1:2–25, 123, 125, 170, 211
3:10–11, 125
5:1–8, 79, 123, 125
5:18–23, 8, 102, 109, 115
6:1, 114
6:10, 16, 79
7:1–17, 99, 124, 133
8:16, 124
9:6, 159
10:5–19, 7, 124, 133
11:1–14, 5, 7, 9, 22, 25
14:4–27, 54, 100, 124, 158
19:11–12, 8, 25, 109
22:22, 159
28:23–29, 7, 16, 79, 109, 125
29:11–16, 8, 16, 79, 124
29:14, 102, 115
29:20, 194
30:1–10, 16, 79, 109, 115, 124, 126
31:1–3, 16, 79, 109, 115, 124
35:5–10, 49
36:3, 22, 15
40:12–14, 131, 167
41:20, 131
42:5, 7, 131
44:25, 102, 111
45:12, 18, 131
47:9–13, 7, 44, 111
50:4–6, 16
53:3–12, 119, 147
54:13, 16

Jeremiah
1:5–2:10, 16, 114, 133
4:22, 16
7:1–23, 123, 211
8:8–9, 7, 8, 16, 102, 109, 169
9:12, 109
9:17, 7
12:1–13:23, 12, 61, 195
18:18, 4, 22, 109
23:4–12, 169
26:10–16, 109–10
31:29, 4
32:9–14, 8, 16

36:4–26, 15, 103, 110
37:11–38:6, 110
49:7, 25
51:57, 8

Ezekiel
7:26, 4
16:44, 53, 64, 76
chap. 17, 54–55, 81
18:2–4, 4, 145
25:4, 25
27:8–9, 7, 25
28:2–10, 7, 25, 100, 111
28:11–19, 25, 100

Daniel
chaps. 1–6, 20, 95, 112–13
1:4–20, 5, 25, 91
2:2–12, 25, 44
2:30, 96
5:7, 25

Hosea
chaps. 1, 3, 79
2:21, 127
4:9, 60, 64, 76, 127
4:16, 127
6:4, 127
6:6, 104
7:6, 127
7:12, 145
8:7, 127
10:12; 13:3; 14:5–6, 127

Amos
2:6–10, 127, 133
3:1–10, 126–27, 133
4:1–5, 127
5:4–15, 126–27
5:21–27, 123, 127, 133, 211
6:2–12, 61, 127
7:14–15, 114
6:1–6, 127
9:7–15, 119, 133

Obadiah
8, 25

Jonah
4:11, 129

Micah
2:1–5:5, 78, 119, 127
6:8–9, 127, 211

Index of Biblical References

Habakkuk
  2:6, 54

Zephaniah
  1:12, 99
  3:20, 119

Zechariah
  3:1-2, 152

Malachi
  1:6-2:17, 4, 7, 173

Tobit
  chap. 4, 31, 59
  12:6-10, 59, 95
  14:10, 93

Wisdom of Solomon
  chaps. 1-5, 214
  1:1-16, 194, 215
  1:12-5:23, 214
  chap. 2, 97, 194, 214-16
  3:1-19, 215-17
  4:7-5:23, 214, 217
  chaps. 6-9, 214
  6:1-25, 82, 214, 217-18
  7:1-22, 218-19
  7:22-8:1, 85, 131, 219-20
  8:1-20, 85, 130, 219-20
  chap. 9, 213, 221
  chaps. 10-19, 214
  chap. 10, 214, 221
  11:17-12:25, 214
  13:1-15:19, 214, 222
  16:2-19:2, 214

Sirach
  1:1-24:29, 205
  1:1-30, 103, 131, 205, 207, 209, 211
  2:4-18, 208, 210
  3:2-30, 207, 211
  4:3-19, 82, 205, 209, 212
  6:14-47, 205, 208, 212
  10:2-27, 28, 108-09
  11:5-30, 18, 208, 210, 216
  12:10-18, 207
  13:1-26, 18, 59, 208-09
  14:1-19, 207-08, 211
  14:20-15:8, 205, 207, 212
  15:6, 11-20, 211
  16:3, 208
  16:14, 211, 216
  16:24-18:14, 207
  18:32-19:20, 208-09, 211
  20:6-21:20, 59, 209, 211
  22:27-23:6, 205, 209
  23:7-27, 207-08
  24:1-29, 18, 84, 111, 131, 205, 207, 211-12
  24:30-39:11, 205
  24:32-34, 52, 103, 209
  25:1-38:23, 205
  25:1-18, 76-77, 208
  26:1-28, 208
  27:16-27, 30, 91, 209
  28:17-19, 208, 209
  29:22, 208
  30:14-17, 208
  30:25-33:13, 204
  31:12-32:17, 207, 211
  32:24-33:3, 211
  33:7-21, 205, 208, 211
  34:10-19, 18, 203, 211
  35:1-20, 207, 211
  36:1-17, 204-05
  37:7-14, 208
  38:24, 52, 205, 207
  39:1-8, 18, 203
  39:12-50:24, 205
  40:18-26, 208
  chap. 43, 34
  47:17, 54
  50:25-29, 205, 208
  chap. 51, 52, 203, 205, 207

(LXX) Daniel
  chap. 3, 34

Matthew
  6:1-8, 29
  9:13, 28
  13:3-16, 33, 44-47, 78-79

Mark
  1:13, 152

2 Corinthians
  11:3, 97

Epistle to the Hebrews
  11:1, 187

Revelation
  12:9, 152
  20:2, 97